RAGAN

Chronicles of Arowana

Book 1

A novel by

Sylvie D. Parris

Copyright © 2020 by Sylvie D. Parris

FIRST EDITION

Other books by Sylvie D. Parris

Tapestry of Family
Love in the Key of Magic

One

"Why do I have to wear this?" Rinna tried to stand still, but it was hard with people tugging at all the layers of fabric on her. By instinct, she raised an arm to try to stop the heavy head-dress from tilting right off her head.

"Gods above and below girl, stand still, "Lucinda said she neared armed with hairpins. "You know why you have to wear this. You've known this day would eventually come and you would have to be introduced at court as a proper lady."

Rinna winced as her nursemaid stuck hairpins through the headdress to help hold it in place. Once Lucinda stepped back to examine her work, Rinna's hand went back up.

"Don't you dare." Lucinda smacked her hand. "I know its uncomfortable, but it is important to make a good impression to the princess, even it means hairpins poking your scalp."

"Well? Let's see her." Lucinda and the other maids moved out of the way to let Lady Mirabelle through. Rinna's mother examined Rinna with a critical eye. "Turn," she ordered.

Rinna turned slowly in order not to jostle the headdress.

"Curtsey."

Keeping her eyes focused on Mirabelle's distended belly, she did as she was told. Mirabella clucked in disapproval. "you look like an arthritic priestess, not the young daughter of a lord." She demonstrated a graceful curtsy, unhindered by her pregnancy. "Greeting."

Good morning your highness. I am Lady Norrina Tesennae, daughter to Lord Gregor Tessenae, advisor to your highnesses, King Senneck Halson Braun the third and Queen Eileen. I am here to serve as one of your ladies in waiting." Rinna had practiced that greeting every day for two hours after supper all week.

"At least your tongue knows how to work properly." Mirabelle said, "come, your father, Jamil and Emir are waiting."

Rinna followed her mother to the front of the house where they would ride an open-air carriage to the palace. Her older brothers greeted their parents in the formal manner, expected outside their house Rinna waited for them to finish before getting assistance up into the carriage by a groom. As usual, they pretended she didn't exist.

Gregor's connection to the crown, meant that Rinna would become a lady in waiting for the princess. Rinna's freedom came to a crashing halt as she was expected to learn proper decorum, embroidery, and dancing in just a few months. She was also expected to avoid drawing attention to herself to ensure that the princess would never be overshadowed. Today was to be her induction into the inner workings of court life. She dreaded it.

The carriage had not left when a messenger ran towards them. "Lord Gregor," he said, out of breath, "he's here. The heralds' banners have just spotted leaving the forest."

"Damn, he's early," Gregor exclaimed, tossing a coin to the messenger, "thank you. Tell the king we are on our way."

"Why did the emperor come early?" Rinna reached up and adjusted her headdress, alleviating the discomfort caused by a hairpin.

"Norinna." Mirabelle scolded as she handed Rinna a fan, "it is not your concern. Remember, speak only when spoken to."

Rinna waved the woven fan to help cool her mother as the carriage began to move. By the time they reached the palace crowds had begun to gather anticipating the arrival of Esmerelda's future husband.

Upon learning that the emperor had set his sights on the country, Senneck sent dignitaries to appeal for a peaceful resolution, offering Arowana's 400-year-old library, its proximity to the next continent across the sea and its sheltered deepwater harbor. Rinna didn't know more details of the agreement, only that the emperor had demanded Senneck's daughter. She was told that Arowana followed the example of a neighbor who had escaped military conquest.

The emperor's arrival was full of ceremony. Six heralds played a musical cadence as soon as they entered the city gates.

They were followed by pavilions draped in cloth of orange, red and gold carrying what turned out to be the emperor's vizier, a fire magician-priest and his entourage. Soldiers with plumed helmets and short red capes marching in perfect precision followed in row after row. Rinna stood for what seemed hours with her family and the rest of the court on the steps of the palace until Emperor Corbaine was finally spotted. The girls near her all twittered and whispered behind their hands at how attractive the king was. Rinna just wished he'd turn around and go home and leave them all alone.

King Senneck and Queen Eileen waited at the top of the steps, with their daughter. Corbaine dismounted off his black charger standing hand on hips as he surveyed the buildings around the palace and the people gathered. Then he climbed swiftly up the stairs to be greeted by the king and queen. He barely acknowledged their formal greeting. He gave his future bride mere glance before moving on inside as if was his own house.

"Look," one of the servants standing behind Rinna said in a low voice, "Princess Esmerelda is crying."

"That she is," another said, "the queen is the more interesting. Its like she's wishing she could trade places with her daughter."

"A third spoke, "I wonder how long until Corbaine tires of his chubby bride and seeks to add to his harem? I heard…"

Rinna's attention was pulled from the servants' gossip by a sudden chill. The fire magician and those in the religious order he oversaw were climbing the steps. Something about the magician priests frightened her as they passed. No one else but a group of poorly dressed servants followed, something more than one person thought odd. With minutes the procession was over.

King Senneck called his advisors together to decide how to proceed. They had not expected the Emperor's behavior. Rinna sat by her mother listening to the women at court. They were abuzz with their opinions about the visiting monarch, and how lucky the princess was to have such a powerful, virile man as a husband even if he was almost three decades older than the princess. The queen and her daughter had retired to their rooms, minus their usual companions. Rinna wanted to be anywhere else.

That evening, while the court stood waiting their turn to greet the monarch and groom to be, Corbaine ignored his bride standing by his chair, instead squeezed the uncovered breasts of a girl in his lap not much older than Rinna. Where the girl had come from no one knew. The court was scandalized but didn't dare react for fear of breaking the alliance. Since taking the throne barely into his twenties, Corbaine and his armies had conquered a third of the continent.

As Rinna and her family made their way forward, Rinna noticed that King Senneck was trying to ignore the display, his mouth in a tight line, the Queen kept her eyes looking downward and Esmeralda was fighting back tears, a smile plastered to her face. Rinna wanted to smirk at Esmeralda for being knocked off the pedestal she loved to perch from, but she also recognized the open cruelty of what was happening. No amount of deportment lessons had prepared her for such a scenario. She felt bad for both girls sensing that the emperor was enjoying making everyone uncomfortable.

Rinna couldn't help but stare, seeing that the half-naked girl looked dully at nothing while the Lords and Ladies bowed and curtsied, then turned to whisper to one another as they hastened away. She wanted to take the girl's hand and run far away. Esmeralda could come too.

Then it was their turn. Mirabella tugged Rinna's shoulder, holding a grip on the fabric of her court dress to force her into a curtsy as if Rinna wouldn't perform as expected. Rinna's face reddened in embarrassment. As her father spoke, Rinna caught the attention of the girl giving her a slight smile. The girl's eyes widened in surprise then resumed her blank stare as the king moved his hands lower.

"Lord Gregor Tessenae, Earl of Fairshine, Royal Advisor to

your king, your daughter is an interesting creature," King Corbaine's voice was a deep baritone that did not hide his disdain as he named off Rinna's father's titles, "she will attend the banquet tomorrow evening."

Rinna glanced in alarm at Emperor Corbaine. It was a set rule that drawing attention in court was not to be done. She had no idea how she'd gotten his attention other than trying to offer the poor girl in his lap a bit of kindness. She had been standing behind her brothers so she wouldn't be noticed. Rinna started to say something when she felt her mother's painful grip on her shoulder while her father accepted the invitation. As soon as they left the throne room, Mirabelle turned on Rinna.

"What did you do to draw attention to yourself like that?" Rinna's mother hissed as she pulled Rinna down the hallway.

"Nothing Momma, I did nothing. Why didn't anyone say anything about him hurting that poor girl? Couldn't you see the bruises on her?" Rinna shot back, frustrated and afraid for the girl, for the princess, for herself, "is he going to do that to Princess Esmeralda in front of others too?"

To Rinna's shock, Mirabella slapped her across the face, "stupid girl. Have you not heard anything I've been telling you for the past two months?"

Rinna stared at her mother in confusion as tears started to fall. Her mother had never raised a hand to her in anger before.

"Mirabelle. I will handle this," her father said, "I know the day has been long and difficult. Why don't you go rest awhile, have someone bring you some watered wine and those sweets you like with walnuts in them."

"I didn't do anything father. I promise," Rinna tried to set her headdress back upright then pulled it off as she sniffed away her tears.

"I know you didn't poppet," his voice sounded tired. "everyone's nerves are just a bit on edge these days.

"Can you answer then?" Rinna wasn't going to let the matter go. "momma said we are to be chaste, quiet and humble, and yet everyone is pretending nothing is wrong with what he was doing to that girl or to the princess. Lady Glorina told Momma that he keeps hundreds of girls as slaves, some of them not even human, just to make sons from them."

Gregor didn't say anything, instead, he walked to a small room with a balcony. It offered a view that looked south where the salt marshes lay just beyond the horizon.

"The customs of Khaetor are different than ours. They have slaves, we don't. In their eyes, that girl was just a thing. We are going to have to adjust."

"But…"

Gregor rested a hand on Rinna's shoulder, "it's nothing that will concern you Norinna. Be a good girl and try not to irritate your mother."

Rinna knew that her father wasn't going to explain things so remained quiet. Gregor remained silent for a minute, instead looking out at the scene before them. There was the flash of lightening in the distance, briefly illuminating a cloud. He patted the top of her head, "everything will be alright, you'll see."

Gregor left the room leaving a frustrated Rinna to find her way back home by herself. She didn't think her father believed the words of encouragement he had said any more than she did. She knew that he had advised against the alliance, not trusting the Khaetor monarch. Rinna didn't know if anyone else felt like she did.

She found herself seated next to Corbaine's chief magician Rocnor, the high priest to the fire deity Irator at the banquet. He smelled of flowery perfume and smoke. It didn't quite mask an aroma that reminded Rinna of the butcher shop and something that had been left dead in the sun too long. A little older than her father, Rocnor wore flowing robes of orange, yellow and red, and had his hair slicked back with streaks of colored clay that matched the color of his robes. When he moved or walked, his clothes looked like a fire burning. His hands were weighed down with jeweled rings. Rinna caught a glimpse of a strange tattoo on the inside of his wrist. It looked like red-orange hued flames.

She sat at the high table instead of her mother, who had begged off because of her advanced pregnancy, claiming fatigue. Rinna had expected to sit at one of the other tables for lesser nobles or their wives. Instead, she found herself sitting next to a man who horrified and repulsed her. She was the only child at the table. The princess who was five years older, was the only person near her age in the room other than servants. Esmeralda was seated in between her parents placed to the right of King Corbaine who had commanded the head seat. Rinna knew that was another breach in protocol as well as where she herself was sitting, only the magician between her and the emperor. Her father sat on her other side, ignoring the fire magician and her to talk with his fellow advisors.

Rinna spent the evening forced to listen to Rocnor pontificate on the glorious attributes of his deity. A thin, plain looking man, he spoke of how he looked forward to introducing the people of Arowana to Irator's cleansing joy while stuffing course after course into a mouth that never stopped talking.

The people sitting across from her were his, all dressed in red robes with different amounts of orange that Rinna assumed notated hierarchy. No one else but King Corbaine spoke with any of the magician priests who barely spoke at all. She didn't know why, only that they all terrified her. Rinna thought Rocnor was quite possibly thinking of murdering them all, and barely touched her dinner.

When the meal was finally over, she fled back home not waiting on her father. She took off her dress, then snuck into the kitchen where she threw it into the fire that was always burning in the hearth. The fabric reeked with Rocnor's odor. She then went out to swim in the harbor, the cool salty water washing away the feeling of charred flesh.

She was glad she wasn't asked to be present for any other functions involving the foreign king's terrifying advisor. Instead, she was expected to be present and available for the princess. Esmeralda ignored Rinna, the youngest and smallest of the princess's entourage as did the other girls. Rinna found she could sneak away to the library, or to a quiet balcony and not be missed for an hour or two. If she made herself be seen on a regular basis in the same room as the princess, Rinna had the next two weeks to herself.

Four days before the wedding, the princess was late to arrive in the salon where the other girls gathered. She rushed in with a halfhearted apology
for being late. Rinna was hot in her itchy dress and wimple, the only girl wearing one, and hungry because no one could eat until Esmeralda did.

"But I have the most wonderful reason," she said breathlessly, "he came to my room last night."

"That soldier you like to hide with and kiss?" Rinna blurted out knowing Esmeralda was still sneaking moments with the soldier. She'd seen them the day before tearing at each other's clothing in the room where Rinna had chosen to hide with a book. She had managed to leave without being noticed. Esmeralda and the other girls gasped.

"No, you stupid, ugly little mongrel," Esmeralda had risen to her feet, towering over the much smaller Rinna. Rinna heard the titters of the other girls. "Don't ever speak in my presence again, is that clear?"

Gladly, Rinna thought, cursing her inability to keep her mouth shut, "yes, your highness," she said instead.

"It was him, Emperor Corbaine," Esmeralda gushed, having already forgotten Rinna, "he said he had to show my father that he was an emperor and daddy just a mere king, but it had been so hard to not want to swoop me up and marry me on the spot and do to me what he'd done to that girl who had sat on his lap. Then he did just that, and more, more than once. It was wonderful."

"What about that girl?" one of the other girls asked, "what happened to her?"

Esmeralda's eyes gleamed, "oh, she belongs to that magician, the tall scary looking one. I told him that it upset me to see him with a harlot. Corbaine was playing a joke on his chief advisor. He said they play silly jokes on each other all the time, and not to worry. I'll never have to see her or another girl on his lap ever again."

Rinna found the need to escape too pressing to ignore, horrified that the princess and the other girls believed King Corbaine's blatant lies. While Esmeralda waxed poetic about the sexual prowess and physical appearance of King Corbaine with details Rinna did not want to hear, she made her escape. The salon had a small curtained balcony. Rinna slipped out onto it then used a variety of handholds to climb down to another balcony a floor below. It was a skill she had managed to keep secret from everyone, one learned by her time exploring in the forests beyond the city. She'd even taken a dress with her once to learn how to maneuver with the many layers of skirts, something that had proven beneficial more than once.

On the day of the wedding, Rinna left the house before dawn. She had packed some bread, a hunk of cheese, a handful of sugared nuts, an apple, a small knife stolen from the kitchen and three books she had taken from the library. She had no problems leaving the house in the predawn hours, sneaking past the servants and the guard she knew she would find dozing at his post. Everyone who was awake, was busy in preparation for the wedding, something Rinna wanted nothing to do with. She was a little surprised to that the city gate was unmanned but shrugged it off as something to do with the events of the day.

She was delighted to be told she would not be attending the ceremony due to space restrictions but had demonstrated disappointment and remorse because it was expected of her. Rinna was going to salvage as much of the day as possible with books, sunshine, quiet and fresh air before duty called.

Two

Rinna saw him just as she settled into her favorite tree and her book opened. It had taken an over an hour to get from her house to her hiding spot and he had already found her. He was trudging up the hill on Butters. Rinna could hear his grumbling well before he got close enough to see her. Sighing, she tucked a scrap of ribbon to mark the place in her book and waited, one leg swinging idly off the branch she was sitting on as she leaned against the trunk of the tree. She thought about climbing a few branches higher in the giant oak then climbing over a few trees using the interlinking branches, but then the scolding would be that much longer when she returned home.

Garrett reached the top of the hill and the tree she was sitting in. She'd been easy to find, his having ferreted out all her hiding spots by the time she was seven. It was only a matter of figuring out which one the child had chosen to hide in. Garrett was glad he'd found her at the third location he looked but was still unhappy she'd picked the one furthest away from home. He'd missed breakfast thanks to her insubordination.

"Your father will have you beaten for this Norinna. Get down out of that tree right now."

She scoffed at the idea. Neither of her parents paid much attention to her and had ignored her in the past two weeks except to make sure she was present at required court functions and dressed properly. She was the only daughter in a family of five sons. The only thing she had in common with her siblings was the mass of curls that on Rinna were tumbled well past her shoulders in wild disarray.

"Daddy won't do anything, and you know it, nor Momma despite her wanting to because she only leaves her rooms to go to the queen," she hated when Garrett sounded snooty. She also wasn't so certain any more about her status with her mother. "I don't even have to be at the palace until after midday."

Garrett was Rinna's father's majordomo, and only slightly more irritating than her younger brothers, who teased her about her hair and how small and skinny she was. It didn't do any good to complain about their refusal to call her by name, instead of The Brat. She was expected to smile sweetly and talk to the children of other dignitaries or sit quietly all dressed up in lace and ribbons pretending to sew on a pillow with the other women, while the men talked about treaties, trade, wars and what the guilds were up to. Rinna always found that more interesting than sewing.

When Rinna had first seen Garrett on Butters, his gentle bay colored mare, she knew that her freedom had ended early and that she couldn't cajole or bribe her way out of it. Her disappointment was bitter, but she could do nothing. He was already wearing his court finery even though the sun had just cleared the horizon. As he neared, Rinna could see sweat beading down his face from his balding head, his cap tucked into his belt. Garrett was thin with bushy eyebrows that he was very proud of, claiming it was how he had won over Lucinda for a wife.

"I had to come all the way out here to fetch you. Your impertinence is taking both of us away from more important duties. You will be attending the wedding of Princess Esmeralda to Emperor Corbaine. Lady Maribelle has fallen ill and as your father's daughter, you are required to take her place. We need to hurry or else you will be late." Garrett sneered up at the girl in the tree. She was wearing baggy trousers and a dirty tunic, her feet bare. Her face had a smudge of dirt and her dark uncombed curls tumbled around her face, looking more like a bramble bush than hair.

"You look like a street urchin, not the daughter of one of King Senneck's advisors. That needs to be remedied immediately," he held out what he'd been carrying. It was a dress, dark blue velvet with layer after layer of lace along with a blue wimple complete with a beaded overlay.

Rinna had to get what she felt out before going back. She'd kept her thoughts to herself after her mother had slapped her and she knew it would be hard to hide what she thought during the long ceremony and the events afterwards.

"Momma doesn't want to have to stand for hours trying to balance that belly of hers. I don't like Emperor Corbaine, and don't think Princess Esmeralda should marry him. He brought too many soldiers, he keeps looking at things as if he plans to steal them, and his magician is evil. He smells of dead things and he scares me."

Lady Maribelle was due in a month. She was using her pregnancy and her daughter to her full advantage. Mirabelle hadn't attended a public function since the day the emperor arrived. Rinna didn't dare ask why.

Rinna wanted the princess to punch the emperor on his very arrogant nose, tell him to take his magicians, his soldiers and go home then marry the handsome soldier she'd seen canoodling with Esmeralda more than once when the princess thought no one was looking.

"Lady Norinna. I will climb up that tree and pull you down if I must," Garrett bellowed, breaking into the thread of Rinna's daydreaming. Garrett's adding the lady part had her sticking her tongue out at the man. He stood staring up at her, his eyebrows fluttering in the slight summer breeze. Rinna thought they looked like mismatched caterpillars. She frowned, putting her book back into her bag.

"Fine," Rinna groused. She hated being called Norinna, preferring the shorter nickname Rinna. She also hated being called Lady. "I'll dress up, and stand in Momma's place, and smile and curtsy like I'm supposed to. I still don't like Emperor Corbaine. He's..." Rinna, tried to think of the right words, "dishonest, mean and greedy."

"This is a momentous day, and don't you forget it. This marriage will help strengthen our kingdom and provide a port for our new allies. We need their strength and what they will bring in commerce, they need our harbor which will help us, especially as we've had problems with pirates," Garrett had heard similar misgivings from Rinna's father. Garrett thought Gregor was too soft on his daughter, giving her far too much freedom.

They both heard a boom which echoed through the trees.

Looking up she tried to see through the canopy of leaves for rain clouds, but the leaves were too thick. Climbing higher, she looked back towards the city.

"Garrett. Something is on fire. I see smoke," she climbed back down, lowering herself to hang off eight feet off the ground. She let go of the branch, her bag of books slung across her shoulder as she landed.

"I smell it. Probably some revelers who got too drunk, got in a fight and caught a brothel on fire," he held out the dress he'd brought for the girl, but she ignored it, being more curious about the source of the smoke. She skipped out of sight. Sighing he followed her. Butters as interested in going back to the city as Rinna was, took the opportunity to graze on the grass that grew in a sunny spot granted by a break in the forest canopy.

The girl has a point, Garrett thought as he followed her. The day was going to be very long with little more to do but watch the celebration from a crowded, distant vantage point. At least he had a full flask in his pocket to help the day drag by less slowly. Lucinda would be staying with Lady Mirabelle and watching from a canopied balcony so wouldn't be scolding him for getting drunk with Alfred, the stable master.

It didn't take him long to catch up. She was standing still at the edge of the woods, her hand resting against the trunk of a tree. The smell of smoke was much stronger, pungent with a mixture with tar. Brambles and a slight rise blocked what had stopped Rinna until he was almost beside her. What he saw made him gasp in shock.

Two of the ships in the harbor were on fire, as was the castle and many other buildings. The library Arowana was famous for was engulfed in flames. From where they stood a mile from the city walls, they could hear clashes of metal and screams. An arch of fire rose from inside the city to hit another ship that was trying in vain to raise its sails and escape. The fire rained down on the ship setting it ablaze. Rinna jumped, as a spire of the castle collapsed, the victim of another blast of fire coming from inside the city. People trying to flee were killed by soldiers who had been waiting outside the gates. Garrett had paid little attention to their presence when he left the city, irritated at needing to find Norrina.

He hadn't been gone that long. How could that level of carnage have happened so quickly, he wondered? He knew that the head fire magician must be responsible, having heard stories of his abilities and that of his order, but he still had a hard time linking the destruction he saw happening to the magic which he'd always been skeptical of.

The approach of soldiers to the northern gate caught Garrett's attention. Even from a distance, it was easy to see the short red capes marking the soldiers as Kheatorian. The city's walls had never been heavily fortified, depending on their sheltered harbor and the mountains with their high passes to protect them. As they watched, a section of wall collapsed with people falling along with the stones. A group of soldiers broke off from those marching into the beleaguered city and began to approach where the wall had collapsed, too close from where Garrett and Norinna were standing. People who had escaped unharmed so far now faced approaching soldiers. Thick smoke hid the view from the other gates. Garrett was certain that the horrific scene before them was being repeated at the other three other gates leading out of Fairshine.

"Norinna. We must go. It's not safe," he tugged on her hand to take her back into the forest. He knew what had happened, that they had been betrayed and Emperor Corbaine was using his fire magicians to destroy the city.

"But Momma, Daddy, my brothers—we need to…"

"I'm sorry child but we need to go before the soldiers see us. We cannot help them now," Garrett's eyes were streaming tears nearly as much as his charge. He didn't know if was from tears of grief and anger, or the acrid smoke that smelled of tar, wood and death, wafting their way; he just knew they needed to get as far from the city as possible and quickly. He helped her climb up behind him on Butters. They rode north staying off the road not stopping until they reached a stream. There Garrett shed his court clothes keeping only his undershirt, trousers and boots. The dress and his clothes went into Rinna's bag, which he carried. Rinna had already pulled out a pair of boots, a pair she had shed as soon as she had reached the tree line overlooking the city earlier that morning.

Garrett knew she had been ransacking her brothers' cast-offs again, as the scruffy boots looked worse for wear, much like the clothes she was wearing. While he didn't understand why a girl would want to dress like a half-starved orphan, her current attire was far more practical than what he had been wearing. Plus, she would be indistinguishable from any poor child in the kingdom. Taking a cue from her, he took a couple of handfuls of mud and splattered them on his shirt and pants, hoping the impromptu disguise would help them hide their social status from the Kheatorians.

Rinna watched Garrett's transformation, her sapphire blue eyes large in her face, saying nothing. He argued for leaving everything behind, but she refused to leave her precious books. Garrett finally gave in, thinking they would be either worth something in trade along with the clothes, or for building a fire.

They rode until well past dark staying mostly off the road leading to the nearest mountain pass, seeing or hearing nothing but the usual sounds of the forest. Rinna remained silent as she rode behind Garrett until they crossed the road for the fourth time.

"Where are we going, and why aren't we staying on the road?" she had her head resting against Garrett's back. She had cried quietly early into their journey, remaining silent until just then.

"There's a town a few days ride from here, but I'm trying to see if there are any houses or places off the road we can stay. Plus, I am checking to see if soldiers are coming."

"Oh," Rinna was quiet for a moment, "bad soldiers?"

"Yes."

Rinna was quiet again. After a while felt her relax against her back, knowing that she had fallen asleep. Garrett wanted to do the same but didn't dare until he had put as much distance between them and Fairshine as he could.

They slept that night under the shelter of a large fallen tree several yards from the road, hidden from view by a stand of evergreen shrubs. Garrett didn't dare light a fire, for fear of being discovered by the invading soldiers. They shared the remains of Rinna's bread, saving the apple and nuts for breakfast. Garrett gave Rinna a sip of the ale in his flask. She made a face as she drank it, then took another on his insistence. He took larger sips, then lay down, glad for the thick carpet of leaves on the forest floor. They slept huddled together, using his court cloak as a blanket.

They stayed on the road the next day, neither of them stirring from their sleep until nearly mid-morning, too exhausted to hear the men and horses passing them by on their way north during the night. They saw no one on the road all the next day. When they came near a clearing and signs of a settlement, Garrett turned Butters into the forest to go around it. Rinna asked why they were avoiding the houses she could see through the trees just before they turned off the road. Garrett only told her he was being cautious. When they both smelled the aroma of decay, he knew he had made the right decision.

Rinna found a blackberry bush heavy with ripened fruit near where they camped, picking as many berries as she could, using Garrett's court cap to hold them. They ate all of them that night, too hungry to save the rest for later. Garrett refilled his flask with water from a small brook, having finished off the contents the night before.

On the fourth day, they crossed hills that climbed higher as they neared the village of Ragan that lay at the base of the high mountains where the road continued past crossing the northernmost pass. They could see the snow-covered peaks in the distance growing larger with every mile they passed. Garrett explained that the village had the same name as the lake it sat next to, and that they were known for their wool cloth and ceramics, the lake for its trout and freshwater pearls. It was late afternoon, the sun dipping down beyond the mountains to their southwest when they crested the top of a hill and saw an orange glow in the distance. Garrett stopped Butters, then turned sharply to the left, leaving the road completely letting the horse pick his way through the wooded terrain.

"Where are we going? Why do I smell smoke?" Rinna's voice trembled.

"Caution," he answered. It was dark when reached the shores of Lake Ragan. They followed along the shoreline, staying within the cover of the trees, the half-moon reflecting off the dark water until Garrett stopped and dismounted. He helped Rinna down. They stood side by side watching the village across the lake burn, hearing the distant crackle and pops of the fires.

"Garrett. What are we going to do?"

Garrett looked down at the little girl who he was certain was responsible for his being alive, "for now, we rest. In the morning, I am going to see if there is anything we can find left in Ragan, and if there are any other people. We need food."

He left the next morning, returning just as the sun was dipping behind the mountains. He had with him a dog, some gardening tools, a sword and a bow with a quiver of arrows.

"I didn't see anyone there. There were some dead soldiers," indicating the sword and bow. He didn't mention the dead villagers not wanting to upset Rinna any further, "I also found some bread and salted fish."

"I found mushrooms, berries and a fishing pole. Their line got stuck in a tree branch," she pointed to the pole leaning up against a tree, "I just had to climb up and untangle it."

Garrett raised his significant eyebrows in surprise, "well, at least we won't starve."

The next day, they found an abandoned hut about a two hour's walk from the burned-out village. It was nestled in a cove with a small beach and an open grassy area. They could see the snowcapped mountains rising on the opposite shore of the lake. The hut surrounded by huge evergreens on three sides was out of view of the village. There was a tiny boat pulled up next to a tree, tipped over to keep out the rain.

Neither appreciated the beauty of the spot, at least not at first, being too intent on turning the hut into an adequate shelter and finding food. Rinna discovered a net under the boat. She stretched it out as best she could trying to understand how it worked. By nightfall she'd had figured out a way that she could manage on her own, catching four fish. Garrett cleaned and cooked them by placing them on hot rocks laying on coals in the hut's fireplace. Even without salt or spices, both thought the fish was delicious. The dog Rinna named Brownie was content with the fish heads.

"Are we going to stay here?" Rinna asked Garrett the next day, "or are we going home?"

"For now, we stay," Garrett answered, "until we know it's safe, we don't dare go home."

"Daddy, Momma, my brothers, do you think they are…?" Rinna couldn't complete the question.

"Unless they somehow managed to escape, yes," Garrett mourned the loss of his wife, the home he'd spent most all his life, and the ordered predictable existence he'd come to enjoy, "I could be wrong of course. Your father is smart. If anyone escaped the fire magician's destruction, he did."

Rinna wanted to believe Garrett but she'd seen the people being murdered as they tried to escape just as Garrett had. She knew that her family was dead and that Emperor Corbaine and the evil magician Rocnor had killed them. She had felt all along that the Khaetor monarch was bad and that his being in Arowana meant something bad was going to happen. She never dreamed he would destroy her home and kill everyone.

That night she climbed into one of the evergreens to sleep too leery of being trapped inside.

"Norinna, get down here and go to bed," Garrett ordered, 'It's dark and now is not the time to play in trees."

"I'm afraid. I feel safer here Garrett," Rinna pleaded, "please let me sleep here tonight. I don't want to be inside where

I could burn up."

Garrett was too weary himself to argue with the girl. Every time he closed his eyes, he saw the flames and heard the distant screams of the dying. He wanted a drink, to dull the pain and the memories, "fine, but if you fall out break your neck, it's your fault."

The next day he took Butters back to the village, returning dragging some half-charred lumber and a box of rusted nails. Scavenging around a burnt out building he found a cellar and a keg of ale. He was able to find some blankets that were not too badly charred, a line of hung laundry that had escaped the flames and some cookware. Over the few weeks he helped her build a platform in the tree she slept in. She agreed to sleep inside when the weather was bad or when it was too cold.

Neither could have guessed that they had found what would become their home for the next decade.

Three

<u>Ten Years Later</u>

Cai looked down at the lake from the last turn of the trail leading down from the pass. There was a small village along one end of the shore, with a crude wood and stone fortress commanding attention. The road ran through the village, exiting by the fortress where it crossed a wooden bridge over a stream that exited the lake. It disappeared into the forest that blanketed the foothills and lower slopes of the mountains for as far as they could see. The lake and the surrounding forest were beautiful, the village an ugly scar on the otherwise pristine landscape.

"We traveled four months for this? If that's a harbor, I'll shave my beard and eat I," Dax was quite proud of his beard which he kept groomed and oiled. Dax was his second, and one of Cai's best friends.

"No. The capital is still a few days ride away," Cai grinned at the thought of his friend beardless, something he'd never seen, "at least we can get a meal, some supplies and hopefully a bed for the night."

They had met when Dax was single handedly holding his own against brigands who had been attempting to rob a small caravan of people transporting grain. Cai had part of an escort for a dignitary. The dignitary insisted on moving on. Cai ignored the orders to proceed, telling the other guards to stay with the dignitary while he went and helped Dax.

Dax had a battle axe and a short sword, Cai his long sword. Cai helped tip the balance ending the assault in a few minutes with the attackers either dead or on the run. Cai had offered to buy Dax a round at the town they were both heading to the same destination as the dignitary screamed obscenities, furious that Cai had ignored him. The dignitary stopped when Dax who was nearly seven feet tall hefted his ax, towered over them and bellowed for the man to shut up. They'd been friends for eight years.

The rest of his group uttered their relief at the possibility of a night indoors, a hot meal and hopefully a decent mug of ale. Crossing the mountains that bordered the province had taken nine days, three longer than expected, thanks to a late spring snowstorm that kept them hunkered in their tents.

Cai was in Arowana to replace yet another Lord Governor sent by Emperor Corbaine who also happened to be his father. He had immediately asked Dax and his cousin Elgin to go with him. They'd picked up the other two along the way, men Cai had met and befriended during his time in the Kheator army. Cai learned that he would be the fourth replacement since his father had conquered the small nation.

Arowana was one of the smallest provinces, its only real value to the expansive Khaetor empire, its deep-water harbor where the former capital named Fairshine lay. The harbor had become a distribution point for a small but lucrative slave trade giving sellers access to customers in nations across the Tarling Sea. Conquering Arowana when Cai was fifteen had been considered a triumph by his father, particularly as it had been so easy. Now it was just another chunk of land that needed to be held on to, while King Corbaine looked for even more lands to take and people and resources he could exploit. During his thirty-six-year reign he had added five more kingdoms since taking Arowana, now holding fully half the continent.

"At least the forest is unsullied," Observed Elgin. A full-blooded elf, he was fair skinned, tall, leanly muscled, with large almond-shaped eyes the hue of sparkling sapphires and long black hair with beads braided in that matched his eyes. He was sold with Cai's mother when Corbaine had purchased the pair on a whim from a slave market. Elgin was too young to remember anyone else but his aunt who'd become pregnant soon after being placed in Corbaine's harem. She had died giving birth to Cai.

Elgin remained in the palace nursery with his cousin until he was five. Someone had suggested all elves were excellent archers and had given Elgin bow and arrows sending him out to entertain the king and his friends for dinner. A lucky shot had impressed the court, keeping Elgin safe from a short life as a drudge. On Cai's tenth birthday, Elgin was given to Cai who promptly freed him.

Cai couldn't hide his mixed heritage. His skin was the tone of leaves on a forest floor that only deepened in the summer with the muscled build of a warrior that he'd gained from his father. His hair was straight and black like his cousin's, instead of the reddish-brown of his father, opting to wear it just long enough to tie into a tail at the base of his neck along with almond-shaped vivid blue eyes that gave proof of his elven heritage.

It was raining and nearing dark by the time the group made their way down the mountain and into the village. As they neared, everyone observed the state of the houses and shops in comparison to the better built fortress sitting on a small rise. Of the dozen buildings half looked unoccupied. They that were in slightly better repair than the empty ones. It appeared that an honest effort had begun on the fortress, but then people just gave up over time, slapping everything else together. It looked functional, and possibly defensible. It also looked out of place for a tiny village in the middle of nowhere.

A short scream and the sound of a slap got their attention. Cai dismounted and walked towards the sound between a dilapidated shop and a smithy, the forge already banked for the night. There he saw a man who was holding a young girl, her face showing the red mark of a handprint. Another man was on the ground, with someone standing over him, a pitchfork poised above the man's groin. They were smaller than the men, causing Cai to think that maybe they were a teenage brother of the girl. The third had a short sword in his hand warily watching the person with the pitchfork. The sword holder had his back to Cai.

"Back away and let her go," although the person was wearing a hood to protect against the rain hiding their features, it was obvious that the speaker's voice was female. "Let her go and your friend here will not need to learn to urinate through an extra hole."

"You will regret this bitch," the man on the ground growled, his voice indicating his fear of the sharp points hovering above his genitals.

"I already do, but maybe now you will think twice before deciding to rape children," she said.

The man on the ground nodded and the soldier holding the little girl let go. The child ran, stopping when she saw Cai and the others watching. She blinked at them a moment, her brown braids dripping rain off their ends as she hesitated, then continued down the street until she disappeared around a corner.

"I hope you are happy," the man who had been holding the girl took two steps closer to the woman, "you made us give up our plaything, so now you get to take her place."

His companion with the sword also moved towards her. The hooded woman didn't hesitate, bringing the pitchfork down hard. The man on the ground screamed, causing his friends to freeze in shock. The woman took their hesitation as her chance to get away running in the opposite direction of the little girl she had just rescued.

"Gods above and below, she skewered him," Dax said in a low voice. He and the others had joined Cai.

"No," observed Elgin, "look."

The man was getting up off the ground while a string of curses spewed from his mouth. The three men turned and stopped in surprise upon seeing Cai's group approach.

"You saw what she was doing, and you did nothing? She tried to murder me," the man who had been on the ground accused.

"If she was trying to murder you, she would have quite easily," Cai sniffed the air, "instead she managed to get you to soil yourself."

"You can't talk to me like that. I'm a soldier of the empire. I can have you flogged for such insolence," the man pulled out a dagger placing his feet in a defensive stance.

"All of us?" asked Dax. The soldier blanched when he saw Dax. Dax had his axe in his hands, and a scowl on his face. Behind him the rest of Cai's group stood, all openly displaying weapons.

"I will make sure Lord Bannister hears of this. We expect order in Ragan, and we don't welcome thieves and outlaws into our lands," the soldier looked for his friends, who had already made their escape. He too turned and walked away as fast as his dignity would let him.

"And I thought we would be bored out of our minds," joked Tolin. The youngest of the five, he was the most recent addition of the group, and the second tallest in a group of tall men at six feet five. He had light blonde hair, a winning smile, a heavily muscled build and an easygoing demeanor.

Cai walked to where the pitchfork still stood. The mysterious woman had brought it down in between the soldier's legs. It had been a daring move, as she had helped the girl to escape only to place herself in harm's way. But it had worked. If women were having to take such measures to protect themselves or children, things were bad, which meant the usual for the lower classes in the Khaetor empire.

They found the tavern with an attached stable to settle their horses. Entering they found the main room noisy and full, a mixture of soldiers and locals. Tired looking women served food and ale, while trying to avoid the grasp of the patrons, the worst offenders being the guards. One woman was on her knees servicing a seated man who was yelling encouragement at one of two men wrestling in a corner. He kept a firm grip on her hair to keep her from leaving until he was satisfied. Another man lay slumped on the floor, his head resting on the hearth of the large fireplace commanding one end of the room. He was wet, dirty and was ignored by everyone despite the putrid smell he gave off.

Of the six tables in the room, one was empty in the corner near the hearth. As soon as they crowded around it, a woman came over. As she took their orders of stew and ale, she kept staring at Elgin, while taking quick glances at the others. She jumped in alarm when she heard a shout then hurried away in that direction.

"This place is a shit hole. I've been in a lot of them, so I know," Tolin grimaced as he looked around the room. He counted fifteen people, not counting them, noticing that most were armed. "

"No arguments, here," Cai had also been in many taverns while traveling wherever his father decided to send him. This one was as expected.

A few minutes later their food was served along with a passable brew. Josiah, the oldest in Cai's group, struck up a conversation with some locals at the next table. Josiah was quite good at getting local gossip and feeling people out. He looked like a kindly father with his cropped beard and hair shot through with silver, brown eyes that crinkled in the corners when he smiled and the languid demeanor he tended to present. Often before they knew it, people would tell Josiah just about anything Josiah wanted to learn. They never guessed that Josiah was also a gifted assassin and spy having earned his surname Quickblade when he was still a teenager. None in his group knew how many knives Josiah carried with him, or how he was able to hide them so well.

Elgin made a face when he tasted the stew, "at least the name of the place fits. The Putrid Boar may also hint at where the meat came from for this stew."

"Dammit Elgin!" Dax growled, "I was eating this swill just fine until you opened your mouth." He threw down his spoon in disgust.

Elgin grinned when Tolin and Cai pushed their half-eaten bowls away, "you'll thank me later. At least the bread is decent."

Josiah didn't seem to be bothered by the stew as he relayed what he had learned. "The place is run by some self-proclaimed lord named Bannister. Came here from Fairshine late last summer. Seems they run through these guys quite often with peaceful breaks in between. This one and his cronies rob, cheat, steal and enslave; typical, provincial lawlessness. He's currently responsible for keeping this lovely village in its current state."

"So Fairshine is just as bad if not worse," Dax wrinkled his nose as someone walked by passing gas, "remind me to write your father and thank him for the lovely province you were given to oversee."

#

What was I thinking? Rinna thought as she crouched in the loft of the stable trying to talk her heart rate into slowing down. She had just threatened three armed men. The only thing in her favor had been the hooded wrap she had worn to keep off the rain and the element of surprise.

The men were strangers, likely new guards for Lord Bannister. Garrett said the man had a problem keeping them. She knew she was breaking the rules by trying to find Garrett after dark, but her concern for his well-being overcame her apprehension. She hoped the cover of night and the rain would make things easier for them both to slip away once he was found.

Why she had picked up the pitchfork leaning against a cart by the smithy and confronted the soldiers wasn't hard to figure out. She was fourteen when she witnessed the rape and murder of a girl not much older. Rinna had become separated from Garrett in the market at the capitol, her only, and his fourth trip to Fairshine since the kingdom had fallen to the Kheator Empire. He never knew what she had witnessed, only that she was adamant about leaving.

Seeing the girl, knowing she was terrified and helpless, Rinna wading in to help without even thinking. She'd been aware of a group of men approaching as she was poised with the pitchfork realizing that her bluff was failing. Yet they too had merely stood in the shadows and watched. She shivered at how close to a victim she herself had come.

Hearing noises down below, she peeked through a crack in the floor of the loft. People were bringing in their horses for stabling, one so tall she could have touched the red hair on the top of his head with a finger poked through the cracks on the floor. Another with long glossy black hair with blue beads braided in paused directly below her. She shrank back away from the crack as she saw him begin to look up. Rinna wondered if they were the ones who'd watched her confrontation. There was no way to know. Now that spring had arrived and the pass opening back up, the stream of goods, and people would be flowing again. She listened as they settled their horses and complained about the quality of the stable.

They soon left talking about being hungry. Rinna waited a few minutes then climbed down from the loft. She looked at the new horses in the stall, missing Butters who they had to sell years ago. Eight horses acknowledged her presence, their heads poking out of the stalls in curiosity. Three were sturdy pack horses hinting that the newcomers had traveled for some time. The other five were the horses of warriors. She'd seen plenty of them growing up. She went to each one, giving noses a gentle scratch, impressed at how well cared for they all were, even if they were a bit thin. She knew that forage over the pass was in short supply this time of year which is why few crossed until later. One of the horses was much larger than the others. He rolled his eyes, his ears flat as she approached.

"I'm sorry I don't have a treat for you, big boy," standing on the board just out of the reach of the horse's teeth she investigated his stall. It was a very tight fit, with his rump and his shoulders both touching the ends of the stall.

"No wonder you are unhappy. You don't have enough room in there," Rinna had grown into the skinny arms and legs she had possessed as a child, her dark curls wrestled into a waist length braid that never quite managed to stay neat. Her body had developed lean muscles thanks to the amount of physical activity she did, but she'd never gained much in height topping out at five feet four, short in a land where most women were at least two to three inches taller.

Jumping down, she reached up and caught the big horse's

bridle, then opened the gate of the stall. The horse's ears were still flat, distrustful of the strange person holding him. He tried to toss his head free, but Rinna had too firm a hold as he pulled her off the ground.

"My Butters used to try that little trick too. It won't work with me. I'll just hang on until you get tired of me swinging off your nose," she reached with her free hand, stroking his muzzle, then standing on tiptoe reached to stroke the horse's neck, calming him, as she pulled the reins over his head. She looped the reins to a post, then dragged out his feeding trough. The big horse nudged Rinna's shoulder as she pulled the trough into place.

"You are welcome," she said giving his nose one more stroke. She knew the men were probably more mercenaries heading to Fairshine and deserved no kindness, she just couldn't stand the idea of the horse spending the night stuffed into that stall.

Leaving the stable, she put her hood back over her head to keep off the rain and headed towards the nearby tavern and the real reason for her trip to Ragan. Over time, Garrett's health suffered along with his outlook on life. The joints in his hands became arthritic, and he started having issues with staying warm. A respiratory ailment a year ago, had robbed Garrett of much of his stamina and left him with a chronic cough. He had always been a complainer, but now it was worse, as the pain in his joints and his cough made it harder to hoe their large garden or tend to the nets. By then trips to Fairshine had ceased, his finally giving up on ever returning to the life he once had.

With the arrival of Lord Bannister, Garrett had insisted she stay, and he make any trip to the village. She'd not been to the village since and when there, had only recognized three people. Garrett kept her apprised of who was in charge and their descriptions. It helped her know who to avoid when she did make a trip. Rinna was fine with the arrangement, until he started returning minus most of the goods he'd intended to trade for.

He had not returned home in two days, which meant that Garrett had likely accumulated a debt again. They had sold Butters, the dog and two of her three precious books long ago for needed supplies. That past winter Garrett begun drinking, his excuse, that it helped with the pain in his joints. It had cost an entire harvest of rare mushrooms Rinna had hoped to sell for new shoes for them both, the last time. Her remaining book was in a pouch she had slung over her shoulder. She grieved for what she was having to do, while being furious at the man who had put them both in such a position. She'd not been able to find him anywhere else, so knew he was at the Putrid Boar.

The main room of the tavern was noisy and pungent, smelling of body odor, garlic and spilt ale, overlaid with despair and death. This late in the day, it was full and noisy, with slave girls serving the customers food, drink or flesh. Rinna looked around for Garrett, finding him after a minute, sprawled over the hearth. Her heart dropped as she saw Donner, the tavern owner, heading towards her his smile leering as he approached. It was reputed that he rarely left his spot behind the bar.

"I'm here to pay that man's debt. How much, how much did he drink?" Rinna looked up at Donner as she pointed towards Garrett. She hoped the pounding of her heart was not visible through the layers of clothes she wore.

"One mug," Donner said as he laughed, "your father drank exactly one mug of ale, before he keeled over dead."

Rinna's eyes widened in horror as Donner relished in her reaction to the news, "dead? How?" she turned to go to Garrett as Donner grabbed her arm.

Donner bent down close; the smell of alcohol strong on his breath, "who the hell knows, but I don't care. I just care about the matter of payment and you'll do nicely."

"You said he only drank one mug of ale," Rinna tried to free her arm without success. *I should have waited until someone came out and asked them if Garrett was here*, she thought as panic built.

"That doesn't count the ale or the lime I've had to throw

on his corpse for two days until you came to collect him, nor the boarding fees for the space he's taken up. It added up quickly, and I know you don't have the means to pay," Donner dragged her through the tavern as she did everything she could do resist. Most patrons recognizing entertainment had since turned their attention to Rinna and Donner. Some, she noticed, bowed their heads.

"But I can pay!" Rinna shouted as she jerked her arm out of his grasp, stepped back and got her book of plants out of her bag holding it out to Donner. "This book was once housed in the royal library in Fairshine. It should more than cover the cost."

The room quieted as soon as the occupants realized what was happening. Donner frowned as he took the book from Rinna, his face reddening in anger. Books were practically non-existent in post conquest Arowana and what Rinna had just handed him was not what he had expected at all. Everyone watched as she backed away from him intending to make a dash for the exit. Donner knowing what she was intending, laughed and threw the book into the fireplace. It immediately began to smolder.

"No!" Rinna cried taking two steps towards the fireplace before Donner grabbed the loose tail of her headwrap and jerked pulling her backwards and onto the floor. She freed herself from the wrappings, as she tried to scramble away. Donner caught the end of her braid then dragged her towards the stairs. Her screams could be heard all the way as she fought for release. A few minutes later, he came back downstairs, and announced that bidding would begin for use of his newest acquisition.

Four

Cai and the rest of his group watched in growing anger at the plight of the young woman and the scheming of the tavern owner. Her presence explained the man laying at the hearth, and of a desperate attempt to save them both. The tavern owner's disregard for the book was unexpected. Fairshine had once been renowned for its library. Any book from there would have been extremely valuable.

Elgin held Cai's arm during the exchange as Cai was ready to do battle to help the pretty girl. "We are outnumbered and stuck in a corner. We can't help her if we get ourselves killed."

"We aren't if we have Rajah with us," Cai leaned back in his chair frustrated and angry.

"You know damned well, Rajah is sleeping off a belly full of prey, cousin," Elgin watched the reactions of those in the room as the young woman was dragged upstairs. He had pulled up his cloak to hide his ears, after the stares from the barmaid, "we aren't likely to see him for two more days."

Dax stroked his beard as he looked around the room, "you know, we could create a diversion and see if one of us could get the girl out another way."

"Just think, I could be languishing in that prison in Beldeene, waiting on my execution," Tolin had been caught sneaking out the bedroom window belonging to the wife of the commandant of the garrison in that town, "thanks, so much for breaking me out."

"You are welcome," Cai took a sip of his ale. He'd met Tolin through Elgin. Tolin had been working as a bouncer in a brothel, Elgin sent there to fetch a tax collector who had absconded with an entire district's worth of tax levies. The tax collector wasn't there having already been thrown out of the brothel by Tolin who took offense to the man abusing the girl he had hired. He helped Elgin find the thief who then took him to meet Cai. In Tolin, Cai found another good friend.

"What do you have in mind Dax?"

Dax told them which had Josiah laughing, "I happen to see a couple of bottles of what may prove to be a better-quality beverage than what the owner serves to his usual customers. We need supplies, I like stealing from cruel assholes. You get things started. I'll meet you back at the stables," Josiah picked up his mug and made his way to the bar.

Cai and Elgin slipped out of the tavern just as Dax stood up and bellowed that the corpse at the hearth was moving while Tolin made some loud moaning sounds. Cai couldn't help but laugh as people almost knocked him over trying to get out of the tavern. He and Elgin separated, going opposite directions around the building to try to find a different way inside. The rain falling in steady sheets, turned the ground into a slippery quagmire of mud and muffling what was going on inside. He turned into an alley looking up for a ledge or a window when he saw movement at the eaves of the thatched roof. He stepped into the shadows and watched as a person climbed up and out of the thatch. They then hung on with both hands as their feet hunted for a window ledge. From there they lowered themselves again before dropping to the ground. There the slippery mud caused them to lose their balance and fall.

Her cry as she fell told Cai that the person must be the woman they were trying to rescue. He watched as she picked herself up and ran into the woods at the back of the building.

A moment later Elgin made his way around the corner where he joined Cai, "there's the kitchen, but it's guarded. I didn't find another way in."

"We don't need to. She got herself out," Cai explained while they walked back to the front of the tavern. There they met Dax and Tolin who were huddled under the eaves of an empty shop.

"That was fun," said Dax, "half the place ran out, afraid that girl's dead father was rising, his shade bent on vengeance, the other started fighting over who had won the bidding war on the girl. It was made more fun by Tolin raising the bet by just a few pennies every time someone made a bid."

"It was profitable," Tolin had two new knives stuck into his belt and a loaf of bread wrapped in a towel under his arm. He gestured at the bread, "breakfast."

They all watched as Donner stomped outside. He spent a moment looking up and down the street then made his way to where Cai and the others stood.

"You. Did you see her? Did you see that thieving bitch?"

"See who?" Elgin asked, trying not to laugh as Josiah strolled out the front door of the tavern with a bundle over his shoulder. Others left carrying items in their hands as they took furtive glances in the direction towards Donner to ensure that he was turned away before hurrying off into the rain drenched night.

"My new slave. She put a hole in my roof and escaped."

"From the second floor?" Dax scoffed, "she was a little bitty thing."

"To you, most things are itty bitty," Tolin's joke made everyone laugh but Donner who turned his back with a murmured curse. He saw that at his patrons were trying to rob him. Waving his arms and shouting, he hurried back to salvage what was left and to throw out everyone who wasn't trapped working for him.

The entertainment over, Cai and the others went back to the stable where they had put their horses, intending to sleep in the loft. He stopped in surprise seeing Dax's horse Devil out of his stall tied to a post.

"What the fuck," Cai heard Dax say behind him.

"What I was thinking," Cai said. Devil let no one touch him but Dax. The horse had not been happy about being put into the too small stall. Someone had not only moved the horse, but made sure he was comfortable and fed.

"Well that tavern owner plans on going after the girl in the morning. After he sobers up, and gets help," Josiah said climbing up the ladder into the loft, "says she and her father had a place somewhere along the lake. No one seemed to know exactly where though. I also stored our new supplies in Devil's stall before going back for a chat with the tavern owner. Glad you moved him Dax. Damned horse is too big for that stall."

"I didn't move him."

"And there is no blood or missing body parts in Devil's vicinity?" Josiah looked down from the loft in wonder, "I'd like to meet the brave idiot who did that and survived intact."

"I'm surprised you didn't slit that tavern owner's neck on the spot Josiah," Elgin was already in the loft, poking at the hay with a foot to scare off any vermin.

"Nah, no fun in that. Besides, right now he's more useful alive. He was complaining about the price of bribes to keep him in supplies going up. Those that live outside the village do their trading on the sly, so harder to catch and tax." Grunted Josiah as he climbed the ladder to the loft, "The asshole offered me a job as a guard. Apparently, he's had a bit of thievery happening when he's not looking. Told him I'd think about it while I was pocketing the tankard I had just finished emptying."

The men all laughed. Josiah was as good a thief as he was an assassin and spy. A few minutes later they had all settled down for the night listening to rain fall outside.

Cai lay awake after his friends fell asleep. As he had many nights since he was ordered to **Arowana** he what was he expected to do here. He had no love for the man who had only publicly acknowledged his parentage after Cai was an adult, and only because Cai had shown skill on the battlefield. He hated the Kheator army, their cruelty, and Corbaine's lust for land and possessions. He'd repeatedly seen the king delight in using oppression and misery to keep the populace in control, and his having no qualms in using fire magicians to commit atrocities to achieve his goals.

Cai thought again of the idea of boarding a ship and going anywhere that was not connected to the Kheator empire or find where his mother's people had fled to after their forest homes were destroyed by Corbaine's greed for lumber and slaves.

Then Cai thoughts turned to the young woman they had encountered twice that evening. She proved to be resourceful and courageous, something he wasn't used to seeing in women thanks to how the social structure of his father's empire was constructed. He knew they would be attempting to help her in the morning.

She wasn't the only one who's lives had been harmed by what his father had done. That number was too high for him to count. Still, Cai felt responsible, even though he knew he wasn't at fault and probably had little chance of making things better for anyone. He wrestled with the decision between staying or going before finally falling asleep, his mind made up.

They were across the bridge just outside the village early the next morning when Cai stopped his horse. The others rode on briefly before seeing that he had turned to look out over the lake.

"Pay up," Elgin smirked as he turned his own horse around.

Tolin grumbled as he handed Elgin one of his new daggers, "I swear you cheat, Elgin."

"Hell, I knew he'd change his mind," Dax patted Tolin on the shoulder as he passed, "he's too honorable to let that poor girl face that tavern owner by herself or to walk away when he could at least attempt to right a wrong, or in this case a village full of wrongs."

"I hope you don't mind the change in plans," Cai smiled as watched his friends return.

Josiah glanced at the others before speaking, "I for one am glad. I rather like this place. It has potential and has this beautiful road where we can control all that comes and goes giving those in Fairshine plenty to fret over."

"You want to stay," Cai wasn't surprised, of all his friends, Josiah had been the one who had most advocated for at least trying to make a stab of trying to settle in. All of them hated how things were done in the empire and had suffered in one way or another.

"I want to stay," Josiah looked at the mountains, watching as the sunrise made the shadows track lower and lower from the upper peaks, "I'm tired of doing the bidding of others, risking my neck all over the fucking empire with nothing to show for it. I had a home once, and a family. I lost them. I'd like it again, and here is as good a place as any."

"This place is pretty isolated, with a small group of thugs controlling people just trying to survive. This should be a prosperous village," Elgin had been immediately drawn to the forest and the clean pristine air. He had never seen his homeland far to the north west, but he'd heard that it had once been something like where he currently stood.

Cai nodded. He thought Elgin would find the environment appealing, "what about you Dax?"

"I'm for staying," Dax scratched his chin under his beard, "besides I don't like ships."

"I would like to break that tavern owner's arms. How he runs that place is obscene," Tolin didn't care either way. He saw in his friends something he admired and respected feeling honored to be included.

"All of you are in agreement with the chain of command if we live through the day?" Cai was relieved everyone agreed. A decision had finally been reached. He watched as the village began their day. He saw a guard on the top of the fortress standing in place watching them. He had a vague idea of what needed to be done here. They would need a strategy. He hoped he hadn't doomed them all.

"Let's go see if we can help the woman from last night," Cai turned his horse Lucky back down the road as the forest quickly surrounded them.

"Think she has family?" Tolin asked, "It would be a tough life if it was just her and her father."

Dax spoke, "I'm wondering where in the hell she got a book from," Once out of sight of the village, they headed into the forest to circumvent the lake, "if it was from Fairshine, then how did she come by it?"

Cai had wondered about that as well. Books were rare and expensive. He and Elgin had been taught to read and write, but only because of their connection to the crown. Unless one was wealthy, a member of the fire magician/priesthood or a scribe few were literate. His own father was illiterate, trusting his advisors to do the job for him. There were a few printing presses scattered about the empire, and some skilled in making paper. Fairshine once had one of the larger concentrations of them, and the biggest library on the continent. Now all that was gone. The woman's possession of something that valuable was a curiosity.

"That idiot tavern owner didn't realize that he threw a fortune into that fire," Elgin shook his head. It had been a few years since he'd held a book in his hands. He missed it. That anyone would throw something so valuable away angered him. "She could have bought the whole damned village with that book and she tried to use it to pay off her father's bar tab."

Josiah voiced what they all knew, "she was desperate, and I doubt it was the first time she'd had to pull her father's nuts out of the fire."

"That asshole knew it too," Tolin ducked under a low hanging branch as they followed along the trail, "who throws ale and lime on a body until family shows up just so the dead guy's debt can get paid?"

"Someone greedy for a pretty new slave," Dax ducked as well. The branches hung low off any trail.

#

Rinna woke up to the sound of a woodpecker hunting for breakfast somewhere near her treehouse. The bird stopped a minute then began again, its quest for food noisy and rhythmic. The ancient pine was riddled with woodpecker holes. She sat up looking around the small space she had slept in off and on for most of the past decade. What had once been roomy as a girl was now cramped. It had taken several hours to get home. Wary of being followed, Rinna had taken a circuitous route, stopping several times to hide in a tree to scout out followers. No one had been to their house in years, but she was leery enough to not take any chances.

Making certain no one was near she had filled the strapped bag she used to gather plants, herbs and mushrooms with supplies, planning on leaving early in the morning. Once she climbed into her treehouse, she was shaking from exhaustion and grief but found it difficult to fall asleep, terrified that people would be dragging her from her bed. She slept wrapped up in her blanket that had gotten damp getting into the treehouse.

She'd slept later than she had intended as the sun's rays were already touching the upper mountain slopes when she glanced out the small window. Rinna knew she could stay no longer. To remain only meant certain slavery, if not by Donner, by someone else in Ragan. She had few options, to go over the pass and hope she could find someplace there safe, to try her luck at the ports for a passage out, or to move into the mountains and hope she could find permanent shelter near the snow line.

All were bad choices, however the third gave her the best odds of survivability. Over the years she had found places to hide supplies and a weapon or two just in case she and Garrett needed to leave their home. One of them was her intended destination, from which she would search for a more permanent residence.

She wiped her eyes with a sleeve wincing as the action made her black eye hurt. She had acquired several scrapes and bruises from Donner's treatment of the night before and the back of her head was sore where he had jerked on her braid. He'd not raped her, but she knew that it would have only been a matter of time and would have certainly faced it at the hands of one of his customers.

I've got no time for tears, she thought as they began to fall anyway. She'd cried all the way back home, not sure what hurt more, how close she had come to being under Donner's control, the loss of Garrett and her last ties to her family, or the loss of her book, one of the main things that had helped them survive the first few years and her last link to her past. Garrett hated Donner, so Rinna didn't understand why he'd ended up at the Putrid Boar. He usually did his drinking with the blacksmith at the Brass Shield, the other tavern in Ragan.

She finally got her tears under control and lifted aside the leather on the floor covering the doorway. She was about to throw down her rope stairs when she saw the cat. It was golden-brown, with taupe stripes, and was at least the size of a fully-grown mountain bear. The cat hearing her gasp, looked up with his yellow eyes. It yawned revealing its teeth with large curved upper incisors that rested on the outside of its mouth. The cat stretched, then trotted off in the direction of the lake.

Rinna remembered seeing a picture of a cat like that in a book when she was a child. The book had mentioned it was native to a land she had forgotten the name of, and that if trained from a kitten made excellent companions, bonding with its owner. They were lethal and quick with a history of being trained for war, their teeth, claws and speed making them fearsome foes. She had no idea why it was under her tree, or where it had come from. She only hoped that it wasn't waiting on her for its next meal and found something else to interest it, far away from her.

She looked out the small window which faced the lake but couldn't see the cat. She was about to look back down through the hole in the floor when she heard horses and then voices.

"There you are Rajah," a man's voice said.

Rinna could hear other voices as men poked around the little house she and Garrett had shared, but she couldn't tell what they were saying. The cat must belong to one of them, she thought. Hopefully they would take the thing and leave.

The voices got closer. She heard two of them commenting on her garden, one of them wondering what one of the plants were. There was only one window in her treehouse, the thin mica piece gleaned from a burnt-out building in Ragan long ago. It looked out over the lake, not allowing her to see down below thanks to the branches and needles of the pine tree. She didn't dare lift the cover over the entrance to her house so couldn't see who they were.

Don't look up, don't look up, Rinna thought as the voices came closer regretting not leaving last night despite how tired she had been. She heard a thud outside her little house.

"Hey Cai. Look what Rajah just found," someone said.

"Someone built a treehouse," said another.

"Think anyone's up there?" a third voice asked. Just then something heavy landed on the roof of her treehouse. Despite her trying to stay quiet, she let out a squeak, as she felt the branch sway under the extra weight.

"Yep. Someone's up there," she didn't even try to hide the screech when she saw a massive paw, batting at her little window.

"Come on down. We are not going to hurt you," a voice called up to her.

"Tell that to your friend who thinks I'm breakfast," Rinna yelled back.

"He won't eat you. I promise," the same voice said.

"I don't believe you!" Rinna wailed as she felt the branch sway under the cat's weight.

Rinna knew she was out of options. She was afraid the treehouse and the cat would all come crashing down, and that scared her enough to make the decision to leave her once haven. Hopefully they'd kill her quickly, or the cat would.

With shaking hands, she took her pack and pushed it down the hole, followed by the ladder. She climbed down halfway, then jumped the rest of the way, landing in a half crouch so she could run the few feet she'd get before the cat pounced. Looking around, Rinna found herself surrounded by five of the biggest men she'd ever seen. All wore variations of leather or plated armor mixed in with regular clothes, were armed and looked like they knew how to use their weapons.

The cat leaped down from the tree landing in front of her. Rinna backed up two steps in alarm, before freezing in place staring at its yellow eyes. The top of Rajah's head was almost to her chin. To her surprise he was purring as he stepped closer, then gently butted her with his head. The movement knocked her off her feet. The next thing she knew she was surrounded by the enormous cat who had put his head into her lap.

"I'll be damned," one of the giants around her exclaimed. Rinna placed a tentative hand on the cat's head behind one of its ears, giving the spot a slight scratch. The purring got louder as the enormous feline tilted its head under her hand pleased with the attention.

Five

One of the men squatted down in front of Rinna, "I'm curious. Did you move a rather large horse out of his stall last night?"

Rinna glanced up at him. It was a question she would have never expected him to ask. He was Kheatorian even though he lacked the reddish-brown hair and brown eyes of the Khaetor king and his people. The stubble on his face was black like that on his head, something she couldn't help but notice as he scratched his jaw.

She nodded disturbed at the sense of familiarity the man gave her, "some idiot shoved that poor horse into a stall that was much too small for him. He was quite unhappy with his accommodations."

The man grinned as he stood, his teeth white against his dark tan skin, "did you hear that Dax. She just called you an idiot."

"She also called Devil, poor horse," laughed one of the other men.

"She's got an affinity with animals. Interesting," the first man spoke again, "Okay Rajah, you can play with your pretty human later. Let her up."

"And plants, if this garden is any sign," said another man with hair the same color of the one the cat seemed to belong to. The cat got up, trotting back to the tree where it used it as a scratching post. Rinna looked up at the man who first spoke to her. She did not understand what he or the other man meant by affinity. She ignored his offered hand, getting herself back to her feet without his assistance.

"Who are you, and why have you invaded my home?" she demanded, pleased with herself that her voice didn't reveal how terrified she was.

"We were looking for Cai's cat, and for you," said the man with flaming red hair and a matching beard. His hair framed kind eyes the color of the sky on a late summer day.

"Donner. He sent you," she whispered remembering seeing him at the Putrid Boar. He stood out being the biggest man in the place.

"You mean that asshole back at the tavern?" the big man shook his head, "no little beauty. We decided he doesn't deserve you."

"No," Rinna was surrounded and had not avenue of escape. She had a knife in her pack, which was too far away. Her bow was in the house and she had one arrow left which is why she had decided to leave it behind. She didn't trust the big cat either. She turned looking from man to man trying to decide which would be the easiest to slip past.

"We have no intention of harming you," a man with a short-grizzled beard and wearing the most leather of the five stepped forward. He held his hands out, palms facing her, an attempt to show he meant no harm. She counted a fourteen knife handles peeking from their resting places on his half-sleeved vest. "I swear by the memories of my beloved wives and my favorite knives."

"Obviously we've bungled things," the first man said, "I'm Cai. The bearded giant is Dax. The fatherly looking man is Josiah, the blonde muscled one is Tolin, and that's my cousin Elgin."

Rinna eyes darted between Elgin and Cai, catching the family and racial connection something she had missed before. She'd seen pictures of elves in books when she was a child. She was too frightened to be intrigued.

"Please tell me why you are here."

"Donner," Cai answered, then quickly explained seeing the look of panic return to Rinna's face, "but not on his behalf. We thought you may want some help."

"Thank you, but I had not planned on staying around long enough for him or his slathering gang of goons to find me," Rinna snuck a glance over to her pack, "I appreciate you going through all the trouble, but it really wasn't necessary."

"Do you have any other family? We can make sure you get

there safely," Josiah could tell she was trying to remain calm as she plotted her best route for escape. He admired her fortitude.

"No, they were all killed when your king decided to murder most of us while pretending to want to marry our king's daughter," she watched as the men exchanged glances, using the opportunity to get to her pack. She pointed towards the nearby mountains. "I'm going that way. Please go a different direction."

She shouldered her pack and started walking. She'd barely made it past the house when she was pulled back by something tugging on her. She turned to see it was Rajah, a part of her pack in his mouth.

"Let go. There's nothing in there you want," she tried to pull it out of the cat's mouth, but he tugged back deciding it was a game. She pulled harder and the cloth pack ripped, her belongings spilling to the ground. The cat tossed the bag in the air then pounced on it, his tail swishing as he played with his burlap prey.

Rinna knelt picking up her things sitting them in her lap as tears streamed down her face. Cai knelt beside her to help. He'd rescued the pack from Rajah while scolding him. He tied the damaged ends together before handing it back to her.

"The five of us decided this morning that we were going to help you," he handed her the items he picked up, "we were impressed at how you handled yourself last night. It's obvious from just the bruises on your face that life just dealt you a lot of pain and loss. For that I'm sorry."

"And yet you did nothing," Rinna dapped at her eyes with a sleeve, "we've had to survive pretty much on our own for the past ten years. I don't need or want your help." She stood, holding her ruined pack close to her.

Cai looked at the woman with the bruised face holding all her worldly possessions in a bag that his cat had just ruined and knew he would do about anything just to see her smile.

"We've got company, Dax announced, "you were right Josiah, they would try to follow us," A group of men appeared out of the woods on the far end of the clearing Rinna had turned into a garden. Rinna stiffened then started to back away intending to run as far as she could. Cai stopped her, a hand on her arm.

"I want you to go with Rajah," Cai gestured with his head in the direction of Rajah who trotted over the end of his tail flicking back and forth, "He will protect you. He will not let anyone hurt you. I promise you that."

He walked back to join his friends, standing at the edge of her garden while the newcomers walked right through it. Rajah nudged Rinna with his head. She hesitated, bemused at the big cat's seeming understanding of what Cai wanted. Purring, he nudged her again, as if to herd her towards the house. A few moments ago, the creature terrified her and had just destroyed her pack, yet she felt she could trust him. She couldn't begin to fathom why.

She rested a hand on his back as he led her into the house she had shared with Garrett. He flopped down on the floor as soon as he entered. She stood at the doorway with Rajah lying beside her and watched as the five men waited on Donner and those, he brought with him to approach. She trembled when she saw Lord Bannister and members of his guard among the group as they trampled her garden.

#

Lord Bannister looked down on the five men from his horse. He initially thought they were escaped slaves. After seeing their sizes and how well armed they all were, Bannister concluded they were likely mercenaries.

"We thank you for securing one of our businessmen's valuable properties. The crown doesn't take kindly to the theft. Your work here will of course be rewarded," Bannister was a short man who had run to fat and the only one of three on a horse.

"The crown doesn't give a shit what happens here," Cai replied with more calm than he felt, "I do find it quite interesting that a tavern owner has to get a dozen men and the local official to help him go after an unarmed girl half his size."

"She also assaulted me," said one of the guards, "she tried to murder me with a pitchfork."

Dax, Tolin and Elgin begin laughing. Dax crossed his arms across his chest, "Yeah, we saw that. Three of you against a child and a young woman, who only managed to draw piss, not blood from her so-called assault."

"She owes me money, for her father defiling my tavern with his corpse," Donner remembered the men from last night. He was certain they were involved in Rinna's escape but didn't know how.

"You mean the corpse that you purposely left on your floor for two days, intending to trap her into slavery?" Cai's voice was cold with anger, "is this how the representatives and subjects of the Kheator Empire act in this province? If so, count your days numbered as it will not be allowed to continue."

"Like you can do anything. You're mercenaries or escaped conscripts and clearly outnumbered. Trying to cause trouble is just going to get you killed. But, if you survive such an ill-advised attempt to harm us, you'll fetch hefty sums in the slave markets. Stand aside or face the consequences," Bannister ordered without patience.

"Funny, I was about to say the same thing," Cai drew the sword from the sheath strapped on his back as his friends drew their own weapons. They took four steps closer to Bannister and those gathered around him.

Three of the men who had come along stepped back including the guard who Rinna had threatened with the pitchfork. They had not been expecting for Rinna to have well-armed protectors. Lord Bannister hadn't either. He just intended to demonstrate his authority to the villagers. The news of the girl also assaulting three of his guards also meant that the tavern owner wasn't getting her back, but Bannister hadn't mentioned that to Donner.

"Just who do you think you are, threatening an official of the crown and his subjects?" Bannister's sneer was weak, alarmed by the weapons and the size of the men wielding them. He was relieved when his men drew their own swords wondering what had taken them so long.

"The new Lord Governor and his council," Dax proclaimed, his voice booming loud enough to echo across the lake.

The men in the group looked back in shock. A couple of them exchanged glances, shook their heads and decided to walk back home. The rest shifted nervously. Donner scowled, seeing his prize perched at the doorway of the house. He was determined to get her back.

"They lie. They sat in my tavern just last night. The Lord Governor would have gone to the fortress, not my humble place of business."

Lord Bannister nodded, "agreed. Kill them." He smiled as he watched his soldiers rush forward to engage the interlopers.

Rinna watch as the five began to fight with the others. It took her seconds to realize that if her temporary protectors had wanted to kill all those attacking them, they could have done so easily. Instead they were disarming or injuring them. She looked down at the cat. He was curled on the floor half twisted so the front half faced up to the ceiling his paws tucked under his chin.

A couple of Bannister's guards had gone back into the forest and skirted around Cai and his men approaching from behind. She spotted them as they approached from the lake side of the house and hid behind a rack Garrett had built to stretch out hides to dry. Rinna poked at the cat with her foot.

"Do something," she hissed. Rajah merely flicked the end of his tail.

The two guards were gesturing to one another as they waited to make their move. Knowing she had to do something, Rinne picked up her bow sitting by the door. She took aim with her one arrow, releasing the bowstring just as the first man rushed Elgin hitting the guard square between his shoulder blades. Josiah turned at the man's scream killing the other guard with a thrown knife to the throat. Rajah yawned, turned back onto his stomach, stretching his paws out in front of him before settling back down again.

The death scream of the man Rinna shot ended the short battle. Those that hadn't run away when things first started, including Lord Bannister and Donner, fled following their companions leaving behind the two dead men in Rinna's garden.

Rinna's bow fell to the floor with a clatter. She'd killed a man. She only killed animals for food, and only did so when Garrett stopped being able to contribute anything to their diet or income anymore. She hadn't thought about the fact that he was a man, only that she had seconds to act and that her target was moving. She backed into a corner as she saw Cai walking towards the house, the others behind him.

"You saved my life," Elgin stood in the tiny house next to his cousin, "for that I am forever in your debt," He bowed slightly, a hand to his heart.

"You. You are all my enemy. You killed my family, destroyed my home, ruined my country," Rinna pointed to Dax, "he's the new Lord Governor, likely as awful as the last four, and I don't know why your cat slept through the whole thing."

Cia took stock of the one room house. It didn't look very sturdy, but it was clean. Bundles of fragrant herbs hung from the ceiling. Two beds sat on opposite ends with a table in the middle. The small fireplace was cold with battered cookware sitting on the tiny hearth. He could tell Rinna and her father had lived a step or two above starvation.

"Rajah was told to keep you safe. He did his job," Cai took a step closer, "we are not the enemy. We are just stuck having to live under the same king. We had all decided to take the first ship we could buy passage for or steal until we walked into that hellhole of a village across the lake."

"He's right, we were planning on leaving," Tolin picked up the bow Rinna had dropped, leaning it against the wall, "As for us being the ones who did any of the things you accuse us of, you are wrong. Most of us weren't much older than you when that happened. Josiah was probably old enough, but he hates

Corbaine ever since the man tried to hire Josiah to kill his own brother. Cai rescued me from a hangman's noose."

Elgin sat cross legged on the floor taking out of piece of cloth to clean his sword, "Dax, well he didn't like the idea of rape and pillage when he was conscripted into the king's army when he was fourteen. As soon as he could, he took every weapon he could carry and took off. I grew up a slave, and Cai's mother was one. His father just happens to be the tyrant we have to call emperor, and Cai, not Dax is the one stuck with the thankless job of Lord Governor."

Rinna took a harder look at Cai understanding why he looked familiar. His father's image was seared into her memory, as was his magician. Cai must favor his mother, but she could see the resemblance to the Khaetor monarch in his warriors build, his skin tone, his nose and mouth and how he stood. She sat on the floor, and pulled her knees up to her chest, wishing she was in a tree instead.

"I don't understand. Why did he send you, and not with an army and one of those horrible magicians? Why did he destroy everything, and just leave a few of his soldiers and officials behind to make things even worse? Why should I believe such a story?"

"My father only cares about the taking, not the taking care of," Cai found her questions interesting, and yet a challenge as if she were testing him, "as to why me? Probably to get rid of me. I was promised assistance to bring order and prosperity to the province. Instead I had the decree delivered to me, told to gather my things and go with nothing."

Rinna tilted her head, "what does the decree say? There should be something there that tells you what the title gives you in power, along with declarations of allegiance to the crown, civil and military orders, the collection of taxes, and plans for improvements or changes."

The way she phrased the question and her knowledge intrigued Cai. *How would she know what's in a decree*, he wondered? The decree is official and minus any such details."

"What do you mean...Oh, never mind," Rinna put her head down on her knees. Things were happening too fast for her to keep up. She'd learned to adjust to quickly changing scenarios since she was eleven and knew it would be awhile if ever that she'd have a normal life. She wanted to run and realized that her chance had evaporated. To show her face back in the village meant her death. Now that he knew where she lived, Donner would return or send one of his men if she stayed.

Yet their story had a ring of truth to it. So far, these men had not harmed her. In fact, they had protected her from a fate she was too terrified to consider. They presented confidence and authority without the overweening mindset she'd come to expect from those in charge.

She stood smoothing escaped curls from her face. Holding her head high, she stood, walked past Cai, Tolin and Elgin and back outside. Rajah had curled up into a ball, enjoying the warmth from a mid-morning sunbeam. She stood outside the house watching as Dax and Josiah began to dig graves for the men she and Josiah had killed in her rows of young squash. The men's horses were tethered at the far end of her ruined garden eating the tops off her carrots. Cai, Elgin and Tolin followed her outside. She turned and looked up at Cai.

"I want to see it Lord Governor. I want to see that decree."

The decree?" Cai didn't understand why the woman whose name he didn't even know yet wanted to see it. It had taken him and the others five seconds to see that she was smart, courageous and resourceful but why would a beaten up, exhausted woman on the fringes of what was barely a society want to see it?

"I assure you it's real, it has the emperor's seal."

"I don't care about the seal. I don't care about the official ceremony granting you the job, how much food was at the celebration banquet or what everyone was wearing," Rinna snapped. She took a breath to calm herself. It wasn't working, "I care about what I and the others who live here get to expect; more of the same, or worse? I want to know if you are lying. I want to know who the hell you people are and what you intend, decree or not."

She watched brokenhearted as her garden entered its death throes as the two dead men were dumped into their shallow graves. She wanted to lay on the ground with her dug up squash plants and dry up and die with them. Instead she channeled her grief and her fear into anger, "as bad as this is..."

She couldn't finish the sentence that ended with the words, *I know worse.* Instead she went to her garden. Picking up whatever the men from the village had dropped, she threw them as far as she could into the lake. Then she started on the squash. She'd had such hope for them, having bartered hard for the vegetable seeds. She had planned on selling them at the market and try to see if she how well they would store over winter, intending on trying several different things. They had just begun to go from seedling to small vining plants reaching to entwine each other and she had no seeds left.

She pulled up a trampled plant and walked to the lake's edge where she threw it. She watched it float in the mild current wondering if it would make its way to the stream near town and float downstream to the harbor.

She turned to get another seeing Cai a few steps away. He held out a rolled parchment. Rinna wiped her hands on her tunic so dirt wouldn't mar the paper, "I'll let you look at it if you tell me your name."

"It's Rinna. Norinna actually, but I hate that," her anger fled as she felt the texture of the paper he placed in her hand. She'd not seen any new writing or held any paper other than her books since she was a child. Despite its contents it was of great value to her. She sat down on the grass by the strip of sand along the lake shore as she carefully opened the decree, smoothing it out on her lap. The document was short.

I hereby decree that Prince Cai Sunspear, bastard son of Emperor and King, Corbaine Sunspear, ruler of the Kheator Empire is now and forever Lord Governor of the province of Arowana if he can take and hold the seat.

The seal looked official and it was witnessed by Rocnor Fireweave, Grand Court Wizard. Most Supreme High Priest of Irator, God of Cleansing Fire, Vizier and chief advisor in the service of Corbaine, king and emperor of the Kheator Empire.

"At least you didn't bring him along," Rinna rolled up the parchment and handed it back to Cai who had sat down beside her.

"Who?"

"Rocnor, the evil magician with too many words after his name," Rinna picked up a blade of grass, peeling off slices, "you've been sent on a fool's errand. Emperor Corbaine didn't intend on you succeeding much less surviving."

"No, he didn't," He watched her quietly concentrating on the task of reducing the blade of grass to a sliver impressed with her accurate assessment. She held it out letting it go to drift away in the breeze, "how do you know who Rocnor is?"

"Because once, in a far different life, I had to share a meal with him," Rinna's voice was so low, that Cai had to lean forward to hear her, "he sat no further from me than you are now."

Cai had been terrified of the man as a child as were most children. He knew that fire magicians fed off other's fear among other things. He'd been fortunate never having to be any closer to fire magicians than the balcony of his father's expansive throne room.

"Whoever sat you next to him was being cruel. How old were you?"

"Eleven. I know it was cruel," Rinna stared at her hands in her lap, "Emperor Corbaine must have noticed me looking at the slave he was fondling as my family and I were being formally introduced. I was more interested in her than him. I felt awful for her, mad that no one said a word as she was being abused in front of everyone while the king ignored the princess, he was supposed to marry standing right next to him."

"Sounds just like something he would have done. He was probably amused that you were probably the only one to dare challenge him even in such a mild manner. You being a little girl doing it insulted him. Your seating arrangement was intended to terrify you," Cai was curious how she endured it, "how did you manage it?"

"I recognized him and your father as dangerous. So did my father. I listened to Rocnor's veiled threats wondering why the king had someone so obviously insane as an advisor, then decided to do what I always did when my mother lectured me about my many deficiencies, ignore him," Rinna shuddered at the memory, something she had forgotten, "the longer I pretended to forget he existed the more heat he gave off."

Cai's admiration of Rinna's courage went up significantly. Rocnor would have roasted her on the spot anywhere else. He must have been ordered to restrain himself until the appointed hour.

Dax neared, "the horses are all watered and ready to go, and if someone will wake Rajah up, we can get back to that village and give that fat lord something else to run away from."

Rinna didn't move as Cai stood. Staring out at the lake, she said, "the name of the village is Ragan as is the lake. The fat lord is named Bannister. The fastest way to get rid of him is to poison his food if you can get close enough as it is said he is always eating. I have something in the house that would do the trick."

She picked up a blade of grass and started to demolish it as she had the first, "no one remains of the original population, being killed by Corbaine's soldiers. Some are slaves, some just trying to survive, people who are hiding from someone meaner, or agents of the current Lord Governor. Trust no one. In fact, it's probably easier to kill most and start over. It's been done several times before, but the results have always been what you see now. Better yet, stick to your original plan and get on the first ship that will let you."

"Rinna?" Cai didn't understand why she didn't get up, didn't realize that he was trying to help her.

"Just don't--don't die."

Six

"Now we'll be having none of that little beauty," before Rinna could respond Dax had swept her up into his arms and was walking back to the nearby horses.

"Put me down! Dammit, put me down!" she stopped yelling as she was set sidesaddle atop Devil. The horse turned its head and nickered a greeting.

Dax climbed up behind her, "don't you worry. I'm not going to let you fall off. Riding a horse takes a bit of getting used to."

"I know how to ride a-- Oh!" Rinna clung to Dax as he reared Devil back than directed the horse into a gallop.

Dax's laughter echoed through the forest as they rode through the trees. Rinna kept her eyes closed and her face in Dax's beard after seeing the speed at which they rode. She'd never been able to take Butters faster than a trot.

It seemed like only minutes later and they were in the village. Rinna opened her eyes when they stopped. To her dismay they were in front of the fortress and had gained the attention of the guards and most of the villagers.

"You can let go now little beauty," Rinna realized she had not only a tight grip on Dax's shirt, but also part of his beard.

"I'm sorry. I wasn't expecting the ride to be so—fast," Dax's laughter was loud but warm.

"That was just Devil showing off. He likes you," he dismounted taking Rinna right with him, ensuring that her feet were steady underneath her. He put Devil's reins in her hands, and her torn pack over her shoulder, "keep him company for a minute."

She stood in the space under Devil's neck who had moved so his head was over her left shoulder. She stroked his muzzle absently as she watched the rest of her five companions arrive then have a very animated conversation with the guards. Cai and the others had their weapons out and were doing a good job of intimidation. Most of the residents of Ragan had stopped what they were doing, watching things unfold with interest.

Hearing a disturbance behind her, she peeked around the

big horse as Rajah approached, people scrambling to get out his way. The residents dispersed seeking a safer vantage point to watch. Her lips turned upward as the saber cat plopped down a few feet away and began to wash a paw. The animal was big and terrifying, and yet with similar mannerisms to a house cat. She felt quite safe in the presence of the horse and the cat, assured that neither intended her harm. The realization was unexpected yet a relief.

A few minutes later Elgin separated himself from the rest. He held out a crooked arm to Rinna, "my lady. We have acquired accommodations for our stay."

The guards had lowered their weapons and had sidled off into the village, something Rinna found interesting wondering what the newcomers had said to have them concede to easily.

"Please don't call me lady, Lord Elgin, I never liked it, and Lord Dax told me to stay here with his horse," she took Elgin's arm anyway not knowing what else to do.

"Your response tells me there is much more to you than meets the eye Lady Rinna. Despite your dislike for the title, it very much fits," he smiled at her tossing a title right back at him as they walked towards the entrance of the fortress. No one had ever called him a lord before.

"More like less," Rinna scoffed. She looked in interest as they passed through the gates of the fortress. Garrett had worked on the construction when the village was being rebuilt. It was the first building started and the last finished and the only one that had any amount of stone. She had never seen the inside, despite Garrett working on it off and on for over three years.

Entering the courtyard, she saw Lord Bannister at the far end where the keep stood, speaking to one of the members of his council who ran the nearby quarry. Bannister was sitting on a large high-backed chair built wide enough to fit his bulk. Others who controlled all the commerce and land in Ragan ringed around him in a show of unified support. Rinna noticed a few people milling around the edges, while guards stood at the entrance to the inside of the fortress, and at intervals all around the inside of the courtyard. She glanced up expecting to see more guards up on the walls surrounding the courtyard but didn't see anyone.

Cai who had walked on ahead had taken an assessment of where everyone was and was also surprised at the lack of defenders on the wall, something not missed by the rest of his friends. The buzz of voices in the courtyard, some angry some curious died off without warning. His gaze was drawn to the entrance of the courtyard seeing what had stolen everyone's attention.

She had one hand in his cousin's arm, the other holding Devil's reins. Rajah trotted beside them. She looked regal even wearing a ragged tunic and torn pants, her feet bare. Her bruised face was one of calm confidence, her hair a crown of velvety curls, that was barely held under control by a long windblown braid. Elgin stopped once he reached Cai. He released Rinna's arm bowing slightly to her before stepping aside.

"Did you know you brought Devil in here with you?" Cai asked as he bent close to her. He took Devil's reigns out of her hand then tucked her arm in his. Rinna looked behind her, sure enough, Devil was there, Rajah beside him.

"No," he watched her mask of confidence slip, while Elgin failed to hide a smile.

"Put that arrogant queen look back on your face and pretend you intended to do exactly what you did," Cai tugged her closer, "walking in here on the arm of a full-blooded elf with an oversized war horse and a saber cat in your wake, just made one hell of an impression."

Rinna glanced warily over at the lord and his courtiers and saw them staring at her, Bannister's mouth was gaping. Hovind who ran the woodcutters into early graves looked an odd shade of grey. She tilted her head up straightening her shoulders, giving herself as self-important a look as her black eye, unshod feet and ragged clothes could give her. Her mother would have approved, she thought realizing that those lessons in deportment and court manners had a purpose after all. Cai chuckled softly as he observed her shore up her outward demeanor.

Rinna knew she had just thrown her lot in with Prince Cai and his friends. It was probably one of the stupidest decisions she had ever made, but for the first time in a decade she felt safe. It was ironic because they were in anything but a safe situation. She blinked as Cai nudged her out of her thoughts. They had stopped at the steps in front of Bannister and his advisors. Bannister's expression was haughty, looking down at her with a gleam. She had no doubt what that look meant, shivering at the thought.

Cai glanced down at her, then Bannister, not missing the exchange. He turned her to face away from the fortress lord. Rinna noticed that Dax was beside her, Josiah to his side, Elgin and Tolin on the other side of Cai.

She jumped when Dax spoke, his voice echoing against the walls of the courtyard, "all hail, His Highness, Prince Cai Sunspear, Lord Governor of Arowana, son of Corbaine Sunspear, King and Master of the Empire of Khaetor. The Lord Governor and his council of elders greet you," Rinna looked around at the people in the courtyard gauging their expressions. She heard Bannister's gasp of outrage, seeing in the faces of those in the courtyard a mixture of shock and distrust.

Dax continued, "this is the Lord Governor's first decree. Lord Bannister and his courtiers are banished from the fortress and will need to petition to gain reentry, as are the guards and soldiers under his command. Failure to vacate immediately will be on their heads. Prince Cai, our Lord Governor and his counsel will listen to petitions, complaints and suggestions from the people of Ragan tomorrow. Until then the fortress is officially closed."

Bannister, his face red with fury stood as he shouted, "you cannot do this. We outnumber you. Guards attack!"

Rinna cringed into Cai as she began to turn in reaction to Bannister's shout.

"Don't look back my love. He's not worth it," Cai said, feeling her tremble as she did as he asked. Tolin had drawn his twin swords, Josiah daggers, and were facing the men on the steps. Facing the courtyard, Dax had a sword out almost taller than she was and Elgin an arrow notched into his longbow. Cai only held Rinna's hand in his arm not having moved to face the former leader. He had a commanding look on his face, his head turning slowly to observe how people in front of him reacted.

A few ran forward swords raised stopping in their tracks as Rajah roared. The saber cat then crossed the distance between himself and the soldiers in a single leap landing on one of them, where he crouched over the man holding him down with a paw. His companions needed no further motivation. They turned, running out of the courtyard as fast as they could.

"Some of you have already seen that we are not to be taken lightly. We've buried two of your members after their unprovoked attack on us and a member of your community. Lady Rinna and this village are now under our protection," Cai's voice was a rich baritone to Dax's melodious bass. "My patience grows short. Leave now, or the next man Rajah pounces on will not live to tell the tale," Rajah's tail flicked back in forth as he crouched over the trapped man.

It didn't take long for Josiah and Tolin to usher out the soldiers including the man Rajah had held pinned down. Bannister wanted to go inside and retrieve things, shouting red faced as he made his demands. Dax and Tolin let him rant for a few minutes while blocking his way into the fortress's keep. Then they shoved the man into a nearby barrel and carried it with Bannister screeching insults all the way out of the fortress. They brought the empty barrel back inside setting it down near the stables. They then closed and barred the heavy wooden doors where Rajah remained, having discovered a patch of sun to curl up in.

"Well that's everyone but those inside," Elgin observed. He, Rinna and Cai had moved aside to stay out of the way while Tolin and Dax had their fun tossing out the fortress lord and his advisors. Josiah stayed by the gate tossing a knife into the same spot on one of the gate doors until they closed.

Cai nodded after a moment, "wait here."

He released his hold on Rinna's hand. He went with the others to unload then stable their horses. Rinna sat down on the steps not trusting her legs to support her weight as she watched them work, talking among themselves, seeming to be at ease. If she hadn't seen it with her own eyes, she would have never believed five men and an enormous cat could clear out the courtyard with so little effort. Rinna had no idea what she was doing here, why they kept calling her lady, when retaliation was going to start. She rested her elbows on her knees, head in hands as she looked around the courtyard. It looked slovenly and smelled of manure and something rotten.

She wanted to go home. *Maybe I can salvage some of the garden*, she thought, then remembered that Donner and Bannister were out there and very unhappy with what had happened. Now that they had seen her with the new Lord Governor, her home was less safe than ever.

"Lady Rinna?" Rinna looked up seeing Cai standing in front of her, "we have things to do inside." He held out a hand to her.

Rinna again ignored the hand as she stood up dusting off her tunic, "why am I here?"

"Isn't the reason obvious?"

"You could have left me outside, or at my home. I already had plans for my own future," Rinna was impressed at the display of strength and authority by Cai and his friends but knew the treachery of Bannister and his ilk, "besides once they rediscover their courage, there will be retaliation. Have you considered that?"

"I am making this up as I go along."

Rinna blinked in surprise, "you're joking."

"No, little beauty," Dax said, "he's not. We have a general idea of what needs to be done here. It's the details we are lacking."

Despite herself, Rinna's lips twitched in amusement as she saw Dax wink at her.

"We're all going to die."

Cai laughed as tucked her arm in his, "absolutely, but not today."

Rinna tried and failed to pull her arm away, "you didn't answer the question."

"I know I didn't," Cai walked inside the others following behind. They passed a short hallway into a large main room with tables and benches set up, one table on a platform with chairs lined up on one side. A slave ran up to them, then prostrated himself before them.

"What the fuck," Tolin stepped back, "please, sir, man, whatever your name is, stand up."

The slave got back on his feet, looking to each of the men before settling on Rinna, his eyes confused and pleading. He was middle aged, his height all in his upper body, a gifted leatherworker Garrett traded with. Garrett had mentioned not seeing him in a while. She now knew why. She wasn't dressed any better than he was, so was surprised that he looked to her for guidance.

"Hello Patrick. Could you please bring some food and, uhm, ask everyone to come in here?"

"Yes, Rin--Lady Rinna," Patrick stammered as he glanced quickly between the big men with Rinna. He left the room as fast as his legs would take him.

She tugged at her arm in Cai's, who had not let go of her. She noted that the top of her head reached his collarbone, "I... That was what you wished for?"

Cai nodded, "unless I'm wrong, we will have food and everyone who is inside before us shortly. So yes, I believe you just made a difficult task much easier."

Rinna suspected that he had anticipated more conflict and the need for hostility, something she knew they could accomplish in fierce and efficient order already having witnessed it once. Dismissing the memory of the short battle and her role in it that had destroyed her garden as something she'd deal with later, she instead looked about the dining hall with a critical eye.

Garrett would have been appalled to see the level of squalor in the home of a lord. They had possessed almost nothing of value, and their home had been built from mostly scavenged materials, but he had always insisted on things being as neat and in as good order as they could make it. Garrett had also constantly drilled her on manners, diplomacy, the management of a household. She had fiercely resented his lessons, not understanding why they were necessary. She remembered how just a few days ago he had lectured her on the protocol of guild leadership and structure.

Garrett had always irritated her with his snobbish demeanor and his difficulty to adapt to their new life. She missed him, imagining him complaining in horror at the state of the room while feeling guilty for never appreciating what he had given her.

"Lady Rinna? Are you alright?" Cai had his arm around her waist, a concerned look on his face. Rinna had been so lost in her thoughts that she didn't even feel the tears tracking down her face.

She nodded, dabbing her face with the hem of her blanket as she pulled away realizing for the first time, she still had it draped around her. To her relief he let her go, "I'm fine."

"I don't believe you, but we have other things to discuss," he watched as slaves set out food on the high table. They waited until the slaves were done and gathered together. Cai counted twelve men and women, all wearing rags, many also with bruises. He looked at Elgin whose eyes revealed the pain and anger on behalf of the people before them. Of the five only Cai and Josiah had not once slaves. Rinna had been a heartbeat from it herself, and he suspected was well familiar with the same brutality, the results of his father's destructive conquests.

"Lady Rinna, these are your people," Cai spoke in a low voice, never having moved further than a few inches away, "you advised me to trust none of them. I ask your advice again."

Seeing Patrick thin, a healing burn on his hand, minus his usual air of confidence made Rinna's heart ached for the man and fear for his family. She didn't hesitate to answer Cai, "free them."

Cai nodded, resting a hand back on her waist, he looked to Elgin who stepped forward.

"We know that you have all been treated poorly here. That will not be allowed to continue. You are free. Those of you who wish to leave can do so immediately, those of you that wish to stay will be considered waged staff of this fortress and treated thusly."

Rinna wondered at how they planned on doing that. Most in the village had no coins, doing trade by barter. She knew that a main source of income were fees imposed on travelers along with some lumber and small blocks of stone, all sent to Fairshine. She'd not seen a single coin in years.

"But you are Khaetorians. He's a Prince and the Lord Governor," said a woman pointing at Cai, "he wasted no time making her his concubine, so why should we believe you?"

Rinna started to protest at what the woman was implying but Cai tightened his arm around her, "you are not my concubine," he whispered.

"Fuck this. I'm hungry," declared Dax, "you brought out enough food for everyone here. Get some of it if you want or leave if you want. If you stay, we can explain what no longer being a slave means to us." He walked to the table and started filling a plate.

"That's our Dax, thinking with his stomach," joked Tolin. He too went to the table filling a plate. Rinna watched as the woman who had spoken edged her way to the table. When Tolin handed her a cup, then poured ale into it, the rest wasted no time getting food for themselves.

Rinna stayed where she was, Cai next to her, waiting for the men to fill plates up with food alongside those who had prepared it. The big men were jovial, the rest apprehensive. She waited until most had gotten what they wanted before approaching the table. She selected some bread, and a bowl of watery soup. Cai took the bowl out of her hand taking it to the high table. Her eyes flashed in irritation as she got another bowl to fill it with more soup for herself.

"That was your bowl," Cai had returned, "come sit down before you fall over."

He led her to a chair next to where the others were sitting watching with interest. Deciding to ignore the men she was seated next to, she stared at the bowl as she tried to remember the last time she had eaten. It had been the evening before she had come to Ragan to get Garrett. Thinking of him made her want to cry all over again, but she didn't dare break down in front of people. She'd not slept more than a few hours since before Garrett had left. The smell of food hungered and exhausted her.

She broke off pieces of bread and dipped them into the

broth before eating them. She lasted six pieces before she fell asleep, her head resting against the heel of one hand propped by her elbow, the other lay beside the bowl with a piece of bread still in it.

"Well, she lasted longer than I thought she would," observed Dax, "the little beauty has had a very rough couple of days." They had the high table to themselves.

"What are your plans for her cousin? We've gone through a lot of trouble to get her," Elgin bit into a piece of meat, grimacing at its toughness.

"If you don't want her…" Tolin teased then took a sip of mead. It was too sweet for his taste.

"You lay a finger on Rinna, I'll…"

Dax snorted, "told you Tolin. Rajah decided Cai's fate."

"That's just a myth," Cai protested. Reaching over, he pushed the bowl away from Rinna, so she wouldn't accidentally spill it.

"And you've hovered over her since she climbed down from the treehouse Rajah was guarding, delighted with his pretty little prize," Elgin grinned as he watched his cousin try to pry the piece of bread out of Rinna's hand without waking her, "I agree with Dax, Rajah found your mate. You should have seen your face when that woman accused you of making her your concubine. It was a mixture of outrage and pride."

"And if you hurt her, make her cry, or do anything but treat her like a princess, you'll answer to me," Josiah's threat was mild. He had liked Rinna the moment he saw her, finding that he could easily consider her a daughter.

"I'm not going to have this discussion right now," Cai growled, "we have more important things to discuss. Like how we keep these people from murdering us in our sleep, much less taking an entire kingdom."

"That one asleep beside you seems to be a fount of information," Elgin glanced around the room. Most of the others had slipped away as soon as they had gotten their food to disappear back into the bowels of the fortress.

"I think she grew up in the court at Fairshine. She told me she had met my father and had sat next to Rocnor at a royal banquet," the reaction from the others was not unexpected.

Elgin coughed as had choked on his mead, hearing the news. He caught his breath, "Rocnor, your father's advisor, destroyer of everything he touches? That Rocnor?"

"They sat a child next to that bastard?" Tolin exclaimed, "she was how old, ten?"

"Eleven. She apparently managed to piss him off when he was expected to behave himself by deciding to ignore him," Cai's voice held a margin of pride, "no doubt he was waxing poetic about his deity and how great he was as its chief advocate."

"It's a wonder he didn't reduce her to charcoal on the spot. Rocnor's not known for his patience," Elgin thought a moment, "if she was connected to the Fairshine court, then that would explain where a book came from."

"And her ability to read," Cai stood. He picked Rinna up, moving her to the hearth where he lay her down using Elgin's cloak as a blanket. Rajah who had slunk in at some point, immediately curled up around her.

Cai scratched the top of the saber cat's head, "watch over her."

He and his friends spent the rest of the day attempting to put the courtyard into order concentrating on the stables and an area to meet the residents in the morning. The inhabitants of the fortress watched from a distance with curiosity. After nightfall, several slipped away through the kitchen doors that led to a garden area overlooking cascades and the small mill that sat at the top of the spillway. Cai and the rest took turns on watch, accessing the defenses offered to the fortress from the roof and wall walk around the fortress. They saw those that left, counting those that remained as they spent the night keeping an eye on the village.

Through it all Rinna slept, the toll of grief, terror and exhaustion demanding compensation for the difficulties of the past couple of days. Rajah never left, perfectly content to act as a living pillow, sensing her need for recuperation.

Seven

Rinna woke up by the hearth discovering that Rajah was acting as her pillow and a strange cloak was thrown over her. Sitting up, she was surprised at how rested she felt. Seeing sunlight filtering through the dingy half-shuttered window at one end of the hall, she suspected she had slept through the night and into the next day. She hadn't slept that long since she'd been sick with a rash and a fever when she was fifteen.

"Thank you, Rajah," she scratched the big cat's head, not understanding why the animal who could easily bite off her head didn't frighten her. She stood folding the cloak and draping it over a nearby chair seeing Patrick hovering nearby. She took off the blanket, which was still somewhat damp, draping it over another chair.

"Good morning Patrick. Is there something you need?" Patrick was a familiar face, something that gave Rinna a bit of comfort in her strange surroundings.

"Y-yes my lady," Patrick blanched when he saw the big cat stretch then stroll out of the room. He relaxed visibly once the saber cat was out of view. He and the other just freed slaves had given Rinna and her feline companion a wide berth as they both slept.

"Lord Governor Cai ordered me to see to your needs, but that's all. We are uncertain what he expects of us."

You would not be alone, Rinna thought, "I understand Patrick, it's a lot different for all of us. Erm. Can you point me to the privy, then gather the rest of the staff?"

"Yes, Lady Rinna."

Rinna closed her eyes briefly, "please do not call me Lady. It's just Rinna."

When she emerged from the privy, Rinna was certain that food would never pass her lips again, the stench was so foul. It was obvious that no one had cleaned it or made sure the waste was treated in a long time. She and Garrett might have lived in a one room shack, but their chamber pot was cleaned twice a day. In summer they had a variation of the theme with an impromptu bench and a crude shelter they could easily move.

She returned to the dining hall to see a knot of people

standing by the fireplace. She counted eight people. She was certain those missing had taken Elgin up on the offer to leave. They all prostrated themselves when they saw her, "stop that! Everyone, please get up."

They got up resettling on the benches of the nearest table. Rinna saw that several of them had bruises, one had a festering cut on their leg, all looked malnourished and terrified. Rinna understood just how privileged her life had been by living away from the town, and out of the attention of Lord Bannister and his friends. Thinking of Garrett had tears threaten again, but she pushed them back down knowing she was going to have to try to bluff her way through trying to earn these people's trust while having no clue what was expected of her, or what their new benefactors intended. She hoped she was guessing in the correct direction.

"I know that everyone is confused at what is going on, so we shall try to clear things up together," Rinna felt her stomach growl. She remembered beginning to eat, but not finishing her meal, "but before that, is there any breakfast left? I seem to have slept through a few meals."

The men and women looked at one another.

"Well that is the first order of business. I know I'm hungry. I'm certain all of you have eaten a long time ago."

"But we are not allowed to eat until the master has had his fill," explained a woman.

"And Lord Governor--Prince Cai hasn't eaten yet either, has he?" Rinna considered a moment, "Lord Bannister. Those were his orders?"

The woman nodded.

"Lord Bannister will be dining elsewhere in the foreseeable future, so I think it's safe to assume that his ridiculous rule went with him," Rinna replied. To her relief, several of the people before her laughed, "I am curious how none of you are dropping dead of disease after seeing the state of the privy."

"Oh. We don't use that one," Someone blurted out, as Patrick also tried to shush them.

Rinna narrowed her eyes at Patrick, "I know you think I'm the enemy. I am not."

"But you are still the Prince's concubine," Patrick straightened his shoulders, speaking in a scornful tone, "that makes you his property. And we will not be taking orders from you."

"And yet you didn't leave with the others," Rinna leveled a look at Patrick. "I wonder why? I also haven't ordered anything of anyone."

"The others didn't leave," Said the same woman who had spoken earlier. The woman was about her age, a good three inches taller, very pretty with blonde hair, hazel eyes and golden skin common with the people of her nation. She was too thin, but everyone was, including Rinna.

"Lord Dax recruited them as guards," the woman's revelation was a pleasant surprise.

Patrick, now that he had rediscovered his spine, assumed the demeanor Rinna was used to from him, "as for the privy. We have our own. The one I showed you is for the masters of the fortress."

Rinna sighed, "I see. Thank you for the insight, Patrick. The same offer stands. If any of you want to leave, if any of you don't want to work here, if any of you prefer life under your former masters, there is the door. I suggest you walk through it."

No one moved, "well then, I'm sure all of you have jobs that you do here, or feel that you would prefer doing, being stuck in a role you are unsuited for or just hate. Can you at least tell me what that is, so we can all eat?" Rinna found in her irritation and uncertainty that she had slipped into a role Garrett had been trying to prepare her for. He would be thrilled to see her doing what he'd trained her to do. She surprised herself to discover that it didn't feel as unnatural as she expected.

A few minutes later, the pretty blonde woman brought Rinna a bowl of berries and a chunk of bread as she learned what everyone's jobs had been. She dismissed them to whatever they wanted to do for the day asking them to check in with one of the others by nightfall if they chose to remain. They all viewed her with suspicion, so she excluded herself from one of the people to check in with.

She wanted to go home, then realized it wasn't her home

anymore, at least until she didn't have to worry about Donner. The idea of trying to survive in the higher mountains frightened her. It was a last, desperate resort, one she didn't want to attempt. She wanted to go in a corner and cry until she had nothing left but the setting in the fortress was too unfamiliar. She didn't know what she was doing at the fortress, why she had been brought, why she'd been left to her own devices, why it was assumed she was Prince Cai's concubine. She had too many questions, and not a single answer.

She decided to go to the lake, her favorite place to try to sort things out. She walked out into the courtyard, noticing that the space had people milling about. Prince Cai and his friends seemed to be holding court near the gates seeing them standing on an impromptu platform with people gathered around. She began to run when she heard her name called not stopping until she reached the shore of the lake. The shoreline at the spot she ran to had about a five-foot drop to the water. She knew the water would be frigid this time of year but didn't slow down as she dived in fully clothed.

She swam until she tired, then flipped onto her back and floated. There she stared at the sky not paying attention to the dark clouds gathering, a sign of an incoming storm and let her emotions free, crying wracking sobs that threatened to pull her under. She cried for Garrett, for her books, her ruined garden, for the guilt of killing the man who was attacking her benefactors, for being afraid, alone and having no idea what to do. Finally, drained and cold from the water that originated in the snow-covered mountains, Rinna swam back towards shore.

Cai had been listening to petitioners since daybreak. He had slept in the stables after spending a few hours on the wall watching for trouble with Dax, before switching out with Josiah. He'd sent Tolin and Josiah to look at the nearby quarry. Lord Bannister and his council had been the first in the door, demanding that they be included in the matters of government, and for Bannister to retrieve his slaves and personal property. Cai had refused, on all but personal property asking Bannister for a list of what items he needed, and it would be arranged for him to pick them up the following day.

Bannister had been furious, making demands and threats until Dax moved to stand in front of the corpulent Lord shouting, "Next!" right over Bannister's head. Dismissed, Bannister watched in helpless fury as his friends were given the same brusque treatment. None of them had been allowed inside with any weapons, including the eight men he had acting as his personal guard.

The next three hours saw a litany of personal griefs, feuds, demands and attempts at bribery. Absent from the petitioners were those without power. It confirmed that the village had existed in a state of near anarchy, with those with power and property tending to keep it until it being taken by force from someone else.

Cai learned that now that the mountain pass was reopened that goods headed inland, others to the coast were due any day, and that tolls, bribes and other concessions would be expected, being the largest source of income for Ragan, or those that controlled Ragan. Everyone they had spoken with that morning wanted to keep a share of that pie. Cai was ready to burn the place to the ground and send the inhabitants over the mountains to complain directly to his father when he saw Rinna walk by. Josiah who had just returned with Tolin called out to her, which only caused Rinna to run out the gate.

Cai stepped off the platform as Elgin announced the end of petitions for the day, "your mate has got a good head start on you cousin," Elgin said with a grin.

"Taking your horse," Cai ignoring Elgin said to Josiah. He mounted and rode out after Rinna. He found her just as she dove into the lake. He sat on the horse watching as she swam out towards the middle. It was a large enough body of water that she stopped well before reaching it. He heard Rajah's low growl, seeing the big cat crouched nearby also watching Rinna. Cia dismounted and walked to Rajah where he sat down next to the saber cat.

"So, tell me," Cai rested a hand against the cat's back stroking Rajah's fur, "is the myth true? Did you choose her as you did me? If so, then your taste is wonderful even if your timing is terrible. She thinks I am her enemy, the murderer of her people.

How in the hell am I going to convince her otherwise? I don't even know how I'm going to fix what my father has done here." While Cai petted Rajah, Rajah rested his head on his paws, his ears twitching on occasion as the occasional sound of Rinna's sobs broke through the noises of the village behind them.

He knew she was swimming back to shore when Rajah's head lifted. She was heading to a spot closer to land than where he was, so he walked to where he thought she would come ashore, leading Josiah's horse. He waited several yards away to watch, and to ensure he had space and time to protect her if needed. Rajah stretched then bounded off into the forest his duty done.

When she began wading towards shore Cai's mouth dropped open. He had known she was beautiful the moment he saw her clearly in the tavern. The dripping wet fabric of what had been shapeless layers of tunic and trousers were now clinging to the curves of her body revealing that she was very much a woman and one that he wanted under him crying out his name in pleasure.

The suddenness and ferocity of his lust shocked him. He'd never had any desire to force himself upon a woman, and he wasn't about to start. The bruising on her face displayed the cruelty she had suffered at the hands of another man had him want to protect her.

He didn't care if the myth of saber cats helping people in their care find mates was true, he knew he wanted Rinna, and he intended to keep her. Knowing Josiah had some oilcloth he kept for temporary shelter tied in a roll behind the horse's saddle, Cai went to retrieve it. He took the oilcloth and shook it open as he walked towards Rinna, she had seen him and had stopped several feet from shore, poised to swim back out.

"Please, get out of the water. I know you are freezing. I can see your teeth chattering from here," As soon as her foot touched dry land, he wrapped the oilcloth around her. It was large enough that he was able to wrap it around her twice.

"I can't move my arms," Rinna complained trying to wriggle free, her teeth indeed chattering from the cold, her lips almost blue.

"I can't have a member of my council getting sick on me because they let themselves get too cold," Cai tugged her hair out from under the oilcloth. Holding the heavy wet braid, he wrung it to get out as much water as he could. Once done, he readjusted the oilcloth, so she had more freedom of movement. He then pulled her into his arms relieved that she hadn't resisted.

"I'm not a member of your council. I'm not even a resident of Ragan. Garrett is dead, my livelihood turned into a graveyard, and everyone thinks I'm your concubine," Rinna didn't think she had any tears left. Yet they began to slip down her cheeks while her shivering body welcomed the warmth of Cai's. She didn't consider pushing him away, something she would mull over later.

Cai began speaking as her shivering began to slow, her head tucked in under his chin, "when I was a little boy, everyone knew I was a bastard son of the king, one of many and one with a non-human mother, not the only one of those either. Corbaine's daughters were either killed at birth or sold as soon as they were weaned. I learned quickly that to survive I either had to become invisible or indispensable. I went for invisible while learning everything I could just in case I could become indispensable one day.

I served in his army which is how I met Dax, Tolin and Josiah. Being merely a half-breed, I was disposable. All Corbaine's sons are, but half-breeds must work harder to stay alive. I was ordered to guard prisoners, hunt deserters or clear out a den of pirates at one of the ports.

One day my father brought a saber kitten he had captured having successfully killed its mother. He called all his living sons of age intending to grant the one who could control the kitten the choice of his own province to rule, and an army to hold it. Some were too far away to get the message in time. There were fifteen of us in that room. Within two minutes, two of the sons had killed three of their brothers, intending to take the kitten for themselves. When another son tried to pick it up, the kitten attacked him so fiercely the man bled to death before he hit the ground.

While everyone else was either still fighting or trying to restore calm, little Rajah climbed into my lap and licked my half-brother's blood off his paws before falling asleep. During the entire time, Corbaine was fondling his newest slave girl, completely indifferent to the outcome. He left before things got sorted out. I was given this province and was told that half breeds born to women who didn't survive a son's birth couldn't choose which province they wanted or get his own army."

"Why are you telling me this?" she heard the tone of his voice change as he told his story demonstrating the anger and the grief that was present.

Cai stepped back loosening Rinna's arms that had found their way around his back. He held them lightly through the oilcloth at her elbows, "I thought you deserved to know. I had intended on getting as far from my father's world as I could, but you changed my mind."

She looked up in surprise, seeing nothing but honesty in his face, noticing for the first time just how beautiful his eyes were, "Me? How?"

"You defended a little girl armed with nothing but a pitchfork. We arrived too late to do anything to prevent what was happening but in time to step in if needed and to be impressed by your courage. Then I watched later as you climbed through a roof after being beaten and escape as it was the easiest thing in the world," Cai smoothed wet tendrils away from Rinna's face.

"When I was about that little girl's age, Garrett and I were in Fairshine. I watched as four men raped and murder another girl, not five feet from where I was hiding. I don't go often to the village, and never alone because I know how dangerous it can be for women and girls here, but I had no choice, I had to come. Garrett hadn't been home in a couple of days, He isn't—wasn't well, and I worried about him." Rinna lowered her head, concentrating her view on a leather tie on his vest, "I didn't even know I had a pitchfork until I saw myself standing over that man and being quite willing to hurt him," she closed her eyes, the memory a painful one, "and then yesterday..."

"And yesterday, you defended us with honor and skill.

Taking lives is something that must be done sometimes. It should not ever be taken lightly, which is the opposite of what my father thinks," they both looked up as thunder echoed across the lake.

"Rinna, I know nothing about governing, and little about your country. You were born here and seem to have knowledge we lack. My friends and I have decided to try. I need--I would like your help."

Rinna looked no higher than his chin, which had a few days' worth of stubble, "I have nowhere else to go except into hiding, and I'd prefer to live. I'd not last too long in the higher mountains. Winters here are cold, up there they are brutal. I knew yesterday where I was throwing my lot which is only slightly less hopeless than any other option."

She paused when he laughed, "just tell people to stop calling me Lady Rinna and--tell them that I am not your concubine."

"The title fits you quite well, so you are stuck with it," Cai squeezed her elbows, "know this, you are not, nor ever will you be my concubine. I want you by my side, not as my slave. I know nothing about you and yet I need..." his lips touched hers, tentatively then with more confidence.

Rinna had no experience with the physical delights between men and women. She knew what people did in such situations; she had no idea what to expect from the kiss. It had not been that his lips were soft and warm, that his stubble would tickle or that she would want him to keep going and for his hands to move somewhere else but the bend of her elbows. She was disappointed when he stopped, yet afraid what would happen if he continued. She backed away, her heart beating faster.

"Those were not the actions of a man who doesn't want a concubine," she accused.

"No, my love. Those were the actions of a man in the presence of a woman he finds beautiful and appreciates the value of," he grinned down at her then took her head in his hands and kissed her hard and quick, "I promise on the memory of my mother and your father, that you will never be my concubine. I make no other promises about what else occurs between you and I.”

She was behind him on Josiah's horse a few minutes later when she said, “Garrett was not my father.”

“Garrett? You mean the man who died in the tavern?” Cai had never gotten a decent look at the body slumped across the hearth. Dax and Tolin had gone back and retrieved the body, dumped outside the back door of the Putrid Boar then buried him in the nearby forest. They intended to show Rinna the location so she could practice whatever funeral rites she wished.

“Yes. He decided a long time ago it would be safer for me if everyone thought I was his daughter,” Rinna didn't say anything for a couple of minutes, “in hindsight, he was right. He was right about a lot of things.”

“Who was he?”

“He was my father's majordomo, sent to fetch me for the king's wedding,” Cai took a longer route back to Ragan to give Rinna the time to tell her story. It had started raining as soon as they left the lakeside.

“You had three books?” Cai asked.

“Yes. I had a habit of sneaking copies out when the librarians weren't paying attention.” Rinna answered. The three books she had taken had proven to be invaluable. The one on plants had allowed her to find everything in the area they could use and eventually make a small livelihood from. Another had been on leather and how to tan and prepare pelts for use.

“We didn't have the means to make leather, but we could clean pelts, and trade them for things we needed,” Rinna smiled at the memory, “Garrett tried to make a vest out of some once. He was as bad at sewing as I was.”

“The third book was on diplomacy,” she noticed they had stopped under a canopy of pines within view of the village. The needled branches helped shelter them from most of the rain that had begun to pour in earnest.

“Garrett was beside himself in delight when he found I had that book. He memorized it, and every night, until right before he died, I had lessons on diplomacy, Arowanian history, how guilds work, household management, craftsman specialties, trade agreements, along with ethics, mathematics and philosophy. He never adapted, complained constantly and never stopped railing against our enemies."

"But he made sure you got the best education he could give you."

"He did, and I never appreciated it till this morning."

"He considered you the heir to the throne, so tried his best to prepare you," Cai, noticing the rain was letting up, urged the horse forward.

"He did what?"

"Was Garrett able to find any survivors of either your family or the court?" Cai stopped outside the fortress stables and dismounted. He then helped Rinna get down. Together they walked inside the stables.

"He didn't. Every time he returned; he was despondent for weeks. The last time he went was two years ago. Garrett had vowed to not go back. He got sick that winter," Rinna sat on a bench as she talked watching Cai take care of Josiah's horse making sure the animal was comfortable and with fresh food and water. She knew that it was odd for someone of royal blood to perform such tasks. She could tell that he was used to it, yet he carried himself as someone familiar with command and life in the palaces of his father's world.

"He thought you were the last remaining link to the throne, especially if there was relation by blood," he got a scoop of grain and poured it into the trough.

"My father was a cousin."

Cai, having confirmation, continued, "I bet my sword he hoped to find a way to restore his old life through you, even when he realized how impossible it was."

"I don't believe you. He told me once that I was a bastard, that my father brought me home after my mother had died soon after I was born. It explained a lot of things, why the princess called me a mongrel, why my brothers didn't like me, why momma didn't bother with me until it was decided I needed to be presentable for court or why I didn't look like anyone else," Rinna folded up a piece of straw upon itself then released one end. "I never belonged and knew it, but not exactly why."

Finished with the horse, Cai turned, leaning against the

stall. He liked that they had one thing in common, even if it was something most people frowned upon. He also liked how at ease he felt with her, "did he ever tell you who your mother was?"

Devil nickered from his stall. Rinna slid off her bench and stood on the gate of his stall to give his nose a scratch. Cai suggesting Garrett was preparing her to rule sounded like something Garrett would do, yet it was so audacious that she refused to accept it.

"Someone gave you the right sized stall. Good, I won't have to yell at your owner," she said to the horse as it moved forward enough for her to scratch a favorite spot on his neck.

"No," she finally said, keeping her attention turned to Devil, "he was drunk when he told me I was a bastard and we argued, which was common when he was drunk. It was three weeks ago and hadn't dared bring it up again. Now I can't."

"If he knew that your mother was someone else, then why did he teach you like he did?" Cai watched Rinna move on to the next stall, stroking the nose of his own horse Lucky. He still thought his theory made sense now that he knew Rinna's origins.

"I have no idea," Rinna gave Lucky one more pat before turning away, "maybe he thought I could pass down our history. He never gave me a reason, just got snooty and told me I'd appreciate it one day."

Eight

Cai and Rinna left the stable heading towards the keep. Dax was standing in front of a dozen men, some of them younger than Rinna, all of them soaking wet from the rainstorm that had just ended. He was grinning, hands on his hips, water glistening off his beard.

"Meet our little army. They are all green as can be. Half of them have only run away from men with swords, but they all volunteered. All of them hate Lord Bannister and his henchmen more than they hate the Khaetor Empire and us."

Cai's curiosity piqued, walked to stand by Dax, Rinna beside him, "they all volunteered today? You've been busy."

Cai turned to the men lined up in two rows, "do all of you know what you are getting into? That our enemy for now could be our neighbors, and whomever else wants to come along and upend us?"

All of them answered loudly in unison, "yes sir, Lord Governor."

"Are you willing to train, follow orders, obey the laws the governor and his council put into place, and be soldiers intended to protect our land and our people with honor, and dignity?"

Again, the answer was, "yes Sir, Lord Governor."

Rinna watched the exchange with interest then shook her head smiling as she went to go inside, as Dax had them demonstrate different defense stances. She wanted out of her wet clothes and some hot tea, wondering if there was anything worth brewing to have. Walking through the doors, she was met by Elgin.

"What on earth did you say to them?" he asked as he bowed slightly.

"Who?" Rinna didn't understand what Elgin meant or why he was looming over her in the entryway.

"The former slaves. What did you say to them?"

She frowned in confusion, "I reminded them that they were no longer slaves, that if they wanted to leave, they were free to do so, that you wouldn't expect them to go without food or other basic needs. Then I gave them the day off. Did I overstep my bounds? No one told me what to do."

"You tell me," Elgin stepped aside. Rinna walked into the great hall and gasped. The tables had been pushed to the walls along with the benches. All had been scrubbed clean as were the floors. It would take time to scour away years of soot on the fireplace, but it already looked better. There were three windows along one wall, shutters thrown back and opened. The space smelled much better, with the breeze from the open windows bringing in the smell of rain and pine from the nearby forest.

Eight people stood. They looked tired, but less fearful and distrustful. Rinna walked to stand in front of them. Eyes shining, she took a cue from Elgin and bowed to the group, "I-we are honored by your hospitality. You didn't have to do any of this, and I wasn't even gone that long."

The woman who had called Rinna a concubine the night before stepped forward; she was a curvy redhead named Anna, "we all talked about it after you left. We know that it was you who saved little Greta from being raped the other day. Patrick even admitted that neither you nor your father ever tried to cheat him, often throwing in a few things for free."

Patrick stepped forward to join Anna, "these men. None have tried to molest or harm us, have made no demands and gave us our freedom. My family have been in hiding because Lord Bannister tried to sell my son and his sister to the slavers… my son is standing out there in Lord Dax's new army. My youngest daughter is in the kitchen sleeping in my wife's arms. I saw her today for the first time. My older daughter is peeling potatoes."

Patrick coughed, choked by his tears, "I never thought I'd get to see any of them again."

"We decided to stay, because maybe we have a future here. If not, at least we have something to try to fight for," said another woman, the beautiful blonde Rinna was certain would have had her choice of suitors in the salons of Fairshine.

"We will do everything in our power not to give you cause to regret your decision," Elgin glanced to Rinna's right, "isn't that so, Lord Governor?"

"We succeed by working together. My intention is to succeed. You've proven your capability and we have a great deal that needs to be done. We hope to earn your respect and your friendship," Cai lightly rested his hand on the small of her back, "Lady Rinna, suggestions on how to proceed?"

She huffed at the title, yet her head was already planning, the question familiar ground. She had been the one responsible for ensuring she and Garrett had everything they needed for years. This was the same but on a much larger scale.

"You know what is in this fortress, every bed, every scrap of linen, every onion, weapon, tool, coin or bit of wealth. How hard would it take to do an inventory?"

Patrick grinned, "not long. And I apologize for my former behavior."

"None needed. It's been a difficult time for us all," she thought for a minute. "I don't know if the Lord Governor or his council have toured the keep yet or not, but I think that is necessary. Such buildings are intended to act as a defensive shelter in case of attack. Knowing how many it could hold, what repairs or improvements are needed, what supplies are here or could be stored, potential weaknesses and strengths are important to know. Am I correct?"

Cai was so pleased with her insight he wanted to kiss her senseless and deal with her outrage later. He'd never encountered a woman with that kind of knowledge before and he found it appealing.

"Yes, Lady Rinna. That is their intended purpose," he grinned at the glare she threw him, "knowing how defensible this building is, and all that it contains is very important for us to know."

A few minutes later, Rinna was walking ahead with the blonde woman they learned was named Marta, while Elgin and Cai followed, "you are calling her Lady Rinna on purpose. I thought she didn't want to be called that."

"She also doesn't want to be called my concubine," Cai said as they walked into the first bedroom which had belonged to Bannister.

"Cai. I am not going to allow you..."

"You have nothing to worry about. She's mine or will be

as soon as I can talk her into it, but in an honored position," he looked around the room, "pigs live better."

"Dammit Cai." Elgin started to sit on the bed but thought better of it. He went to look at the chests shoved against one wall three deep.

"She is somewhat aware of my intentions and did not tell me to fling myself off the nearest cliff when I kissed her. I take it as a good sign," Cai looked out the window and its view of the bridge that crossed a stream that fed off the lake, "it's going to be torture until I win her over, and I've never intended to try to win any woman over."

Elgin laughed, "then I wish you luck as I doubt, she will make it easy for you."

"The man everyone thought was her father was her family's majordomo. Her father was one of the late king's advisors and a relative. She and the majordomo escaped the carnage at the Arowanian capital only because they were outside the city walls at the time. She said that was far as they knew, no one connected to the former king survived the attack that was swift, brutal and extensive."

"Sounds just like something Rocnor would do. He so does love making things and people burn, but then that's all fire wizards are good at," Elgin made a face as he poked a lump of cloth with his boot, "He must have been allowed to run amok while Corbaine and his money counters plundered the treasury."

"Gods above and below, what a shithole this place is," Josiah walked in followed by Dax and Tolin.

"Except for the slave's, or former slave's quarters, and the kitchen. They had no power, but they did everything they could to make this place as unpleasant as possible. My papa would have fit right in," Tolin's father had been a slave for a commander in an outpost in Freygor to the south. one of the coastal provinces. He and his fellow slaves had managed to drive out a commander a year due to making the living conditions so unbearable that the commanders had begged for a transfer.

The five left the bedroom and completed the tour of the fortress ending up on the roof where they settled down, leaning on the parapet or sitting on one of several benches. The keep itself was two stories, the second floor devoted to bedrooms.

"It's defensible. There's problems, but none that can't be fixed, the biggest is the pile of squalor outside the gates," Said Josiah, "the bigger houses right against the walls all have to go, someone needs to do something about the state of the other buildings and either build a new privy or clean up the mess that's the current one."

Dax added what he had learned from his new troops, "there's a cabal of men who run everything, the quarry, the mill, the taverns, the shops and what passes for law. It's a pecking order where only a few have beaks, and those that do have them well sharpened. There's maybe fifty people in and around Ragan including those in charge. Bannister and five guys are controlling all of it, with about a dozen underlings who mete out the will of those in control with glee and malice."

"I wonder how much of what they were controlling as far as coin and weapons are in this very fortress," Cai wondered aloud.

If Lord Bannister's bedroom is any hint, I'm going to guess a great deal of it," Elgin crossed his legs at his ankles as he leaned against the battlement.

"Well I'm not sleeping in any of those bedrooms until they've been thoroughly cleaned and maybe ritually purified by a handful of water priests," Tolin said. The rest laughed, agreeing that cleaning out sleeping quarters would be a priority.

Rinna was more interested in supplies so was taken to the food stores and other supplies needed for the household. She wasn't surprised that the pantry, buttery and larder were well stocked, if for no other reason than that the fortress also housed the guards, but there was too much. She noticed several things were already going bad. She was impressed by the kitchen which was clean and well maintained and met Patrick's wife, a woman named Ysanne. Ysanne who held a sleeping infant to her shoulder was keeping a watchful eye on a girl who was sewing.

"We were told it was safe to keep our children here," Ysanne smiled in satisfaction hearing a healthy burp from her infant daughter. She put the baby in a basket at her feet then reached for a sewing project of her own.

Rinna picked up a piece of bread, breaking off pieces and munching on them. She watched the girl as she sewed the expression on her face of concentration and calm. *She is enjoying that*, Rinna thought remembering how much she hated anything involving needle and thread as a child. Her opinion of the craft had never changed.

She noticed the door leading outside, "I take it there is no garden here."

"No," Patrick had returned, bending down to kiss his wife on the neck, "none of us know how to grow anything, and…"

"You weren't given the time or opportunity to do so," Rinna completed Patrick's thought, "I will see if there is anything from mine that is salvageable. If we can move some things, I can start you one here, and teach someone to help tend it. That is, if you would want something like that."

"You are asking permission?" Marta asked. The kitchen was her domain and had been pleased with the compliments of its state.

"This is your home. You should get a say in what it will take to make it function better. If its walking outside to pick some herbs for seasoning, or to dig up an onion, instead of having to haggle for some at the market, which would you choose?" Rinna watched as Marta comprehended what was being suggested.

"But then you put the shops out of business," Patrick complained.

"Patrick you sold finished leather of a superior quality. Garrett and others supplied you with pelts, so you had the materials to work with. I traded you fish to help feed your family because you make damned good shoes and fishing would take time from your work. I was hoping to barter for a pair from you when you lost your freedom. Mine lasted through this past winter, barely, because I couldn't replace them."

Patrick grinned, "point taken. And there hasn't been a decent scrap of leather in the place since Bannister decided I had cheated him."

"Well carve out a space and start making it or reopen your

shop," Rinna suggested, pleased with the look of happy anticipation that crossed his face, "from what I understand that is the goal of Prince Cai and his friends, to allow people to live and work where they are best suited. I'm sure someone can provide you with the raw materials again, and you'll be begging for apprentices to help with the workload. At least I hope so."

"Ah, little beauty! There you are," Dax made the kitchen seem much smaller with his large frame, and melodious bass voice, "you are being summoned by the Lord Governor." He winked at Marta who blushed behind her hand.

Rinna hurried after Dax, having to take three steps to each of his one. They made their way to the roof of the fortress. Rinna was thinking of racks to dry herbs and even clotheslines being set up on the open space that made up the keep's roof as they got to where Cai and the others were. That thought had her stopping in place for a moment. She had taken charge and it had been easy. It was an unexpected revelation. She hoped she hadn't made a grave error.

Someone had dragged some benches to the roof once upon a time. Dax led her to one, where she sat down, noting that the wood was still damp. She shook out the oil cloth she'd kept over her shoulders like a shawl draping it over a section of the wall to dry. Then she sat and unbraided her hair so that it would dry as well, attempting to undo the tangles with her fingers.

"Are there enough stores here to survive an extended assault?" Cai asked without preamble.

Rinna froze, fingers embedded in the locks of her hair, her face paling to almost white, "are we expecting…?

"No. We are merely trying to consider every possibility," Josiah said, "try not to terrify her on the onset next time, Cai."

While Cai stammered an apology to the amusement of his friends, Josiah sat next to Rinna.

"Here Let me help. One of my wives had hair like yours. Beautiful thick curls that tangled if she didn't keep it brushed and bound," he took the hair out of Rinna's hands and began working on it, his touch gentle and soothing.

"We have plenty of food, too much actually. I think we need to let the villagers have some or it will simply go to waste, and we should be much more self-sufficient. The fortress is taking almost everything produced by the village or that passes through here that Ragan may need. That means the people of Ragan are having to fend for themselves with what is left over. There are not enough craftsmen, the shepherds have resorted to hiding their flocks because of flagrant theft. It's getting harder to find game because Bannister and his men kill for sport," Rinna picked at the edge of her sleeve which was becoming frayed, "I could go on, but I think you get the point. Yes, you could lock the doors and survive the onslaught if one came, but you would doom the people outside."

"Did no one try to do it the way you envision?" the question came from Elgin, impressed at her insight.

"Yes, at least at first. Someone suggested the fortress as a means of protection from attackers, from who, I have no idea. It was just finished two years ago. Garrett initially tried to help them restore things the way they were before the soldiers burned everything. For the first few years, it looked like they would succeed, then the slavers started bringing cargo from across the mountains, and sending back gold, cloth and other goods back over. It didn't take long for corruption to set in," Rinna remembered when he given up hope which had been on his return from his last trip back to their old home.

"I know what you are trying to do, and you've already done more than Garrett ever dreamed, but there is no more Arowana, no more province. We've become a wilderness of despair," Rinna said sadly.

Dax watched as Josiah finished combing out Rinna's hair, the dark curls blowing about in the afternoon breeze, "you don't think we can succeed in rebuilding Arowana, do you little Beauty?" She shook her head.

"Then we make Ragan succeed," Cai gestured with his head for Josiah to move. Josiah grinned at his friend, knowing that his caring for Rinna's hair had made Cai jealous, something Josiah suspected Cai hadn't quite figured out yet.

"How?" she asked as Cai took her hand, pulling her to her feet. He walked with her to the parapet on the lake side of the fortress.

"In just a day, we've had people join us. Tomorrow more will. They've figured out what we are trying to do. They also know the odds. I asked if anyone has tried to fix things here. There's been talk, but no serious attempt, because they were quickly shut down," he imagined how beautiful she would look in a gown, and the bruises gone.

"And you believe you will succeed where others have failed?"

"I do, my love, I do," he slipped an arm around her waist, "it will take time, a lot of hard work, and setbacks now and then, but I believe we can make something here."

They watched a flock of duck glide in for a landing on the lake's surface. Rinna found the scene beautiful never having seen the lake from that vantage point.

"Lady Rinna?" Tolin was next to her, leaning against the parapet, "besides trying to rob everyone blind, what do people do around here?"

Rinna turned her attention back to the lake. The ducks had settled in among some reeds by the lakeshore, "Garrett told me there was once a market for freshwater pearls and they caught trout. Some wool, pottery, mostly ceramic tiles and bowls was the rest. Now it's some lumber, and stone blocks going to Fairshine. Then of course the tolls and bribes on travelers and what the taverns can squeeze out of travelers."

"I'm of the mind of not sending anything to Fairshine," Cai too watched the ducks, finding the setting peaceful, "We will need those commodities for ourselves."

Rinna glanced up at Cai, her heart tripping as she saw him looking down at her. She didn't quite know what to do about his proximity. It wasn't unpleasant, just very different. She'd let few people get this close to her since she was a child. She thought of his kisses, then shoved it aside until later, "you are considering cutting off trade?"

"Remember, I'm making all this up as we go along, but yes. Let's make Ragan a healthy community while not giving those in charge in Fairshine a thing," he shot a glare at Tolin who was grinning, then dropped his hand from Rinna's waist.

While Rinna could see the wisdom in the idea of the plan,

execution was something else. Most caravans had guards with them, especially the slave traders. She didn't know how they would overcome that obstacle.

Bannister and his cronies left three days later. Bannister and his closest ally Hovind made a show of it, taking five guards and a wagon stuffed with as much as they could plunder from the houses closest to the fortress. Both men complained to anyone within earshot about how they felt cheated and were going to demand justice, taking it all the way to Khaetor City if needed. Bannister was furious that Cai decided to only return any clothing found strewn about in the former leader's bedroom. Others left in the middle of the night taking whatever they could steal, which wasn't as much as they wanted thanks to the men Dax was training.

The five friends began demolishing the two houses built up against the fortress. Most of the material was stored for later, the rest given to repair the houses and shops of some of the villagers. People watched in curiosity as the five worked, enjoying an easy comradery that involved laughter and practical jokes, usually between Tolin and Elgin.

After most of the two houses were demolished Cai, Elgin and Josiah went to Fairshine. They expected to see homesteads or small communities along the way. There was evidence of former habitation, but none occupied.

"I don't care if Corbaine's soldiers did a clean sweep of the place a decade ago, you still would expect that people escaped, hiding deeper in the forest until the danger has passed," Josiah poked his head in the door of a house. It was within sight of the road and being taken over by nature.

"You are right," Cai found a crumbling outbuilding. Whatever it had once held was long gone, "there is something preventing people from resettling. I suspect that between Ragan and Fairshine, no one felt safe."

"We know your father didn't want you to succeed," Elgin had taken a cursory look. He was more interested in the forest and the rolling terrain of the foothills they were crossing, "he made sure to give you a province that is devoid of what is needed most, people."

"I'd be tempted to reverse the decision to stay," Cai began.

"If it weren't for a woman with dark curls and elven eyes who captured your attention," Elgin laughed when Cai scowled.

"Yet you seem to be avoiding her," Josiah wasn't going to let his friend off the hook. Cai had become more solemn and withdrawn since being handed the decree. He knew the odds were stacked against him yet took the responsibility seriously as he did most things. Cai didn't say anything, but Josiah knew it weighed heavily on his friend's shoulders. Encountering Rinna had helped shore up Cai's confidence and purpose which had been strained.

"I've not been avoiding her," Cai stared at the ground for a moment, "she's either surrounded by at least three people, sleeping or elbows deep in that garden she started. And I-well, she's mad because I made her take one of the bedrooms upstairs."

"I thought she had the room next to Marta," Elgin's attention had shifted to his cousin and away from his surroundings.

"She did, but it's too small. There's barely a room for a small bed. I thought it was a better space to put all those chests that were in my room," Cai glared at his friends who were both grinning, "she got mad when I told her then yelled at me. She told me that she wasn't a piece of furniture to set where I pleased. I was just trying to give her a better place to sleep."

"Cai, I admire and respect you, but you are an idiot," Josiah said.

"He thinks most women aren't interested in him because he's half elf, or that he's a bastard prince with no power or riches so he doesn't even try to get their attention. Now he finds one he is interested in and he's out of his depth," Elgin understood how Cai felt. An elf anywhere in the empire was uncommon; a free one was very rare. Other than one uncomfortable incident the day he met Tolin, women didn't seem interested in him. Like Cai, he'd never met anyone who piqued his interest.

Cai didn't want to discuss Rinna or his absent love life, "I've been rejected enough by women in my father's court and all over the kingdom to know that it's true. Rinna is--well I am being cautious."

He urged his horse into a cantor to end the conversation. Elgin watched Cai disappear around a bend.

"Cautious my ass," Elgin snorted, "he told me he's already kissed her, and she didn't punch him in nose for the trouble."

"Or search for the nearest pitchfork," Josiah grinned as Elgin burst out laughing, "I am now convinced it was a good idea to come here, just for the entertainment value."

Nine

That afternoon they saw two wagons with accompanying riders heading in the opposite direction. Both groups were curious enough about the other to stop.

They were told that they were returning to Beldeene after dropping off a cargo of grain two weeks prior being one of the first over the pass for the season. They were taking back five barrels of salted fish and three baskets of pomegranates.

"I am curious why you are returning mostly empty handed," Josiah asked the lead driver.

"We weren't told to obtain anything to ship home," the man answered with a shrug, "just get to Fairshine as soon as possible. What we have is to cover the bribes going back. Ragan will get the most of it, bloodsucking bastards."

"There's been a change of leadership," Cai glanced over to Elgin who coughed a warning. It had been decided not to reveal who they were on this trip, just to see what lay on the other end of the road.

"Great. Hope they aren't worse than the last lot. It's almost not worth making the trip these days," the driver pulled his cloak closer to help keep off a misty rain.

"Ask for a man named Dax. Can't miss him as he is the biggest thing in the place," Josiah drawled, "he could help smooth the way a bit. He's a friend."

After Cai asked if there was anyone looking for sellswords, the group parted ways. After a few minutes Cai's curiosity got the best of him.

"Why did you tell them to find Dax?"

"Because Dax will send Tolin for a look first, and Tolin will probably spot the false bottom in the second wagon. They didn't risk going over the pass so early in the season with a shipment of grain," Josiah continued, "I also know that we were the second group over this season. The first was a quartet of men looking for work. They didn't have much, a small cart and a pair of mules. They lost the cart to bribes."

"It never occurred to me to even ask," Cai was grateful for Josiah's keen observation skills.

"Which is why you were wise enough to bring him along,"

Elgin handed Josiah a water skein as they rode, "who do you think those men were?"

"Slavers of course. They likely wintered in Fairshine and are now taking the proceeds of their sales back to their bosses," Josiah smirked at Cai's look of surprise.

"I've spent too much time in the army or escorting some of my father's dignitaries and tax collectors all over the empire. I would have never guessed that," Cai responded.

"No, cousin you wouldn't have, but then you are not the type of man who goes for the subtle and underhanded. You don't even like traveling incognito because like it or not, your title does open doors that won't for us," Elgin retorted.

Cai barked out a surprised laugh, "you are right. Being a prince does have its advantages even if it means having to be connected to my father."

"Like coming here," Josiah retorted.

"With no generals making stupid decisions that kill platoons of soldiers, no escorting dignitaries with disgusting personal habits, no spending months in a tent hoping that our asses thaw out one day," Elgin took back the water skein after it had passed on to Cai, "I'm not going to complain. I happen to like the idea of sleeping in a real bed and not having to be a soldier anymore."

"So, do I," Cai saw the trees thinning out ahead, "looks like are getting close."

Once they saw Fairshine, no one spoke for several minutes. Blackened stone shared space with trees. The city's walls stood intact in places, damaged in others. A large section near the closest gate was strewn in pieces along the ground. Almost no original structures were left unscathed from the fire caused by Rocnor and his associates.

The husk of a large building stood taller than the rest near the center of the city. Cai assumed it was once the palace. He could see two blackened towers. The population was concentrated were at the harbor which stood near where they were, the rest near the other city gates. There was little land being used for farming or livestock, at least on this side of the city.

"How many people used to live here?" Elgin had dismounted and was leaning against a large maple.

"Rinna told me about ten or eleven thousand with maybe another thousand spread throughout the kingdom. The mountains and forest always kept the population down, with most people living here." Cai was horrified at the near destruction displayed before him. The harbor had most of the new construction, being devoted to warehouses, homes and shops. No care was considered for the quality of the build, something obvious from over a mile away. They could see some repairs done to structures further in, but not their purpose.

"I knew your father likes to gut a place when he's decided he wants what it may offer, but this is extreme, even for him," Josiah had decided to sit on the ground. Cai had not moved from where he had gotten off Lucky, still holding on to the horse's reins.

"Not for Rocnor," Elgin's anger showed in his voice, "he would have relished the chance to cause major destruction while bringing about massive amounts of death and pain to feed his power."

"My father never took him again on a conquest. Maybe because Rocnor did too much damage. I also heard that he didn't bring any of his lesser priests back with him. Probably killed them so he could take their magic," Cai was just as angry, "the only reason I can think of why Rocnor came along was because of the library."

"Because according to him, only the devotees of that obscenity he calls a god should have the right to an education," Elgin snarled, "we are damned lucky we got to learn to read and write at all."

"Only because it was useful to those who used us," Cai took a breath as his fingers fidgeted with the reins in his hands, "I knew this was bad, I just didn't believe..."

Josiah interrupted, "That a certain woman detailed thing accurately?"

"Got me. She was eleven and I thought that what she remembered had been made worse by her fear. I would have never dreamed Rocnor and his priests could cause this much damage at one time, or that my father agreed to it," Cai turned away, walking back up the road leading Lucky.

"We aren't staying?" Elgin hurried to catch up. Josiah followed more slowly, "I thought the whole point of this trip was to learn what we can about this place."

"We were. I've seen what I needed," Cai stroked Lucky's neck.

Josiah. I should have listened to you and just let you come on your own. I know you are itching to see what you can find out."

Josiah smiled, "no need to apologize. I didn't expect what we just saw either. It's horrifying, and it has me rethinking how to proceed and who I want to recruit to help. I do want to see just who is in charge and what opportunities there may be for our short and long-term plans. I need good scouts and you two are not it. I know you can't help it, but neither of you are good at blending in."

"You know who is worse at it?" Elgin asked

"Dax," all three said together before laughing.

*

Rinna and Marta found that they both had similar ideas of how things should be managed. They soon became friends spending hours reorganizing the fortress's supplies and working to clean the bedrooms upstairs for occupation. Rinna was angry that Cai had ordered her room transferred into storage and her be given one upstairs. She'd given Cai her thoughts on the matter wanting to throw something at him when he just stood there and waited for her to stop yelling at him before telling her that the decision was already made and then walking away.

"I don't need one of those rooms. It should be saved for guests or to give the men on guard a place to rest," Rinna complained when she found Marta putting fresh linens on the bed in Rinna's new room, "I didn't ask to be brought here, but I accepted it. But to have my perfectly functional room turned into storage so he can have more room in his is unacceptable."

"Sweetie, you have to admit this room is nicer, it is quieter than downstairs, and you can have a little table in here and still have room to walk in and out," Marta smoothed the covers on the bed than sat down.

Rinna plopped down next to Marta, "I know it is. But the man could have at least asked me, and I was fine in my old room. The last time I was ordered about and treated like a piece of furniture, I was a little girl.

Marta's laughter tinkled as she reached over and hugged Rinna, "I heard the furniture part. Most of the fortress did, but I don't think he was trying to treat you like a chair."

"Probably not. He's a prince so---" Rinna stood up noticing that a cloak was on a hook by the door. She hadn't put it there.

"He's a prince and--very handsome, smart and not a complete asshole," Marta grinned at Rinna's glower, "I never met any princes or any noble before he came along. I didn't think they demolished buildings or go help thatch a roof."

"They don't," Rinna admitted, "he's not horrible, none of them are."

Marta stood, "good. Now that's settled, can you help me peel potatoes before Dax shows up? I swear the big giant exists just to be in my way."

Rinna smiled. She knew Marta didn't mind Dax being in the way as much as she said she did.

There was enough fabric found to give all the staff new clothes plus enough to use to make new bedding and other necessary linens. Several times Ysanne offered to give her a freshly sewn dress. Every time Rinna refused.

"I will take nothing until I know that everyone else's needs are taken care of first. Besides, I'm just going to get a dress dirty. Once we get things settled, then I'll get something new." Rinna gestured at herself. Her tunic had dirt smudges on it and her sleeves were becoming frayed. Her trousers had a new tear in the knee. She still didn't have shoes.

"What you have on isn't going to last much longer, Lady Rinna," Ysanne smiled when Rinna wrinkled her nose at the title.

"I know that. At least let me get the garden set up and finish stocking the still room. Oh, and we need to get someone to cut some hay. Tolin mentioned that we were getting low this morning. I need to figure out who to ask"

"I understand you are busy. We can talk about this later," Ysanne shook her head as she left the stillroom Rinna was organizing.

Patrick and Ysanne moved back into their old home, as well as two others all glad to pick up their lives again, shrinking the number of full time residents in the keep down to ten, with another dozen trading shifts as fortress guards, sleeping in barracks built in the courtyard. When the new soldiers were not on duty rotation, they resided in the village. They were often recruited into helping move things into new storage locations, fetch water, hunt for meat, or be handed a fishing pole and sent to the lake.

Rinna spent every spare moment not helping cleaning and organizing the fortress retrieving what she could for her new garden. Rinna earned the respect of the four people who stayed as staff when they saw she was happy to stay out of their way trusting them to know what they were doing while working as hard as they did to try to get the fortress clean and well organized. At first Rajah tagged along when she went to her old garden spending the time trying to catch fish or napping on the porch of Rinna's old house. When Cai, Elgin and Josiah left, Rajah did too. Rinna found that she missed the big cat's company.

As night, Rinna would climb into bed exhausted but found it difficult to sleep. She missed her old life, hard as it was. She felt responsible for the four people who ran the day to day operations of the fortress and the men who acted as guards. She fretted about making a mistake and mourned the loss of Garrett who would have been thrilled to act as an advisor. She wanted to escape, even for just a little while.

One morning, Rinna was in her new garden when she saw two wagons and several men cross the bridge near the village's entrance. It made her curious and somewhat apprehensive knowing Cai, Josiah and Elgin had gone to Fairshine. She took a few minutes to wash her hands and face before going to the front of the fortress where she saw the wagons.

The travelers were doing a lot of yelling and posturing with weapons. Dax had his soldiers in near proximity while Tolin was throwing sacks out of one of the wagons. The caravan left soon after with a small escort of Dax's men to the beginning of where the road rose up through the mountains.

Tolin found Rinna and dropped three sacks that clinked when they landed at her feet while Dax rolled in a barrel and another man carried a basket of pomegranates.

"Lady Rinna, the travelers have paid their toll and have departed," Tolin told her.

"You think it's fine to rob them like that?" Rinna's temper flared, "what makes you any better than Bannister?"

"Because those assholes are slavers," Dax watched with amusement as Rinna processed the information, her anger fleeing, "they had a false bottom on the wagon. That money is from the people they hauled to Fairshine last fall. We left them a few sacks and took half the bribes they were intending to give us."

"How did you know?"

"I saw the false bottom on one of the wagons," Tolin picked up a pomegranate sniffed it than tossed it back into the basket, "it wasn't even well done, so I knew they had something to hide. When I pointed it out, they got pissed and made some threats."

"They could have killed you," Rinna ignored the sacks at her feet.

"Eugene remembered them because he had to re-shoe one of their horses last fall, and they paid him by breaking his nose," Dax added. Eugene was at least sixty and was the village's blacksmith, "I think he deserves a reward."

"Oh," Rinna glanced down at the sacks at her feet, taking a step back away from them, "I'd rather not know what happens to those."

"They'll go in the storeroom for now," Tolin flashed a grin as he bent to pick up the sacks, "or maybe I'll see if we can use your bedroom. The storeroom is a bit full."

"You would regret it," Rinna retorted as she turned to go back inside. She knew Tolin was teasing her and earning a reputation as a prankster. Marta wanted to get back at him for hanging all her ladles off the branches of a tree in the garden so had conspired revenge with Rinna. Tolin gave both women a hug and pats on their heads the next morning.

"Well played ladies," Tolin picked up a hunk of bread from the basket on the kitchen table the next morning, "I would have never dreamed of waking up to find my room full of dirty chamber pots."

"I grew up with brothers," Rinna winked at Marta, "they were always doing things to each other. The adult nobles at court were even worse. Some of their jokes could be cruel."

"And you most certainly are not," Tolin placed a hand over his heart, "I promise never to put ladles in trees or threaten to turn your room into storage ever again."

Rinna knew that it was nearing time to gather the berries and plants she collected and dried every year, so gathered what she needed for the trip. She had tried without success to grow the berries that grew close to the ground in her garden but had never managed to keep the plants alive long enough for the journey. She had no better luck germinating the seeds. She hoped for a horse that would make the trip into the high mountains for the desired berries far quicker. The horse would also fulfill another item on her wish list. She had discovered an abandoned grape arbor the summer before and hoped to bring some vines back with her.

Cai was training with the fortress guards when she went to ask for the horse. He'd stripped down to just his pants and boots, his upper body glistening with sweat. Rinna couldn't help but admire the rippling muscles as he sparred with one of the guards. She caught a glimpse of a scar on his left shoulder as he pivoted to escape a blow from the guard's practice sword. Cai then kicked the guard's legs out from under him, holding his practice sword at the guard's neck.

"If you hadn't been ogling Lady Rinna you would have had me. Remember the lesson. Distractions can be deadly," Cai reached down and helped the guard to his feet, clapping the man on his back. He'd seen her approach. She was wearing the same rags from the day they met, and she looked tired.

"Your pretty little concubine works too hard," Tolin told him over a shared bottle of ale last night.

"She is not my concubine," Cai growled.

"I know that," Tolin laughed, "it's just funny to see you get pissed about it."

"Stuff like that doesn't usually faze you cousin," Elgin reached for the bottle, "we are merely enjoying you getting defensive over the lovely Rinna."

Cai ignored the teasing, "why do you say she works too hard?"

"Have you seen her since you got back?" Dax reached for the bottle but was beaten by Josiah.

"We just got back a couple of hours ago, and no."

"For a woman who spent the past decade living on the edge of starvation in a one room shack with the man pretending to be her father, she sure knows how to run a keep," Dax sitting on one of the benches of the keep's roof, leaned back against the battlement so he could stretch his legs.

"Some of the villagers are coming around thanks to her as well," Tolin stretched out on the floor. The evening was pleasant with a mild breeze, "she doesn't demand anything, merely asks. It's funny."

"What is funny?" Cai saw Rajah climb over the battlement wall. He strolled over to near where Cai sat there the cat flopped down on his side to wash a paw.

"One of the villagers, I think a former guard of Bannister, took offense when she asked him to help cut hay for our livestock. He started insulting her," Tolin watched Cai's expression, amused at his irritation, "I was about to go beat some respect into the idiot when she walked to the stable door near where they were standing and picked up a pitchfork."

Dax laughed, "the guy, who is of a darker hue than you and Josiah turned three shades lighter. He backed down and agreed to help and no she was never in any danger. If Tolin hadn't been able to get to the idiot in time, I would have."

Tolin joined Dax in laughter, "you could tell she was mad, but kept her temper until he left. She then went and attacked a plot of ground with a vengeance using that pitchfork. She planted something in that spot a few days later."

Cai thought back to that conversation as he took a cloth from a nearby table, using it to wipe sweat off his neck and face as he walked to where Rinna stood. Tolin and Dax filled him in with some of the work Rinna had done or overseen including the prank she and Marta had pulled on Tolin. He stopped when he was inches away, forcing her to look up.

"You've been avoiding me, my love."

"That's not true and you know it. I've been working from dawn to dusk, trying to help turn this place into a functioning fortress. I've barely seen any of you. You, Josiah and Elgin went to Fairshine which I had to find out about from Marta after you left. I didn't even know you had returned," Rinna saw a line of sweat running down his neck to curve around the lightly furred muscles of his chest. She wanted to catch it with a finger and see what it tasted like. She shook her head at the unexpected distraction and took a step back.

"I need to gather some things we will need for winter, so will need to borrow a horse for a while."

Ten

"What is it you need to get?" Cai remembered their last conversation with her yelling at him for his decision to move her to a better room. Cai was more than ready for a few hours of distraction with someone he found entrancing. Her request offered such an opportunity.

"I go every year to get bilberries, and then some herbs and plants found in the higher elevations. They should be ripe by now and will be quite welcome come winter when fruit is impossible to come by. I found an abandoned grape arbor last year. I couldn't get any cuttings, as I didn't have the means to carry them back safely alive," Rinna explained, "a horse will cut down on travel time by at least a week."

"A week?" Cai was incredulous, "absolutely not. I take it you intended to go by yourself too."

"I've gone by myself for seven years. I don't see what the difference is this year. I even have a full quiver of arrows again thanks to Elgin, so I can at least scare off a bear. They are greedy creatures," Rinna could see from the look on his face he was going to refuse, so gave up, "if I can't take a horse, then I won't. It will just take the usual month instead of three weeks. I thought I'd at least ask."

She didn't make it five feet back towards the keep before she found herself slung over Cai's shoulder. She yelled at him to let her down, as he stormed past people in the great hall and climbed the stairs to the second floor, not stopping until he reached his bedroom. He slammed the door shut, then tossed Rinna on the bed.

She climbed down off the bed that was taller than she was used to and turned on Cai, "you can't treat me like this. Now get the hell out of my way, I have a lot to do before morning."

"Morning? You were going to leave in the morning?" Cai wanted to shake her, his voice rising as he spoke, "just when were you going to tell me this?"

"Well you've not been here to ask, so as soon as possible or have Marta pass it on to one of you, which I was doing before you lost your temper and treated me like a sack of grain," Rinna yelled back, "I would have asked one of the others for a horse which is hard as I never know if one of you are coming or going. If none of you were here, then I would have walked as I usually do. I have a short time frame to work with."

Cai walked forward forcing Rinna backwards until she bumped into the foot of the bed. He leaned over her as she ran out of room to back up, "you are not going."

"Why not? We will need the fruit come winter, and I can't ask anyone else to go when they are already so busy," Rinna didn't understand why he was so angry. They hadn't spoken since the day he left for Fairshine and only exchanged a few brief words before that. The only exception was the day he had kissed her.

"There are other people who can go."

Rinna shook her head, "I don't know anyone else knows what a Bilberry plant looks like. I've been all around the area, gathering plants, and herbs we need, like I always have, except I've taken a helper. Besides, I've gone back to my garden by myself three times to get more plants and into the forest to gather mushrooms, some bark and roots."

Cai's face showed his anger and was inches away, "and when did you do this?"

"The last time was yesterday. Sometimes Rajah even comes with me, but not since you've been gone. No one has had a problem with it," Rinna tried to push him away, but he wasn't budging. She was having to crane her neck to look up at him. "Back up, Cai."

"No. I don't think I will. Right now, I'm too angry at you for taking such risks for your safety," he leaned over further so that she was forced to support her weight with an elbow on the mattress she was leaning against. His hands supported his own weight on either side of her.

"Just because things seem safe in here, doesn't make it so out there. In fact, our presence has made it less so."

"I'm aware of that, which is why I wasn't intending on making anyone go with me when they are obviously needed here. Now that Bannister and his friends are gone, things are much better and Donner is too afraid of all of you to try anything, so I knew it was safe to do what was needed," Rinna kept pushing at his chest with one hand. She may have well pushed at the wall for the success she was having.

"We need as much food as we can get to survive the winter. I always much gathered more than Garrett and I needed selling the excess. Now I must think about a lot more people. I also am quite used to being on my own and have always had an escape plan in place. I know what I am doing."

Cai's anger had left the moment she placed her hand on his bare chest trying vainly to push him away. It was replaced by other emotions that had nothing to do with berries or horses, "that does not mean you are allowed to leave the fortress without permission."

Rinna's eyes narrowed, "I've been in and out of this fortress for over three weeks and no one demanded permission until now. Dax didn't even mind yesterday when I went to check my nets. I merely told him where I was going and when I expected to be back. He even let me take Devil."

"Probably because the big idiot followed you or had his soldiers do so as a training exercise," Cai boosted her up onto the bed, pushing her down onto the mattress, then lay so he had her caught partially underneath him, "did you know we shut down Donner's tavern late last night?"

Rinna shook her head, confused at the sudden change in topic and mood.

"He murdered one of his girls yesterday, right in front of his customers. She didn't get his pants unfastened fast enough. He broke her neck, tossed her into a corner and made one of the other girls do the job."

"Gods," Rinna eyes grew large with sadness and horror.

"He could have done that to you," Cai's hand stroked the side of her face, "the bastard ran off before we could get him, taking a few friends along. My guess is that he went to the capital, following Bannister, his council and several others. What is the name of the crony of Bannister's with the greasy beard and a missing little finger?

"Petyre. His name is Petyre."

His body was found a few days ago near the quarry. His killers were not gentle," He wrapped a strand of her hair around his finger feeling her tremble beneath him.

"He and Donner hate one another," Rinna said in horror. She had been near the quarry recently, digging up a patch of lemon balm to replace the plants that had been destroyed in her own garden, "why did no one tell me any of this?"

"We've been busy, and I assumed you had been staying put. I found out about Petyre from Dax last night as we were clearing out customers from the Putrid Boar and finding a place for the girls to stay."

"I would have considered how I did things differently if I had known, at least taken a weapon with me," Rinna lied as she fought her rising panic at the risks she'd taken. After the first week helping to get the rooms of the fortress cleaned out, she concentrated on getting the garden going and gathering the plants she had wanted, taking for granted the added safety Dax, Cai and the others represented.

"I hope that they got their throats slit as soon as they came in sight of the first pirate, but I suspect that Bannister went straight to one of his benefactors. That means trouble is coming. I'm not splitting our defenses to guard you as you traipse across the countryside," Cai put a finger to Rinna's lips as she started to protest. He hadn't missed the panic she was trying to hide, "I'd be insane to let you go alone and find my suspicions of where Donner went is wrong."

Rinna didn't get a chance to ask where else Donner might be before Cai was kissing her. He shifted so that he could slide an arm under her back, the other he had tangled in her hair. She reached up placing a hand at the back of his neck pulling him down closer, the other was trapped under him. His tongue teased at her lips encouraging them to open. Once she did it entered with a vengeance, causing sensations that left Rinna gasping when he broke the kiss to begin a trail of kisses down her neck.

He heard voices pass down the hall, bringing Cai's attention away from Rinna and what his libido was suggesting. Sitting up he got off the bed bringing Rinna along with him, keeping her body close to his.

"Know this. You are going to have someone watching over

you all the time. You so much as step out of the door of the fortress, you will have at least myself or two other people with you. Your safety is very important to me, Lady Rinna."

Rinna was too frightened about the danger she had put herself in and trying to process the physical reaction she'd gotten from Cai kissing her to answer.

He let her go, hand on the doorknob as he prepared to leave, "one more thing. I notice that everyone has gotten new clothes but you. The next time I see you, you better be in either a new gown, or nothing at all."

Rinna forgot her fear with the new demand, "a gown? I can't wear a gown. I'll just get it dirty, which Is why I insisted on not getting anything new yet. I still have..."

Cai was on her in an instant, her feet off the ground as he picked her up by the waist and set her on a chest of drawers her knees on either side of his hips, "you have no idea how much I want to tear what you have on into little pieces, because you are too stubborn to wear anything else but rags that are literally falling apart. But if I did that, we wouldn't be leaving this room for at least a couple of days. Like it or not, you are Lady Rinna, a member of my council, so you need to start dressing the part."

He looked as if he wanted to say more, but instead stormed out of the room. Rinna's face was flaming as she realized what he had suggested, and furious that he had shoved through her defenses as if they were nothing and at herself for not fighting him harder. After hearing about Donner, she knew he was also right, she had been foolish, taking the presence of Cai and his friends for granted, but being forced to be placed under constant watch was unacceptable.

Frustrated, she left the bedroom seeing Tolin sprawled across the top of the stairs, "where to Lady Rinna? Your faithful guard awaits."

"Shut up, Tolin," Rinna snapped marching down the stairs to Tolin's laughter. She still wanted to take the trip, she just needed to rethink how to go about thanks to a man who was far too possessive and had a way of distracting her in ways she found intriguing yet disconcerting.

She went was almost through the kitchen door to the

head to the garden when Ysanne stopped her. She, Patrick and their children had been able to move back to their old home, where Patrick happily picked back up his leather working trade to the delight of the people of Ragan. Ysanne, a gifted seamstress had been one of the people recruited to help give all the former slaves new clothes.

"These were made for you, so you cannot turn them down," Ysanne had clothing wrapped up in a bundle. Patrick was with her holding their infant daughter and a smaller bundle.

An hour later Rinna was in a simple kirtle of a soft gray, with a cream-colored chemise underneath that had sleeves she could tie up out of the way. A second kirtle in blue with a darker blue chemise lay on a chair in the corner Of her small bedroom. Patrick had surprised her with a pair of soft shoes with a promise of practical boots in a few days, earning him a kiss on a bemused cheek.

While she worked to adjust a seam, Ysanne listened to Rinna's complaints about the clothes being impractical for work, Cai's demands, and of her loss of freedom of movement then proceeded to side with Cai.

"You've worked hard helping us, and I know everyone appreciates it. But you are a member of the Lord Governor's council, the lady of the fortress, and unless I'm missing the signs either his lover or soon to be so," she laughed at the expression on Rinna's face.

"I heard about the concubine thing. They were wrong. But you haven't seen how he stops whatever he is doing when you are in sight. It's been one of the subjects of gossip all over Ragan. That man wants you in a mighty way, and you are wavering."

"I didn't ask for any of this," Rinna countered, "I was doing just fine on my own and he and his friends swooped in and made me come here."

"You were not doing just fine and you know it, none of us were. Yes, they swooped in and made you come here, and we are grateful they did," Ysanne stood, resting a hand on Rinna's shoulder.

"My husband told me that he gave you a hard time when

you first arrived with them. He also told me that he knew you had no more control over the situation than he had, but you handled things with impressive grace and dignity," she helped Rinna out of the clothing in order to try on the other gown.

"It didn't feel that way," She pulled the second chemise over her head as Ysanne folded the gray kirtle, "I was terrified, and completely out of my depth."

"From what I was told, you acted like a queen, even with a big black eye and no shoes. You walked in on Lord Elgin's arm leading the biggest horse any of us have seen, and that monstrous cat as if you were born to it. I know Lord Bannister about pissed himself. You have been the source of happy gossip for weeks, as was you not retaliating on Anna when she threw out the concubine bit at you."

"Anna was Bannister's..."

"Concubine, yes, and the girl was right jealous that you had the new man in control looking at you with favor, after she'd been stuck having to lie under the old one," Ysanne smiled at how Rinna looked in blue as she helped tie up the laces on the kirtle, "lord Cai is quite nice to look at, they all are, you just won't get Marta to admit it. Cai treats you not only as someone rare and precious, but also he is wise enough to make you an advisor."

"I am mad that he thinks I have to be under constant watch. I understand why, and I don't really disagree in principle, it's just that..." Rinna shook her head in frustration, unable to put it into words.

"It's just that you are not used to having other people look after you," Marta walked in, carrying Ysanne's baby who was asleep, "I'm going to lay her down on your bed Rinna, if that's okay with you. Patrick went back to the shop."

Rinna looked at the tiny girl curled up on her narrow bed, "That must be it. I've always been on the fringes, having to look out for myself and Garrett. Even when I was a little girl, I was mostly ignored unless I was having to play dutiful daughter, or in trouble again. It's an adjustment."

"Good. We will help," Marta admired the gown Rinna was wearing, "now tell us, how much of a fight are you putting up with Prince Cai? There was yelling then everything got quiet."

"He's making it hard to resist," Rinna admitted, which only had Ysanne grin and Marta laugh.

"At least you don't have a big giant sweet talking himself into your space every time you turn around," Marta huffed, "I keep having to throw him out of my room."

"You keep letting him in," Rinna retorted, which had all three women laughing. The budding romance between Dax and Marta had been fun to watch. Both were attracted to one another, both pretended not to be, yet were failing.

"Back to clothes for a minute, then I need to go home. My own man seems to think he needs a supper every night," Ysanne had needle and thread flying as she adjusted the hem of the kirtle.

"I'm going to have to wear these more often, aren't I?" Rinna asked.

"You need to dress the part of your status and you need to fully assume the role you've been handed, which is an important one."

"And stop working yourself so hard," Marta added. Ysanne nodded in agreement.

"If you want clothes to get dirty in now and then, I will simply rework something from one of the men's clothes," Ysanne stood to admire her handiwork, "that means you delegate more, dress the part, make wise decisions and keep all those menfolk in line."

Rinna looked down on her gown, smoothing the fabric over her hips, "I haven't worn women's clothes since I was eleven years old, and I hated every minute, because it was always something with too many layers of lace, embroidery and ribbon. I also had to wear a wimple to court functions, lessons, and anytime I was near Momma. This is comfortable, practical and pretty. Thank you Ysanne," the woman beamed at the compliment.

When she walked into the great hall for dinner, everyone stopped talking. Blushing as she realized that everyone was staring at her, she spun to run back up the stairs to her room. Dax stepped in front of her.

"Don't run away, little beauty. We are merely stunned into silence by the goddess in our midst."

"It's just a gown," Rinna knew her face was red as Dax's hair as she walked with him to the place set for her beside Cai. It was the first evening in since they had arrived that all five men were in residence, making dinner a more celebratory affair, instead of the usual setting out food and everyone eating when they could.

Cai was delighted in what Rinna was wearing. He leaned closer, picked up her near hand and flipped it over so he could kiss the inside of her wrist, "I was half hoping I could make good on my threat, but this will do as well. You are exquisite, my love."

They spent the evening meal catching up on progress in the fortress and without, along with news. With the exit of Bannister and the cabal members, the town was becoming less averse to the idea of the transition, especially when Dax and Josiah took over the quarry, kicking out the overseer and reorganizing the work force and purpose of the place. The site had once been used to gather ingredients to make the ceramics Ragan had once been known for but had been recently used for gravel and stone for the fortress and other projects. There were two ceramic makers still in Ragan, who although older and unable to do the work like before, were willing to train some of the younger people the trade.

"What are we going to do once the slave caravans come?" Tolin asked. Travelers have been trickling through, but none carrying goods to or from Fairshine other than the one that had the wagon with the false bottom. "they will know things have changed as soon as they get here."

"Lady Rinna, what did they used to do when they came?" Cai asked, giving her hand, which he had held off and on the entire evening, a squeeze. She had been quiet, listening to the conversation, but not participating

"I have no idea. I only came here when I had to, and almost always with Garrett. We both avoided the place when the caravans came through, Lord Governor," Rinna was starting to get used to everyone calling her by the title, but she was going to make sure Cai know she still didn't like it.

Cai smirked at the tone of the end of her response. He knew she was much more comfortable and relaxed now, but he'd not yet seen her smile. It was on his list to make happen along with spending time focused on her. He listened as one of the guards was asked the same question. The caravans had gotten used to being catered to, with the drivers and guards allowed to act however they wanted, if they paid bribes to Bannister or his friends.

"It wouldn't take much for us to invite a lot of trouble if we handled it wrong," Josiah observed, "if we choke off the slave caravans on this end, then the pirates and traders at the port will come investigate, and there are a lot more of them than us, and well-armed." Josiah had spent time learning all he could from the locals.

"And if we do nothing, then we lose any ground we gain," Elgin added, "I've talked to enough here to know that they feared both the slave traders, the pirates, and whomever the powers that be in Fairshine sent this way but were helpless to act. They knew that one move would have them end up either dead or they and their families on one of the caged wagons heading to the slave markets."

"What if, no never mind, it wouldn't work," Rinna fiddled with her empty cup, thinking of how nice a cool mint tea would have been with dinner instead of the heady mead. She was glad she had salvaged a patch from her garden to run wild just outside the walls of the fortress.

"Lady Rinna?" Cai took the cup out of her hand, "we don't know if it won't work until we know what you are thinking."

"Well, I know that Marta, Patrick and the others here did everything they could to make Lord Bannister's life miserable," Rinna started, "I just wonder if we could do something similar just make it seem as Ragan is the last place the slavers want to pass through; terrible ale and food at the taverns or they closed all together, all the girls coughing and sporting rashes, few townspeople to harass, any supplies to buy of poor quality. I just wish we had a pack of anemic dogs lurking about to give it a real depressing feel."

Rinna saw that she had everyone's attention, so also shared her misgivings, "having us look like we are no threat could make it easier to spring trouble on them and free those poor people in the cages. It could backfire, once word got to the coast how bad things are here. Fairshine could decide to replace us all again. Most of us here know that has happened several times, but it could also be a way to set up a nice little pirate killing ambush if they did like last time and only send a few dozen people.

Then there is the Khaetor Empire. I don't think they care about Arowana at all, despite sending Prince Cai and his men, but the slave trade getting disrupted will."

She shook her head, "never mind. There are too many things that could go wrong."

"Cai if you don't kiss that woman right now for possessing such a devious, brilliant mind, I'm going to do it, and she'll spurn you for my superior abilities," Dax's voice boomed across the hall.

Rinna stared in shock at Dax who was sitting on the opposite side of her from Cai. The big man had the audacity to waggle his eyebrows. The next thing she knew, she was lifted out of her chair and into Cai's lap. He kissed her, his hand on her hip, the thumb stroking back and forth over her hip bone.

"Dax can't have you," He whispered in her ear, "but he's right. Your mind is brilliant and devious."

"Everyone is watching us, aren't they?" Rinna whispered back her arm resting loosely around his neck.

"Yes, my love," Cai kissed her ear.

When Rinna tried to get back up, Cai wouldn't let her, "you are going to sit here, drink mead and relax as we put teeth into this brilliant idea of yours."

"I've already had some mead," Rinna protested, blushing as she saw everyone watching, several with smiles on their faces, "more than a cup, I get tipsy."

Cai took her cup and poured mead into it, "I don't believe you."

"Fine. Don't believe me. But you are responsible for holding my hair out of my way if I throw-up that second cup," Rinna glared at Cai as she downed the contents, then set the cup back down.

"I bet she lasts six cups," Tolin declared with a grin.

"Nah, she's a bitty thing, four," someone called from the next table, which prompted a flurry of wagers.

Rinna had never cared for mead or other strong drinks, especially when they were as strong as this batch was, preferring herbed teas. The effects were swift as she felt her limbs relax and her mind get fuzzy. Cai had a hand on her hip and was playing with a curl escaped from her braid as he and the others talked. The sensations had her feeling relaxed and content. It had been a long day, she was tired, Cai's lap was much more comfortable than she would have imagined, the effects of the mead dragging her eyelids downward. She rested her head against his shoulder, soon oblivious to the people around her.

Eleven

She opened the door to her room to see Cai on the other side, holding a steaming mug. Rinna took the mug out of his hand and tried to close the door back. He merely smiled as he stopped her and walked in. His smile turned into laughter when he saw Rajah spread full out on her small bed.

"I take it you are responsible for that," Rinna sipped her tea holding on to the mug with both hands, "I woke up shoved up against the wall."

Her braid had become unraveled, and he could tell she had a headache from the lines on her forehead. Cai thought she looked adorable and was looking forward to spending a few hours with her. Rajah got off the bed, rubbing his flank against both Rinna and Cai before leaving the room.

"No, my love. When I tucked you into bed last night you were quite alone," he took her mug out of her hands and set it aside, "I also lost my part of the wager as I was certain you would last at least three cups."

He turned her to attempt to comb tangles out of her hair with his fingers. He had not expected her to fall asleep in his lap and had resisted letting the connection linger by putting her into his bed.

"What are you doing? Ow!" Rinna tugged her hair out of his hands, "thank you for the tea, now get out. I'm grumpy, I have a headache. I don't need your help," she snapped as she picked a brush off her small storage table. He plucked it out her hand, holding it out of her reach.

"I will let you have it back for a kiss, freely given," Cai gazed down at her outraged face. He didn't know why he wanted to tease her, but he was pleased to see her reaction, "you also need to teach me how to use this."

Rinna blinked up at him, "you want to learn how to brush my hair? What is wrong with you? I just had Marta cut a foot off it because it had gotten impossible to keep the tangles out. Marta had to talk me out of cutting it to my scalp." Dry, her hair currently reached just past the middle of her back. Wet it reached her hips.

Cai stepped closer, "about that kiss."

Rinna blew her breath out with a huff. His playfulness unsettled her. Everything about the man did, yet she couldn't deny she was attracted to him. Putting her hand on his chest for balance she stood on tiptoe as if to kiss him, intending to get the hairbrush instead. Just as she was about to make a grab for it, he stepped back, causing her to stumble.

"I'm sorry, lost my balance there. Mind trying again?"

She repeated the process only for him to step back again, "you are doing that on purpose."

"Yes, I am," he grinned as he kept dodging out of her grasp until he had a clear access to the door, "because you are trying to cheat you are going to have to catch me."

With a laugh, he was out the door and headed towards the stairs with Rinna right behind him. He made it to the bottom of the stairs and turned to head to the kitchen when Rinna dropped to the ground in front of him. Cai glanced up seeing how she had used a tapestry and a couple of uneven boards to shimmy down from the second floor.

"Sneaky."

"You don't play fair. I don't play fair," she held out her hand her headache forgotten, "hairbrush."

"Kiss."

"Keep it," she turned to go to the kitchen.

"I'll give it to Marta and tell her to clean the privy with it," Cai grinned as Rinna whirled about, eyes blazing.

"You wouldn't dare," she walked back towards him, "give me back my hairbrush!"

He tucked the brush into the back of his belt, "give me a kiss."

"Give me my…" Rinna launched into Cai causing him to stumble back into a table just as her lips closed over his. He caught her hands searching for her hairbrush holding them to her sides as he took what she offered.

"That my love was well done. You continue to surpass my expectations," he murmured after he decided to stop kissing her back.

"As truly entertaining as this has all been, we have more serious matters to deal with," Cai dragged his attention away from Rinna to who had interrupted their interlude. Rinna attempted to move away, but Cai turned her then held her back to him his arms resting loosely around her.

"What is it Elgin?" Cai was a bit annoyed at Elgin's interruption but Rinna in his arms made it not matter as much.

"A caravan has been spotted making its way out of the pass."

Cai felt Rinna stiffen, "how long do you think it will take them to get here?"

"Oh, at least a day," Tolin strolled in. He grinned when he saw Cai and Rinna, "what lover's play did I just miss?"

"Something about a hairbrush. You should have seen Rinna climb down from the balcony. She must be part squirrel. It was worth the look on Cai's face when he saw that she had beaten him downstairs," Elgin smirked.

"Tolin, Elgin. The caravan?"

"Last night, Dax and some of his boys decided to install a bit of a delay in case we needed more time to prepare," Tolin fixed a plate of food from the platters set out for everyone's breakfast, "you remember that small rock fall before the last switchback, it's now a lot bigger. You can get over it if you want to do a bit of climbing. A horse can manage if one takes their time with it, but wagons will find it quite impossible until they clean it out."

"When do you expect Dax back?" Cai was pleased with the news.

"In a few hours," Elgin leaned against the sideboard and began to eat from his own plate, "it's too late to call Josiah back. He will just have to miss all the fun."

"Where did Josiah go?" Rinna didn't understand why the men were so calm about the incoming caravan.

Cai kissed Rinna on the temple, "he took a few woodcutters south, my love. They plan on damming up a stream so that it floods the road, or at least makes it harder to pass."

"About the caravan," Rinna was more concerned with it. The one that had come from Fairshine bothered her. She felt guilty that they had the profits of ruined lives in their storeroom.

"Three caged wagons, about eight guards," Tolin helped himself to breakfast, "they had just started down the second switchback when we spotted them. They didn't see us. It was early morning, drizzling rain and there was a mist. I hope summers here at least get a lot warmer."

"I'll gather everyone, say fifteen minutes in the courtyard?" Elgin said.

"That works," Cai released Rinna, "is your staff prepared to take in more people, including sick and injured?" He went to the sideboard, picked up a hunk of bread, tore it in half, handing Rinna a piece, along with a chunk of cheese.

"You intend on freeing the slaves?"

"I do. What Tolin and Dax discovered about the slavers who were just here confirmed what Josiah had suspected when we encountered them on the road. If you hadn't insisted on drinking that second glass of mead, you would have been awake for the guards and every person in the room insisting we allow no more slaves to the coast if we can help it," he picked up a couple of slices of bacon, handing them to her before getting more to place on his bread, folding everything together.

"That's because most of them are former slaves themselves and do not take for granted what you gave them," Rinna returned to the table, leaning against it as she ate her food letting the comment about her capacity to hold her mead pass, her mind already whirling on housing newcomers, and supplies. She wished she had pen and paper, as it was easier to keep track of things instead of charcoal on the walls and floors of the fortress storerooms.

Thoughts about the retaliation when it was discovered

that they were attempting to quell the slave trade here crept in. Those thoughts along with all the other possible dangers she forced to the back of her mind, they too terrifying to consider. She knew that they would have to deal with ramifications when they came. Instead she concentrated on planning on extra mouths to feed and whether they had enough cloth for blankets and bandages.

She was pulled out of her thoughts by Cai's hand on her chin, tipping it up so she would look into his eyes, "you were trembling and so far, away. Are you alright?"

"Of course, there is just so much to consider and I don't even know how many people or what they will need, or how long we will have to house them," Rinna wrapped her arms around Cai laying her head on his chest. He was warm, strong and represented stability, something she'd long lacked and found she wanted. She wasn't going to mention it though. There were other things on her mind.

"Then there is wondering what the people in town will do, will they help, will they hinder, will they join forces against us. And then there is…"

"Rinna, love," Cai couldn't believe his good fortune as he stroked Rinna's hair thrilled she had willingly initiated the embrace, "breathe. You have people to help you. I have people to help me. Try not to worry."

Rinna disentangled herself, "oh, I know that Cai. We are as ready as we can be, scary as all this is," her face lit up with her smile, "I just needed to steal my hairbrush back." Laughing she went to the kitchen to find Marta.

"Brilliant and devious," Cai said to himself. She'd won the game, he got to see her laugh.

A few hours later, everything that could be put into place, was. The small population tended to shrink further as summer took hold, to tend crops or flocks away from the village. Rinna and Garrett weren't the only ones who used the summer months to gather materials and foodstuffs for the long winter ones. Less people in town meant that it was easier to make the place look far less prosperous.

Ysanne convinced the girls from the Putrid Boar to come inside the fortress for the duration or to stay in one of the empty houses. With the tavern closed, the other already shuttered, due to the owner leaving without warning, it was easier. Parents were also encouraged to either take their children away from the town or stay indoors until the slavers left.

About an hour before nightfall two men on horseback were seen coming into town. They slowed at the Putrid Boar, noticing that the building was dark with no one inside. They then rode through the town stopping before where the larger of the now dismantled houses once stood against the fortress walls. Tolin was just outside the fortress gate watching everything with seeming disinterest. As planned, Tolin was the first person the two men saw. Everyone else was out of sight as instructed. Elgin was above him on the fortress wall walk along with Dax. A roll of thunder announced an incoming rain shower.

After some deliberation, the two newcomers went to the gate. One of them addressed Tolin.

"You there. We need to see Lord Bannister."

Tolin, leaning against the wall examined the wood carving he was working on, "can't."

"What do you mean can't? I'll skewer you if you don't get Lord Bannister," the man's temper was already short from the delay of the rockslide.

"I can't get Bannister cause he's gone," Tolin purposely made himself sound lazy and uncaring. Meanwhile he was looking for weak spots in the men's defense.

"Gone? Where? Who's in charge here?" demanded the other man.

Tolin stood and scratched his groin, "don't know, don't care. They just pay me to watch the gate. It's still here don't see it leaving anytime soon either. If you want to talk to who's in charge, knock on it. I'm going to go take a piss," the two men watched as Tolin stumbled in the direction of the lake.

Elgin who was watching from the roof shook with suppressed laughter, "Tolin is a master bullshitter. I forget how good he is at it until he dazzles us again."

"And he's probably already figured out what weapons those two are carrying, their shoe size and how much coin they have on them," Dax turned with Elgin as they walked towards the stairs, "I keep wondering why Josiah hasn't tried to talk Tolin into becoming a spy."

"He has tried, not sure why Tolin hasn't agreed," Elgin nodded at the guards as they passed.

Grumbling, one of the men at the gate dismounted and knocked on the fortress gate. Rain had begun to fall, gaining in intensity as they waited for someone to come to answer.

Cai answered, opening the door just wide enough for the two men to see him. He had dirt smudged on his unshaven face, his dark hair untied and hanging in damp strands past his shoulders. His clothes were worn, fitting poorly.

"Can I help you?" Cai glanced into the faces of the man, then down again.

"We need to speak to who is in charge. Our caravan has encountered a rockslide and we need you to move the rocks out of the way, so we can proceed to the coast. We also need food and drink for our men and cargo," said the taller of the two men. He had reddish brown skin tone, a shaved head with a patterned tattoo going down his neck.

"Wait here," Cai closed the door before they could respond.

A few minutes later Cai opened the door again, "the price is ten gold coins and six of your slaves."

"That's a third of our slaves! We are not paying ten gold. Your master is a fucking thief," the man yelled at Cai.

"Suit yourself," Cai closed the door back.

The man waited a moment then pounded on the door. Cai opened it a crack, "have you changed your mind?"

"Six coins, silver, we don't have gold, and two slaves," the man demanded.

Cai closed the door back. A few minutes later he opened

it revealing himself and ten others. They shuffled out carrying tools, "master says deal."

"That's the best you got?" the second man asked, "gods above and below, it will take this lot two days just to get to the rockslide. Don't you have a wagon to ride in?"

Cai merely shrugged waiting for the two men's reaction. The one with the tattoo ordered them forward sealing his and his companion's fate. Cai and his team waited until they were well clear of the village before making their move. Tolin and Elgin joined them with horses, armor, weapons and Rajah whose ears twitched in anticipation. They rode until getting close to see the rockfall, then walked the rest of the way.

"Don't come any closer," The disembodied voice shouted. Night had fallen, and the rain had ended, leaving a light fog. "Who are you?"

"Sent up here to help. Looks like you need it." Tolin yelled back.

"Where's Callus and Birch?"

Cai and Elgin were already navigating on foot over the rockslide as Tolin answered. "Tavern."

They had set up tents for themselves, the people in the caged wagons had no shelter from the rain. The six guards were waiting, weapons out. "If you think you can sneak up here and steal our cargo, you are wrong, soon to be dead wrong," one of them snarled.

"You have a choice," Cai had his sword in his hand, Elgin his bow, arrow notched, but not raised. "you can free the people in those cages, turn around and leave, or you can try to stop us from freeing them ourselves."

"Easy choice," the guard said as he ran forward, short sword already raised, the others not far behind. By then Tolin, Josiah and the rest they'd brought with them had made it across the slide. One guard decided to try to clamor over the slide from a different spot only to encounter Rajah who was watching things with half-closed eyes. He got back down just in time to face Josiah, a dagger just leaving his hand.

Those on the wagons huddled together, scared by the brief fight and what it meant to them.

"You are safe now," Tolin told the first group as he undid the lock of their cage. "I promise, no one is going to be allowed to hurt any of you."

Cai and Elgin handed out blankets and some food they had brought with them. The rescuers did what they could to make everyone comfortable. It would be at least a day, before they could get everyone home.

*

Rinna had sent everyone she could to bed stating that everyone would need their rest. They had done all they could to prepare for their pending visitors. All they could do now was wait and that was starting to grate on everyone's nerves.

Fighting sleep as she curled up on her dining chair, the spot she'd chosen when she needed to delegate when she heard voices. She was halfway to the door when Cai walked into the room carrying a teenage girl. He set her down on one of the benches.

"Hello, my love. They are hungry, terrified and exhausted. Some have injuries," turning, he went back outside to help usher in more. He missed her sigh of relief knowing he was back and uninjured.

After helping get everyone fed, injuries tended and places to sleep, Rinna was about to drop on her feet. She'd given up her room to a pair of young sisters who were too afraid to let one out of the other's sight. It took time to convince them to take the room; only after Rinna gave them each a dagger from the weapons stores.

"If anyone barges in without your permission tonight, you take these and poke a hole or two in them," she then showed them how to move her storage table to block the door until they wanted to leave the room.

Rinna had a blanket and a small pillow and just found

a comfortable position to sleep in her dining chair when she sensed someone was standing over her. She peered up seeing Cai looking down on her with a disapproving glower. She noticed that his armor was gone and had bathed, his hair was still damp. Rinna hoped to take a bath herself in the morning.

"What do you need Cai? I'm tired, breakfast is in a few hours, we are out of blankets and I want to go to sleep. G'night," Rinna closed her eyes waving her arm listlessly at Cai.

"There is an available bed."

"No there isn't. Even doubling up, we ran out. The only one I didn't fill up was yours, and that was just in case Josiah and his group returned and needed a place to sleep. I hope he isn't mad that I gave people his room for a few days. You'll just have to share if they get back tonight. I'm glad some didn't mind sleeping there," Rinna pointed haphazardly in the direction of the fireplace where there were several sleeping bodies curled up under their blankets. She squealed when she was pulled to her feet.

"There is an available bed," he held on to her wrist, pulling her behind him until they got to his room. He stopped just inside, "this bed is big enough for both of us."

"You want me to sleep with you?" Rinna squeaked. She backed into a corner as Cai took off his shirt, tossing it aside before he sat on the bed and pulled off his boots.

Cai stopped with a boot in his hand seeing her in the corner, the candle sitting on the chest of drawers near her illuminating her blue eyes large with alarm and her face expressing her near panic.

"Rinna, love what's wrong?" as he stood to walk to her, she tried to back herself further into the corner, "why is my brave courageous love standing terrified in a corner?"

"That," Rinna pointed to the bed.

Cai realized what conclusion she had drawn. He had just been annoyed that she had again left herself out of taking care of someone's needs.

"I would never in a million lifetimes never force myself

on you."

"I know. I'm still scared," she looked down at the floor, "I don't know what to expect, what you intend, if it will…"

"Hurt?"

Rinna nodded, tears pooling in her eyes.

"Come sit down by me," she did after a moment's hesitation. Cai scooted her back, so he could take off her shoes, "hurting you is the last thing on my mind. Have I yet?"

"No."

"And I don't intend to start," he tugged on the ties of her kirtle, "take this off. Tonight, you and I are going to share a bed, as we are short of them. We are going to sleep because we both need it."

He stood, blowing out the candles sitting on the chest of drawers, then removed his clothing down to his undergarments, "tomorrow you are going to teach me how to brush your hair and everything in the beautiful brain of yours to help me be a good leader. We are going to take the time to learn about each other and explore further on what us being together means."

He sat back down beside her, moonlight from the window casting a weak shaft of light across the bed, "I'm also going to also teach you what you need to know to defend our home and lead those under our care when I cannot."

"I've had to be wary since I was eleven years old because your father destroyed everything I loved, or thought was valuable. Then those that came in their place ensured my home would stay broken. I should hate you as you are his son," she looked up into his eyes trying to ignore how little he was wearing, "I can't. I trusted you and your friends almost immediately. I don't even know why, as you are all big and can be quite terrifying. I don't think you were prepared to trust me either, yet you did."

Rinna put her hand on his forearm, noticing how pale in comparison it was to his darker skin, "I cannot ignore any of this, you and me. I've not--before I met you, I'd never kissed a man before. My world, my life has changed so fast I can't even keep up. Please understand that."

"I do. I'm not in the habit of asking women to share my bed, but it's wrong to have you sleeping in a chair when there are more comfortable options."

Twelve

She undressed, leaving on her chemise, then climbed under the covers. Cai had already gotten in watching her carefully fold her kirtle and set it on the chest of drawers along with his shirt and pants. He let out low rumbling laugh when he reached over and felt Rinna close to the edge on her side.

"There is plenty of room, my love," he pulled her close, her back to his chest, an arm draped over her waist, "better," he murmured as he kissed the back of her head.

Rinna waited for something to happen, not quite sure what it would be when she felt him relaxing. She began to relax as well finding that lying curled up against him felt just like sitting in his lap, comfortable, natural, like it was where she was supposed to be. She was almost asleep pondering the whys of that when she heard him.

"Rinna? Why were you in that little tree house when we went to your place?"

He asks the strangest questions, she thought, "I always slept there when Garrett wasn't home. We had built it when I was younger because I felt safer. I was afraid of being trapped in the house while it burned."

"Because of what happened to your home?"

"And here in Ragan. It was on fire when we arrived. A few had escaped but not many. I was afraid of being burnt up for a long time."

Cai didn't say anything, just held her, understanding the fear. He'd seen fire magicians in action. It had been on a far smaller scale than what Rinna witnessed. It had still scared him enough to stay clear of them. He found one of her hands, linking it with his.

She spoke again, "for some odd reason being in the tree didn't bother me. Garrett helped me build the tree house so I wouldn't freeze to death sleeping in a branch with just a blanket or fall out of the thing in the middle of the night.

We discovered by accident that it made an excellent hiding place if someone came along to cause trouble, which only happened a few times in the beginning," she inhaled, "no one had ever thought to look up in the branches of that tree until Rajah showed up. Why?"

"I was curious for one. We probably would have never seen the tree house either if it hadn't been for Rajah."

"I thought for sure he was going to eat me," she yawned; her eyes already closed, "then I thought he was going to break the branch the tree house was on, crush me, then eat me."

Cai snorted a laugh, "I'm surprised you dared climb down. I'm also wondering if we could use something like that defend our southern border."

Rinna turned over to face him. What was suggesting intrigued her enough that she forgot all about their nearness or how tired she was, "do you mean like a watchtower? If so it's an excellent idea and it would at least be a way to see what's coming from a greater distance if you could build them high enough. If there was a way to figure out how to send messages, you could have them set up almost to the tree line at the coast."

Cai began laughing, "I'm in bed with a beautiful woman in my arms, and we are talking about improving our defenses."

"You think I'm beautiful? Marta is the beautiful one. She is the right height, has blonde hair that doesn't tangle in the slightest breeze and the right colored eyes. Dax looks at her like a little lost puppy every time he's near her, and he's not the only one," she was silenced by Cai's lips on her own.

"You would not be here if I didn't think you were beautiful which you are," His voice was low, fingers tangled in her hair, "I don't care that you are not tall. I like your hair and blue is the perfect color for your eyes. Dax treats you like his baby sister, Josiah like the daughter he never had and threatened my life if I ever did anything to hurt you, Elgin and Tolin thought about pursuing you for about five seconds until I threatened to cut off their fingers if they tried."

One hand traced low circles at the base of her spine that sent little chills up Rinna's back, "you are mine, my love, and if we weren't both so damned tired, I would be showing you exactly how much you mean to me."

Rinna didn't know what to say after that declaration, so she draped an arm over him searching till she found the scar under his shoulder. Tucking her head under his chin, she traced the lines of it as she fell asleep. Cai hadn't known how she'd respond. A sleepy exploration of a scar had not been it. He found it soothing and intimate. Content, he fell asleep right soon after.

They didn't see each other for the next few days. Cai, Dax and a few others went early the next morning to move what rocks they could to get the caged wagons past the rockslide. Rinna was still sleeping when Cia kissed her on the shoulder as he prepared to leave. Work was done to make a clear but easily defensible passage, and to slow down newcomers just enough to give Ragan enough time to defend if needed. The job took almost a week, with everyone opting to camp where they were, saving time on the two hours it took each way. When he finally climbed into bed the night he returned, Rinna was already asleep in the middle, Rajah curled up on the side Cai preferred.

"Shoo Rajah, this is mine and Rinna's bed," Cai hissed at the cat. Rajah came and went when he pleased and seemed to prefer Rinna's company when at the fortress. When Cai was gone, Rajah usually tagged along especially if the possibility of hunting was in the offering. People had gotten somewhat used the big cat, knowing that he didn't intend them harm, unless they themselves intended it. Children loved Rajah to everyone's surprise after he discovered they would give him treats and petting.

Cai gave up on trying to move the cat who ignored him, so climbed in bed on the opposite side. He fell asleep to Rajah's purring, as he felt Rinna snuggle up to his back, wrapping an arm around his waist.

She was talking to a knot of people when he came downstairs the next morning. Cai could see that she had been up for a while and was wearing a pair of woven trousers and a man's shirt that had been refitted for her petite frame. It still reached past her knees. She'd tied her hair up into a loose knot with a few tendrils escaping, an interesting change from her usual braid.

"What are you doing?" he asked as he noticed that the four people with her were part of the group they had rescued.

"Good morning. They want to help, so I'm taking them to where some of the good fishing spots are," Rinna explained, "before you ask, I am taking a small escort with me, and my own bow, and no we aren't going far just a bit around the western shore."

"And why, Lady Rinna, do you think you need to be going, when your place is here?" Cai saw her shoulders stiffen in irritation.

And he was so sweet last night trying to get Rajah to move and not wake me, Rinna thought as she turned to face Cai.

"Because Lord Governor, we need meat, and fish is the easiest thing we can get right now. Because it's going to take a lot of fish, and other meat just to feed us, not counting what we need for the winter months, which are rather long. Because I doubt anyone here knows how to net fish except me, so I intend to teach people how. We cannot depend on or trust the people outside this fortress yet, so we must prove our self-sufficiency as well as our willingness to provide for their needs as well."

She stepped closer, continuing in a low voice, "because if I have to stay stuck in this fortress on a day so beautiful, I'm going to start breaking things."

Cai looked at the three men and one woman who were watching the exchange in interest, "Lady Rinna's safety is important, and she seems to dismiss the need for it. I'd drag her upstairs and tie her to the bed, if she wasn't right on all points."

The men looked back in surprise, the woman in approval. Rinna blushed scarlet, "Lady Rinna is responsible for the care of everyone here and she's proven quite good at it. I don't know what to do with a fishing net, she doesn't know what to do with a sword."

"I've used one as a plow before. It worked nicely until I broke it," laughing, Cai pulled her to him, kissed her then left.

A few hours later Rinna was demonstrating how to set

a net for checking later. Directing the woman, whose name was Dana to come forward with a basket, Rinna bent over and scooped out a fish throwing it into Dana's basket. Dana giggling brought her basket forward. The two women talked as they caught three more fish, throwing each into the basket.

Two of the men had gone a few yards around the lake to try their luck with a pole and a line along with a guard. The third, was sitting with his fishing pole beside him. He'd learned the workings of the net earlier. Elgin sat on a hillside watching everyone, while two more guards kept an eye out nearby.

The day was hot with no clouds. Even though the setting was pastoral, Elgin had lived too long in strife and war to trust it, which was why he was on his feet arrow notched when he saw Cai running towards the water. His eyes scanned for any hint of danger seeing Lucky grazing nearby and that Cai didn't have his sword or his leather overshirt on. He lowered his bow with a grin as he heard Rinna's cry when Cai tackled her.

Rinna didn't even know Cai was nearby until his feet hit the water of the lake. She had just enough time to cry out, before his arms closed around her and she felt herself going under. She came to the surface spluttering. Cai grinned down at her, his hands at her waist.

"Hello, my love," he said, kissing her as he slid his hands down to cup her bottom. He lifted her feet off the bottom of the lake, causing her to instinctively wrap her legs around his waist. Doing so made her aware of his erection. Her body reacting to the realization with a primal hunger she didn't know she possessed, startled as well as thrilled her.

She broke the kiss looking almost level to his face, slightly out of breath, "you are a crazy man."

"No, I am a man who very much wishes we were alone," with reluctance he set her down, "I love your hair up like that by the way. I've been thinking of your neck and shoulders all morning. Then I saw you looking like a water goddess."

"And you had to come and try to drown me?" he laughed as held her hand while they walked towards shore.

As she passed Dana and her companion, she warned, "be sure to set your nets away from the hunting ranges of any amorous Kheatorian, or else you'll not catch any fish."

They heard the duo's laughter as they continued up the hill to where Elgin sat. The elf shook his head with a smile. Cai sat down, pulling Rinna down to sit in front of him.

"Next time, cousin, warn me. I came this close to putting an arrow in your back," he teased, "I thought you were supposed to be checking on the progress of the rockslide."

"I was. It didn't take as long as I thought it would. There's just enough of an opening for wagons to go through one by one, if they want to brave the edge of the cliff. It's also an excellent place to pick off an enemy as we can access the cliff above quite easily while there is no such access from the road. I left four men building a shelter near the cliff edge."

"It's a choke point?" Rinna asked. She watched her students. The two who had gone fishing were returning, each with a string of fish. They were talking with their guard. The ones below were sitting on the ground. Dana and the other man, whose name she couldn't remember seemed to a couple.

"Yes, my love. It's a choke point," he untied her hair, combing it out with his fingers, "but it's also our best way out of here in case we need to leave. It's been easy so far. I don't expect that to continue. We need an escape route just in case."

"Looks like our new fisher folk are ready to head back," standing, Elgin smiled knowingly at Cai who wouldn't let Rinna stand, "just get back before dark."

"We need to go back. There's so much to do."

Cai stood, helping Rinna to her feet as Elgin joined the others, "I seem to remember you saying that you needed a day out of the fortress. I caught a glimpse of a waterfall nearby when I was up on the pass. It looks pretty."

"If it's across the road, then I know it. It's a bit of a climb." Rinna liked the idea of an afternoon of idle exploring with Cai. "I don't think your horse could manage it."

As expected, they had to leave Cai's horse, the terrain too

steep for it to navigate. He was happily munching on grass by the stream as Cai followed Rinna. She scrambled easily to their destination.

"Tolin is right, you are part squirrel," Cai had not expected it to be so steep, or her so fast. She was standing, the waterfall behind her, hands on her hips as if she'd been waiting awhile. Cai sat down on a large rock to catch his breath and admire the view.

Rinna pivoted slightly to face the waterfall. "I've been coming here for a long time. This is where I hide my most valuable treasures."

The waterfall was about sixty feet tall spilling into clear deep pool before meandering on the other end down the mountainside in a series of small pools, spillways and cataracts, its destination the stream that exited the lake. The waterfall itself wasn't large, the water falling into the pool in an almost sheer curtain with little ribbons finding their own paths along the mossy rocks until they too fell into the pool. A few rays of sunshine filtered through the trees, but it was clear that the brightness of day was short lived in this grotto being surrounded on three sides by tree topped cliffs. The rocks were covered with moss and ferns with a few flowers scattered about, and dozens of brightly colored mushrooms.

"It's a beautiful spot," he watched as Rinna walked to the edge of the pool, then dove in. Standing, he could see her swim to the bottom then swim back up to the surface. She swam the few feet needed to be able to stand then walked back to shore holding out her closed hand. Cai held his out where she dropped a stone with a green crystal embedded in it.

Cai looked at the emerald in wonder, "is that what I think it is?"

"I think so. I found my first one when I was thirteen. Sometimes I find nothing, sometimes I do. Once I found three, all lying side by side," she gestured at the stone in his hand, "no one has ever known about this until just now. Not even Garrett knew."

"Why are you showing me?"

She was shivering from the cold water, her nipples showing through the thin fabric of her shirt, her hair dripping behind her as it curled before his eyes.

"Because, I trust you. I would have suggested somewhere else if I didn't. There may come a time where riches are necessary. It's not much, but it could buy a few swords or passage out of here."

Cai started to reach for her, but she stepped back, pointed to the waterfall and smiled, "I'll be over there. Follow if you dare," she dove back into the water swimming until she disappeared beyond the waterfall.

Cai waded in, his breath catching as he felt the temperature of the water. Taking a big breath, he dove in himself. If he hadn't been holding his breath, he would have yelled out from the shock of the chilly water hitting his body. He came up on the other side gasping.

Rinna sat on a ledge, her legs dangling in the water giggling, "I didn't think you'd do it once you felt how cold the water is. It took me over an hour to work up the nerve the first time I came here."

Cai found he could stand, the water about knee high. He pulled Rinna to him so that her legs straddled him, "you are very brave and devious, but I think you already know that."

He kissed her neck, his hands at her ribs just under her breasts, as hers went around his neck winding her fingers through his hair. He reached up, cupping both breasts, feeling her chilled nipples through her shirt with his thumbs.

"Cai! What are you doing?" Rinna gasped.

"Showing you that when done right, the art of love is very pleasurable. We are alone, no one is about, and I thought we could teach each other a thing or two." He reached down for the hem of her shirt, pulling it off. He stopped her hands when she went to cover herself.

"Oh, my love, don't ever think that you are not beautiful," laying her back on the ledge she sat on, he bent so that he could take a breast in his mouth.

She arched her back as his tongue ran lazy circles around her areola. She held his head in place as she felt her body thrum in delicious anticipation, something she wanted to escalate. Cai's hands were on her hips, his thumbs stroking her hip bones. She squirmed thinking her other breast felt left out when she heard voices.

"Cai," she hissed.

"What love? If you move your bottom, I can get these pants off."

"Cai, I hear voices," Rinna whispered, "someone is coming." He straightened, hearing the voices as well.

"Fuck. You are right. Someone is coming."

Rinna scooted to the back of the ledge, "did you leave anything outside, anything at all?"

"No. My boots will take days to dry and I left my sword on Lucky," he climbed up next to Rinna, gathering her in his arms.

"Unless they are very curious, then they will never see us," she rested her head in the crook of his neck. They were both cold, the close contact helped warm them. "If they are very curious there is a sword and a bow and arrows to your left."

"I thought I loved you before, now I'm sure of it. You brought weapons here?"

Rinna was trying to get her body to stop shivering, "yes, this is one of my hiding places just in case it became unsafe. Wait, you love me?"

He felt her shivering. He was doing plenty of it himself. The air in the cave was warmer than the water, but not by much. In the dim light, He could see that there was enough space to lie down, and that there seemed to be a breeze coming from a crack in the wall behind him.

"From the moment you jumped down from your tree house. Is that a problem?"

She snuggled in closer, keeping an eye towards the other side of the waterfall. The water flow was strong enough thanks to recent rains to prevent them from seeing through. The day she had first explored the waterfall, there hadn't been rain in weeks, and the spillway was a fraction of what it was now. She was able to see the shelf on the other side which had piqued her curiosity. When she has taken the weapons there a few days later, there was even less water. It had allowed her to swim over holding them over her head and access the space without getting them wet.

"No. I would not have shown you this place if it was."

A minute later they heard the voices again, except louder as two figures appeared at the far end of the pool. There was just enough water between them so that Cai and Rinna could not make out what they looked like, just that they were moving about. Cai was surprised that he could hear them over the sound of water hitting the pool.

"I was certain there would be someone up here, it is that phony Lord Governor's horse down there," one of them said, their voices echoing off the walls of the grotto.

"You are insane," the other one sounded as out of breath as the first one had, "it was one hell of climb getting here, for what, a waterfall? I know you think he took that little bitch somewhere to fuck her, but no woman is worth that climb."

"Well we have his horse, and his sword. He will want it, and when he comes looking for it, we will be minus one asshole. Let's go back to camp. When we get to the farm tomorrow, we can let Donner know what we've found," the first man said. Cai and Rinna listened as they heard the voices fade as the two men left.

"First of all, I did not climb up here just to fuck you. Second, you are worth climbing up here in winter and having to chip through ice to just to hold you for a single minute," Cai tried to give Rinna her shirt. She ignored it as she kissed him, her arms holding him close.

"I know that, and I wouldn't expect you to chip through ice. I have better places to hide in winter," Rinna answered.

"How many hiding places do you have?"

"Three," she disentangled herself crawling to a corner

where she pulled out the sword and the bow and arrows. She moved a bowl out of the way as she worked. Cai picked it up. It was half filled with emeralds.

"Do all your hiding places hide a fortune in jewels?" Cai set the bowl back down as she handed him the sword.

"No, just this one, but both of the others have weapons. One has blankets and some furs. It is my winter hiding spot. The third a net, and blankets. I couldn't keep any of that here because it's too damp."

"I'm beyond impressed. It took some serious planning," Cai looked at the sword in the fading light. There was some rust on it, but it was serviceable.

"It was Garrett's idea. He knew we wouldn't be able to defend ourselves against an armed assault. So, we set up the other two hiding spots."

"You were planning on heading to one of them when we found you, weren't you?"

"Yes. Ragan has changed hands about once every two years until you came. Twice the newcomers went on pillaging trips to try to weed out any possible resistance. They were never subtle, so we could hear them coming a long way off," she slid into the water, her breaths coming fast as she adjusted to the temperature.

"It will be dark here soon. If we want out of here, we need to do it now," she dove under the waterfall coming out the other side, holding on to the bow and quiver of arrows. Cai followed holding the sword and her shirt.

"You will want this," Cai helped Rinna into her wet shirt, "you look like a warrior queen without it, especially with that bow in your hand."

Once the shirt was back on, and Cai had kissed her making her want to return to what they had been doing earlier, she slung the quiver over her shoulder. The bow she kept in her hand. They started down together, her leading being familiar with the way.

She stopped a few feet down, twisting her upper body to

look back up at him, "you look like a god, a deity of vengeance and justice with all those muscles and those amazingly beautiful eyes."

"You think I look like a god?" Cai asked in surprise. No woman had ever complimented him on his appearance before. Her laughter at his expression echoed through the grotto as she made her way down stream, leaving him behind.

Thirteen

By the time Cai reached Rinna, she was sitting on a large rock by the stream. The sun's placement in the sky showed that it was late afternoon. The temperature was also much warmer than at the waterfall.

"You should have waited on me," he sat next to her looking around for any sign of trouble before leaning the sword he carried against the rock.

"If I had, I wouldn't have seen which way they'd gone," she had her knees up to her chest as if she was still cold, her damp hair hanging down her back.

"Rinna."

"They didn't see or hear me. They were too busy cursing and slipping over the rocks to bother looking back," she wouldn't look at Cai. The men had spooked her, confirming the threat they represented and how dangerous Ragan still was. She had caught up to them a lot faster than she thought she would, so remained hidden out of sight as she watched them descend to more level ground.

"I wish Rajah was here. He's big and terrifying, a bit like you, but he is also good and lovable, also like you, isn't he?

Cai put an arm around Rinna's shoulder, "Rajah is a predator and creatures like him are usually trained to be battle cats. He's quick, lethal and doesn't care if people are squeamish about his using his natural instincts. He likes children and you. He's also somewhat sentient."

Rinna rested her head in the crook of Cai's neck. She felt safer knowing he was beside her, "what do you mean?"

"We communicate in a way. He senses when I'm in danger, he guards you because he knows you're mine, and he understands when I ask him to stay away from humans, at least I think he understands. He's never complained. He's still a big kitten. He's just over a year old."

"Cai?" Rinna sat up. She faced him uncertain what his response would be, "that first day, when you told Rajah to guard me. Did you think I was yours then?"

"No. But Rajah did," at Rinna's incredulous look Cai took her hands, "there's this myth that bonded saber cats will choose his bonded's mate. When Dax told me that is what Rajah had done, I thought he was joking. Yet, here we are. I started calling you my love almost immediately and have meant it every time."

"Well I think Rajah chose well."

Cai barked out a laugh as he hugged Rinna, "I know he did. And when we get home, we are going to finish that lesson we started."

Rinna was silent for a moment. Then she looked up at him as a smile crossed her face, "if the rest of the lesson is as wonderful as the beginning was, I'm looking forward to it."

She stroked the side of his face feeling the stubble of his beard as she brought her lips to his. Enchanted, he nibbled on her bottom lip as he drew her body closer.

Cai felt the bump behind him breaking his concentration and the kiss. He turned to see Rajah sitting on the rock, acting like he'd been there the entire time. Rinna saw Rajah and laughed. She reached over and gave his nose a scratch.

"Rajah, I want you to take Rinna home. Make sure she gets there safe," Cai told the cat.

"Rajah pay him no mind. Cai needs his horse and sword and he's not going to go get it by himself," Rinna countered.

"Rinna, these are ruthless people and I'm not going to put you in danger," Cai looked down at her feet, "you also have no shoes."

"I hadn't planned to come here, so didn't wear any. Besides yours are wet," Rinna pulled her hair over her shoulder to braid it, "I've grown up here. I know where every stream is, every good hiding place, where the ground is swampy, where the mosquitoes will eat you alive in the summer. If you want to find them easy, you need me, or else we go home, and you try later with better equipped help."

Rinna slid off the rock to face him, her hands on her hips,

"meanwhile those two men disappear to whatever farm they were going to and we have nothing to show for it."

Rajah decided for them. He yawned, stretched, jumped off the rock and walked a few steps north, before looking back at the humans.

"Devious and brilliant," Cai said as he took Rinna's hand to follow the saber cat.

They found their quarry about thirty minutes later at the edge of a meadow, near a swampy pond. There were five of them and nine horses, including Cai's Lucky. Cai, Rinna and Rajah found a good vantage point on a rise behind some brambles. Rinna was delighted by the hiding spot, quickly picking berries from the brambles and popping them into her mouth, before handing Cai a handful. The berries were juicy and sweet with a hint of bitter sour in a few of them.

"These remind me of the ones you wouldn't let me gather. They are bigger and grow in little trailing plants close to the ground. Seeing those men confirms that you were right to reject my idea to go, so enjoy these while they last, they are probably our supper," she noticed the men occasionally slap themselves.

"They will be miserable after dark. Mosquitoes love standing water like that, and fresh victims," Rinna had learned that lesson the hard way years ago.

"Miserable means less alert. They seem to not be expecting any trouble either. Their overconfidence can work in our favor," Cai picked a twig out of Rinna's hair as she handed him a handful of berries.

They watched as darkness fell, eating all the berries Rinna could pick without being seen. They took turns watching and sharing things about themselves. Rinna shared more about Garrett. They'd made an odd pair, young Rinna was far better at finding food and things they may need, and he was better at organizing, cooking and keeping her from turning too wild.

"By the time I was thirteen, I'd explored most of the area around the lake and all of the streams going up the mountains. Once I reached fifteen, I was supplementing our diet with rabbits and ducks," Rinna was laying on her back as she spoke, "Garrett insisted I learn civilized things too, as he feared I'd become a savage. If I hadn't had my books and his damned lessons in deportment and diplomacy, I probably would have become one."

Cai, who's turn it was to watch, lay on his side so he could see both the camp and Rinna. "I would think you'd not trust people at all," he had practiced making braids on Rinna's head. She now had six on one side of her head, earning him a kiss for each completed braid.

"Blame Garrett. He insisted on dragging me to the market every couple of months, at least when he deemed it safe. I had to learn to haggle prices, demonstrate manners, and recognize when someone was trying to cheat us," she made a face, "I never liked doing that kind of thing. As I got older, I had to do it more and more, as Garrett became more withdrawn. Still I rarely went alone. I'd seen how women could be treated enough times to be wary."

They were both quiet for a few minutes to watch squirrels chatter and posture because they felt Rajah was too close to their nest. The saber cat ignored them. Rinna slapped a mosquito on Cai's arm, "we are too close to the pond. They are going to get fat off our blood."

Cai told about meeting Josiah, "he had been sent by one of my loving brothers to assassinate me. Josiah is very good about sneaking in, killing you, and you not realizing you are bleeding out until after he's thrown back his second tankard of ale at the local tavern. He got quite the surprise when he sneaked into my tent. I was traveling with the army to offer escort to the king's chief treasurer, the intention to count and bring back the loot from a desert kingdom he had just destroyed. Josiah got about two feet in and promptly tripped over Rajah, who had sensed him coming a long way off. Rajah was still a small kitten, and I don't think the brother in question ever thought I'd take him with me."

Rinna tried to imagine Josiah tripping over anything. The man was old enough to be her father yet had a fluidity and grace to him that was mesmerizing. Cai started on his seventh braid.

"I couldn't help it, I started laughing, especially when Rajah sat on the man's chest purring."

"Rajah as a kitten. I bet he was adorable," Rinna thought the look of concentration on Cai's face as he braided her hair was equally so.

"Josiah's' curiosity got the better of him. He ended up telling me that he'd only taken the job because he'd been thinking of getting married again and needed enough money to buy the would-be bride a house. When he revealed that she had two other men also trying to do the same, I asked him if she was worth all the trouble. He said no, that his first three wives put her to shame, and has stuck with me since. That was a year ago."

"Three wives?"

"Yeah. He had three at the same time, adored them all, and they he, the way he talks about them. Lost them to a Khaetor governor who decided that Josiah needed to be his personal assassin. When Josiah refused the governor had his wives executed. The governor didn't live out the day."

"Poor Josiah," Rinna said, "he didn't deserve that."

"He's adopted you as his daughter, you know," Cai dangled the seventh braid over Rinna's nose, before collecting his kiss.

"I know. I think they all have in their fashion," she rolled over, "my turn to watch." While she watched, she braided Cai's head far faster than the seven he had done. By the time it was dark, his entire head was covered in shoulder-length braids. She then took the ones he had made and worked them into one tying it off with a few strands of grass.

None of the men were familiar to Rinna, but then she admitted she had always tried to limit her contacts to the people she and Garrett had traded with. Cai suspected that they were a scouting party, planning on returning to wherever their base. Rinna disagreed, arguing that they had a lot of things with them to be a mere scouting party.

"We need at least one alive," Cai said, "I'm also disappointed Donner wasn't one of them. He I wouldn't leave alive, no matter how much he begged."

They had been looking at different ways either to retrieve Cai's horse and get rid of or subdue the men for the past hour. The best approach was from the meadow, but it was too exposed. There were several large trees, with interlocking branches in the swampy area around the pond with branches hung that over the camp.

"Dark or not, they will see you or Rajah coming from a long way off. We could wait till they are asleep."

"I'd rather not. We've been gone too long already, and we need to learn where these bastards are heading," Cai glanced over at Rajah who was -stretched out half on his back, "I'd send Rajah to scare them, but I don't want to risk their injuring him. I didn't train him for war but to defend and protect."

"We can't let them get away either."

"I know my love. We need a distraction. And I don't see how we can make that happen."

"I think I do," she pointed to one of the trees. It was a massive oak near the edge of the campsite, "I can get up there and shoot one of them. If I angle it right, they won't be able to tell exactly where the shot came from."

Cai hadn't liked the idea, but he hadn't thought of anything better, "I don't know. You need to cross open ground. What if they see you?"

"They won't. It is close enough to other trees that I can get to it and never touch the ground. I'm part squirrel, Tolin said so," they spent the next several minutes discussing strategy which all hinged on Rinna making the first move.

"Are you sure you can do it, shoot a man again?"

"The idea is terrifying. But I know what I need to do. I don't intend to kill him, just give him a surprise and their focus away from you. I'll be out of that tree and in another before they know I was ever there. I know they had intended on killing us, and I suspect that they've been sent to rob or kill people who prefer to stay away from civilization, if you can call Ragan civilized," she kissed him, then gathered her bow and three arrows,

"I'll just imagine my target as a big rabbit."

The slivered moon was above by the time she made her way to her chosen perch. It was about twelve feet off the ground and far out enough on the branch that she had a clear view of the camp below her. Moving slowly so not to draw attention she drew back her bow and fired. She gasped as her target chose that moment to look up, his eyes widening in surprise just as she released the arrow. He moved, causing her to miss the shot, hitting the man in the side of his neck instead of grazing his upper arm as planned.

The man bellowed falling to the ground as blood spurted from the wound. He pointed upward as he held his neck. Rinna began to scramble back up the branch as the other men saw her and began throwing things at her. Something hit her thigh hard enough to throw her off balance. She tried in vain to remain on the branch, but another object hit her shoulder knocking her off completely. Rinna fell to the ground, knocking the breath out of her. She lay stunned, gasping for air as she saw the men approach. The one she had shot remained by the fire bleeding to death.

They never got to her as a beige and brown blur slammed into the nearest man throwing him to the ground in a spray of blood and a cut off scream. Rajah turned to the next man grabbing him by a leg where the saber cat slung the man up in the air, then pounced on him as he landed. Then Cai was there. He engaged with a third man who was wielding an ax. That man was no match of Cai's ferocity and skill. Soon he too was lying on the ground, dead from a fatal wound caused by his own sword. The fifth man attempted to run off, but didn't get far, as Rajah overtook him in two bounds. His screams went on a bit longer before ending. It was over in seconds.

"I'm sorry. I'm sorry," Rinna gasped between sobs, "he saw me just as I shot him. I couldn't get away in time."

"It's okay love. You did well. A bit more of a distraction than I was hoping for, but you did well," Cai's heart settled down to a less frantic level seeing Rinna move. He'd been certain the fall out of the tree had killed her. He helped her turn over seeing a dagger embedded in her thigh, "you have a knife in your leg. I need to get it out, Okay?"

He ripped Rinna's trouser leg to expose the wound which was halfway up her thigh. An inch further to the outside of her leg, it would have just left a gash.

"Dammit to the icy hells of a long dead war god! I'm telling Dax that you are hurting me and then he's going to grind your bones to make bread."

Cai couldn't help but laugh at her reference to a popular children's story, "then he will just have to, because I'm not done. Sorry my love, it's going to hurt a little bit longer."

As gently as he could, he pulled out the knife, then using the torn trouser leg wrapped the wound. He was grateful the knife had not hit an artery, but he needed to get her home for proper care. Rinna found tufts of grass on either side of her and pulled on them as he worked trying not to cry out anymore, tears of pain rolling down her face.

"I'm done, Rinna. I'm done," Cai gathered her in his arms, kissing the tears away, "I'm going to find you a blanket and see about getting us out of here."

Rajah trotted close to her, laying down a few feet away. He began to clean his paws as his tail flicked randomly, seeming to be quite pleased with himself.

"Rajah," the cat turned to look at Rinna. The fire was behind him turning him into a dark shadow, "thank you. I don't know if you understand me. What you did was gruesome, but you saved my life, probably Cai's too." Rajah yawned and returned his attention to his paw.

Cai soon returned with a blanket and a piece of bread, "there's meat on the fire, but I don't trust it, not after Rajah's done battle. He tends to be messy." He sat next to her with his own piece of bread swatting at mosquitoes.

"We should have just let Rajah at them," Rinna said, "I had no idea he was so fast."

"I didn't train Rajah that way. Saber cats trained to kill on command usually end up having to be killed themselves after deciding that hunting humans is too easy," Cai explained, "I didn't want to turn him into a monster. That was the first time I've seen him attack without me already engaged, and in trouble and that's only happened once."

"You are saying he came to my defense?" Rinna was impressed and a bit relieved that Rajah was not the killing machine most of his species was reputed to be.

"He was just a lot faster at it than I was. I should have never agreed to your part in this."

"Well, it worked," Rinna pointed out, "we got your horse and sword back, and five men who I'm sure have been up to a whole lot of evil things won't do it anymore."

"I don't disagree. I just didn't expect you to see things that way."

Rinna huffed, "the man I shot? I recognized his voice from the waterfall. They intended to kill us. They are with Donner, who we know is a murderer and probably planning something bad."

"You've a warrior's heart, my love."

"No. I will think about my part in all this later and that I've now killed twice and cry over it, now that I know I should have gone with my first choice and the higher, less exposed branch. I just know that until we have peace, we will have to fight. I don't like it, but it's that or hiding, or running away. I have too many people I care about in my life to consider either anymore, so I will fight if I must. I just hope it's not for long."

"I stand by what I said. You are a warrior," Cai stood up. "I'm going to ready all the horses. We could use more anyway. Do you mind waiting until then?"

Rinna's leg throbbed in pain, she was tired and sore, figuring she had other injuries they couldn't see in the dark, "I'll be fine. What are we going to do about them?"

"I'll send out a patrol to bury the bodies and to gather up what remains here once we get back home," he stiffened as he saw Rajah stop washing himself and gather up into a crouch.

The big cat quickly charged away from Cai and Rinna stopping again in a crouch, running a few more feet before stopping again. Suddenly Rajah bounded away followed by the sound of voices raised in surprise. Cai was on his feet, sword in hand as he stood in front of Rinna. Seconds later Elgin and Tolin rode into view accompanied by six guards. Rinna could see Cai relax as his friends approached.

"Josiah is going to be pissed," Tolin said, dismounting off his horse, "once again mayhem has been had and he missed it."

"Is he back?" Cai grasped the forearms of Elgin, then Tolin in greeting

"Yes, right before dark, and he has some stories to tell as I'm sure you do," Elgin saw Rinna sitting on the ground. "Lady Rinna."

"She fell out of a tree and has a stab wound. I'd like to get her home," Cai bent over and picked Rinna up.

"Of course, cousin. We will stay here and clean up," Elgin said, noting the gentle manner Cai handled Rinna and her quiet acceptance of his care. *Whatever had happened, their time together has been productive*, he thought.

Rinna felt every jolt of Lucky's trot on the ride home. She gritted her teeth and endured until they reached the courtyard of the fortress. Only then did she give a sigh of relief.

Cai looked down at her, "are you in pain, my love?"

"Yes. I did a bit more then get a hole in my leg," she rested her head on his shoulder as he carried her inside and to Cai's room with Marta in their wake. Despite her insistence, Cai wouldn't leave the room as Marta unfastened the impromptu bandage on Rinna's thigh. She asked Cai to get Eolande who was one of the rescued slaves and a healer. Cai realized he'd been tricked when Eolande hurried into the room ahead of him and Marta slammed the door in his face.

Eolande cleaned and stitched Rinna's wound. Once done she rested a hand over it for a moment. Rinna felt a warm tingling until Eolande lifted her hand and began to wrap her thigh in a soft bandage. The woman hadn't said anything, just worked with speed and gentleness.

"Thank you Eolande," Rinna felt the throbbing pain in her leg lessen, "how did you make it tingle like that?"

"I have the gift of healing. It doesn't hurt as much does it?" she wouldn't look at Rinna's face.

"No. It just tingled and felt warm, then better. Whatever you did, I am grateful."

She touched Eolande's arm. Her skin was a dark brown, her hair tied up in a strip of burlap. As all the former slaves she was too thin and constantly wary. "Your presence here will be most welcome, and you will be quite popular once everyone knows how good you are at your craft. I would love to spend some time with you learning more about what plants can be beneficial for medicine and preparing whatever you would need."

Eolande blinked in shock, "you would?"

Rinna smiled at her, "I will pester you over it, asking tons of questions."

Eolande smiled back. Rinna saw the tension leave the woman's body. Marta who had been holding Rinna's hand while Eolande stitched the stab wound could wait no longer.

"You and Prince Cai. What happened? Did he finally achieve the goal of getting you alone and writhing in ecstasy?" Marta snickered at Rinna's shocked face.

Eolande started to leave, but Marta stopped her, "I know you must be curious. Cai plays a strange game. He kisses her senseless, has her moved into his room, then ignores her for days. Then today he spirits her away, takes her on an adventure then brings her home with bruises and a hole in her leg. I just want to know if she had some fun too."

Eolande looked between Marta and Rinna, already good friends. She was older than them both but recognized the invitation. Sitting on the edge of the bed, she said, "I want details, every kiss, every sigh and just what Prince Cai has under those trousers of his."

Marta, her mouth opened in surprise, stared at Eolande.

She shut it, then grinned, "I knew I liked you the moment I saw you. Now I am convinced."

"I don't know," Rinna said blushing, "but if we hadn't been interrupted, I'm sure I would have found out."

She looked between the two women, one a new friend, and told the story, leaving out the details of the location of the waterfall and exactly what they were doing when they were interrupted.

"I like Cai's hairstyle," Marta teased, tugging at one of Rinna's new braids, once Rinna had told her story.

"He wanted to learn how to help me with my hair. Crazy man," Rinna bit her lip, "he says he loves me."

"And you?" Eolande glanced at Marta who was leaning back on the headboard with a satisfied grin on her face.

"I love him, and I'm scared."

Marta slipped an arm around Rinna, "scared? Why? The man would probably walk through fire for you. Yeah, he tends to be a bit on the protective side, but he's also wise enough to seek your advice, and delegate the job of keeping this place running to you."

"That, that's not it," Rinna sighed, feeling Eolande join Marta putting an arm around on her other side.

"It's the sex, isn't it?" Eolande asked.

Rinna nodded.

"I assume you are still a virgin and have only witnessed what happens between men and women in a negative manner until now," Rinna was astonished by Eolande's insight.

"How did you know?"

Eolande's laughter was low and melodious, "I'm a healing witch. One of the things we are well versed in is sex, dear heart. Our magic is from the earth, nature. Sex is part of nature."

She gave Rinna a kiss on the cheek, "I've seen how the Lord Governor acts around you. I doubt you will be disappointed. But here is my advice. Tell him what you want, what you like, what you don't. It will shock him to the core, and then he will go out of his way to satisfy."

Fourteen

Cai found Josiah and Dax on the roof. They had a jug of ale they were sharing between them. Josiah motioned to a place on the ground next to him, then handed Cai the jug, "how is she?"

"She gave me a scare but will be fine. She's got a dagger wound in her thigh and scrapes and bruises. I should have never agreed to let her help me. Her falling out of that tree is going to haunt me for a while," Cai took a deep swallow of the ale, "Marta and Eolande threw me out of my own bedroom."

Dax laughed, "Don't feel too bad Cai. Marta has thrown me out of her bedroom four times already." The big man grinned, "yet she keeps letting me back in."

Cai relayed what had happened with he and Rinna, omitting details about Rinna's hiding place, only that they had visited a waterfall. He also didn't share any details about the progression of their relationship.

Telling of the attack on the scouts and Rajah's immediate response when Rinna fell, Cai concluded, "I wish we had left one of them alive, but Rajah was having none of it. I could feel his rage knowing Rinna was in danger. Hell, I fed off it."

"You going to tell her of the bonding?" Dax took the jug away from Cai, discovered it was empty so set it aside, "she needs to know."

"She knows. Took it better than I thought, too," Cai leaned back on the parapet. His friends then teased him about his hair, something Cai had forgotten about. He offered no more other than they had found a way to pass the time while waiting for dark, deciding instead to undo Rinna's work. Josiah took the time to tell of his adventures.

"Making a bog was easy. There was a beaver dam that had partially clogged a stream close to a small bridge. We removed the bridge, adding some of the lumber to fortify the beaver dam. Wagons trying to cross are going to get stuck. Horses will find themselves ankle deep in muck," Josiah took one of his knives out to scratch at a spot on his cheek, then replaced it, "it was so easy, we decided to do a bit of spying."

"What did you find out?" Cai was feeling the effects of the long day and the ale so stretched out his legs to get more comfortable. He could hear the small cataract by the mill, and the croaking of frogs from the lake.

"They were expecting a shipment of slaves from this direction any day. Two have already come from the largest pass, Silver Vale I think it's called, to Fairshine have been falling off in the past few years. Nothing has come from the pass next to ours since Fairshine fell or the one furthest south. That is just making tensions worse between the merchants and the pirates who settled on Fairshine as a base, but that's nothing new when pirates are in the mix. There's also been a coup among what functions for government, and guess who landed on top?"

Cai didn't have to guess, "Bannister."

Josiah stretched out next to Cai, "got it in one. The one with the nose is with him and a Khaetorian who resembles you. I saw them strutting about in finery as guards poked spears at anyone who got close."

"You think one of my brothers is here?" Cai had lost count of his siblings some time ago.

Josiah pulled off his boots with a satisfied sigh. Cai already had removed his, his toes still wrinkled from wearing them while swimming in them twice. They would need a couple of days to dry out.

"I wouldn't put anything past that father of yours. There were more ships in the harbor than last time, and plenty of armed men. The place is a mess. It's mostly squalor, hastily built houses, shops and taverns, rickety docks, burnt out districts overrun by rats, feral cats, packs of dogs, and these reptiles. I don't know what they are called; they are just big and mean. There's some new construction for those running the place in charge, of course. That's where we saw Bannister and his new friend go."

"Shit. That means that Bannister and whatever hell

spawn of a brother is there, they know I'm here and what we've done so far," Cai got up and started pacing, "we are not capable of holding off an army."

"True, but unless they have a good spy among us, I don't think they know what all we've done, or that we are aware of them," Josiah stripped off his vest and his shirt. He laid down on the wooden walkway, placing his hands behind his head, "remember, they left a week or two after we arrived, sneaking off with everything they could carry out of those big houses. And we let them."

He yawned, stretching his back, "I've been recruiting my own spies. Those that I took with me, I picked for a reason. I left two of them to keep watch. They will return as soon as they have a bit more information. I told them three weeks, no more."

"That doesn't do us any good here," Dax heard laughter from the far wall walk. Two guards faced towards the mountains sharing a joke. He turned his attention back to Josiah when they moved apart.

"You know me better than that. I've got little sneaks here. I'll be meeting with them in the morning. If we have rats in our grain bin, then we won't for long," Josiah stood, his clothes and boots in his hands.

"I'm going to bed. Dax, If Marta lets you back into her room, please keep the moaning and screaming down to a minimum," Josiah's room was downstairs, next to Marta's.

Dax's laughter echoed off the nearby lake as he slapped Cai on the shoulder. "You should see the look on your face Cai. I'm going to fetch the delightful Marta and take her to my room. We shall see if she can throw me out of that."

Cai laughed, but his best friend wasn't finished. Dax waggled his eyebrows at Cai, "I'd suggest you finally take advantage of the fact you have a certain beauty you've finagled into your own bed. I'm sure you haven't yet, as it's too quiet in there at night, but I think you've damaged her enough for one day."

"I don't think he has either," Josiah deadpanned, "he takes her on a hunting excursion too, when he had all afternoon for other activities."

Cai couldn't help but smile at his friends' teasing as they parted for the evening. Going downstairs he knocked on the door of his room, then hearing her answer entered. Rinna was sitting on the edge of the bed wearing a woven shift. She had her hair over her shoulder brushing it. She looked up when she saw him and smiled.

"Marta was impressed that you knew how to braid hair."

Cai sat down beside her and took the brush out of her hand, completing the task of brushing for her. Handing her back the brush, he leaned back against the headboard, his hands watching her braid the curled length, tying off the end with a scrap of ribbon.

"How are you feeling?"

Rinna laid down, wincing when she moved her legs up onto the bed, "it hurts to move or put weight on my leg. Marta and Eolande counted eight bruises. There's a big one on my shoulder. Whatever they threw at me after the knife is what knocked me out of the tree. I'm sore, tired, and glad to be home. I'll feel it more tomorrow."

"I'm glad to be home too and that you are here safe with me," Cai got up, blew out the lights, undressed then climbed into bed, turning his back to her, "go to sleep my love. We have a lot to discuss tomorrow."

Rinna stared at his back in shock when he didn't move. She threw back the covers and slid off the mattress. She hobbled to the door, her injured leg refusing to do much to cooperate.

"Where are you going?" Cai sat up, "I thought you couldn't put weight on your leg."

"I said it hurt to put weight on it, not that I couldn't," Rinna snapped, knowing that she wouldn't get far. The pain in her leg had increased. She'd be lucky to make it to the stairs.

"It seems that I've done something to offend you, so I'm going to sleep elsewhere," she tried to open the door, only to find that she couldn't.

"You are not leaving. Come back to bed," Cai's voice low,

dangerous and right behind her. He'd moved faster than she thought he could.

"Not until you tell me why you are angry with me. If you won't, then let go of the door," Rinna turned. Cai had both hands above her head holding the door closed as he leaned over her.

"I'm not angry. Why would you think that?"

"Then what is going on here?" Rinna didn't understand, "you leave for a while, then come back polite and distant and act like I'm untouchable. You've not done that since we met."

"You weren't injured before," Cai said, his voice barely above a whisper, "I already caused you pain once tonight. I'm not doing it again."

"I've fallen out of trees before. I was nearly in as bad a shape when you met me as I am now, well minus the hole in my leg, and you didn't mind touching me then," Rinna's voice raised in frustration, "you only saw my face, not the rest."

Cai renewed his vow to end the life of the former tavern owner. He'd not considered that there would have been more injuries on Rinna other than the bruising on her face. He guessed at why she was upset.

"Dammit Rinna. You were sitting there brushing your hair looking beautiful and inviting--you didn't look like you'd almost yourself killed helping me get Lucky back. I had almost forgotten that until you moved."

"Oh," Rinna understood then. Even though she was still uncertain about intimacy with Cai, her curiosity and own desire was stronger.

"Do you have any idea what I want to do to you?" Cai didn't trust himself to touch her.

She placed a tentative hand on his chest, "Show me," she whispered.

"Rinna."

"Please?"

Cai needed no further encouragement. He untied the ribbon at the top of her shift, shoving it off her body as his mouth ravaged hers. His hands found her breasts, as hers wrapped under his arms to cling to his shoulders. She felt a storm building in her lower body as the sensations from what he was doing to her nipples triggered delicious sensations in her vagina.

Cai slid his hands down, picking her up by the waist leaning them both into the door. Rinna got one leg wrapped around him. The other she couldn't lift. She moved her arms to around his neck feeling his hands move further down to cup her bottom. Once he had her supported, he stumbled to the bed, locked in a kiss as Rinna wasn't letting his mouth disconnect from hers. Their fall to the bed was clumsy.

At Rinna's muffled cry of pain, Cai froze, "I'm sorry my love. I misjudged the distance."

He started to move away, but she held him tighter, "everything was fine until we landed."

"And now?"

"I'm naked, in the arms of the man I love, and I was reminded earlier that I don't know what's under your trousers," Rinna started to lift her head to kiss him when he lowered his to the crook of her neck, his shoulders shaking with laughter.

Cai's voice was muffled by her hair, "Marta?"

"And Eolande."

Cai lifted himself up long enough to divest himself of the last of his clothing, then lay back down, resting on his forearms on either side of her. He began by dropping kisses along her collar bone then worked his way down her body, stopping briefly to kiss each nipple before continuing further. He moved her injured leg so that it was bent in as comfortable position as it could be. Her other was already draped around his back. Cai found each of her hands holding them to her sides.

Rinna didn't know what Cai was intending then moaned in pleasure as she felt exactly what he was doing. His tongue found her clitoris running lazy circles around it. Rinna arched her back, trying to free her hands. Cai just held them more firmly as he licked his way down to her vagina, tasting the entrance. She'd had no idea that what he was doing would rob her of any awareness but the glorious sensations he was causing with his mouth.

He had her forgetting her injured leg, that she was naked, or what had happened a few hours prior. All that she could think was don't stop. Rinna squirmed helplessly from the pleasure he was lavishing her upon her. He felt her passion build, and then rise faster as his tongue destroyed all her resistance. He sucked unrelenting with his mouth at her clitoris, delighted in her helpless moans. He then upped the assault as she cried out her orgasm.

"That my love, is just one of many ways we bring delight to one another," he moved so that he was back where he had started. He entered her, watching in the dim light as her eyes grew round.

"This is another," he growled, his hands on each side of her shoulders, her hands gripping his arms. He pulled out, hesitated, then back in, allowing her to adjust to the new sensation.

"Oh Cai. Do that again," Rinna was breathless in wonder, the mystery solved of what it would feel like. She'd heard that the first time was painful so was relieved to find that it was instead like he was a snug fit.

"Don't worry. I intend to. You feel better than I imagined."

He set a pace, slow and gentle at first picking up in pace and intensity, that soon had her keening with each thrust. She tried to hold on to something when he stood up holding her hips off the mattress. Finding it impossible, she threw her arms out to her side as she gave herself to the building storm Cai was creating. They came together, joined completely as wave after wave crashed over them.

"Cai?" he had collapsed on her, his legs and hers draped over the edge of the bed, his face buried in her hair. One of Rinna's arms stayed flayed out to one side, the other on his lower back. Neither felt like moving.

"Yes, my love."

"How many ways are there?" Cai laughed as he stood back up and found a cloth to clean themselves with then moved her all the way onto the bed, before climbing in himself.

He wrapped her up close to him, "I don't exactly know. But I think we can find at least one more before we are too tired to move. I didn't hurt you, did I? I know it can be uncomfortable, the first time. How does your leg feel? I didn't…"

" No. It didn't hurt at all. My leg? I forgot all about it for a while," Rinna had her injured leg draped over his. It throbbed but not as much as she expected knowing Eolande had done something to ease the pain with her magical touch. She felt languid and quite content, assured that Cai loved her and she him, "I love you Cai."

Cai smoothed an errant curl away from Rinna's face, "I love you, my love."

He woke up the next morning quite aroused. That's when he saw that Rinna had laid her head on his chest, her body draped mostly on him as her hand stroked him. She gripped him tighter as she moved her damaged leg, eliciting a groan from Cai.

She lifted her head to look at him, her hand already moved away, "I'm hurting you. I'm sorry."

Cai rolled over taking her with him mindful of her leg, "if that was pain, then I'd like more of it."

Rinna didn't get to say anything else before he was kissing her, helping her shift her body so he could help her finish what she started.

After their heartbeats began to slow. Cai raised up on an elbow to look down on her. Her braid partially undone, lips stiff swollen from their kisses, her legs stretched out with his.

"I did not expect how you woke me up this morning, my love."

"I think that part of you woke up before the rest," Rinna lifted her head to kiss him. She had woken up and seen him, covers thrown off, looking decadent. She had spent several happy moments just looking at him as he slept, memorizing the look of his body. His erection got her attention, having her wondering if pleasuring him was something she'd enjoy. It was.

Cai rolled over, sitting up on the edge of the bed, "I am a very fortunate man and I love you."

Rinna lay on her side as she watched him gather up his clothes, then her shift which had remained on the floor by the door, before sitting back down. She could hear people outside of their room as they passed by on their way to the roof.

"I love you too," Rinna got herself to a sitting position, "damn, I was going…"

"Going to stay put," he kissed her nose that was wrinkled in disgust, "you think walking on that leg was hard yesterday."

"I can't stay in here all day."

"You should, but I get it. I wouldn't either," Cai found the rest of her clothes handing them to her, "I'd be happy to stay in here with you, but like I said last night, there is a lot to do. Josiah is back and hopefully Elgin and Tolin will be soon."

Rinna got dressed taking time to sponge herself off. Cai had her sitting on the edge of the bed for most of it, mindful of her injury. He silently counted her bruises as she dressed vowing to never let her get that close to danger again. He kissed her on the neck after helping her with her shoes ready for them to leave the room. He had it on his mind to get Patrick to make him a pair of shoes like hers as he didn't have a spare pair, something lighter weight for indoors. He'd left his boots on the roof to dry.

"Cai?" Rinna sat on the edge of the bed, feeling the pain in her leg, every bruise along with a bit of soreness from their activities during the night and the morning, "I need to ask you something."

He had been just about to pick her up to carry her downstairs. She had lost the fight to walk anywhere herself for the day, "you can ask me anything."

"Are you expecting me to get pregnant?"

That wasn't a question he had considered, "it's one of the things that can happen when we do what we've done," he sat down next to Rinna.

"I know that, but do you want me to?" Rinna's expression was pensive, and it confused Cai.

"Why are you asking this?

"Because if you don't, I can take some herbs that prevent

it from happening," Rinna looked at the floor not at him, "all the priests used to rail against women using them, saying a woman's duty was to birth sons and the men all seemed to agree. A lot of used the herbs anyway, well except for Momma. She was always pregnant."

"Rinna. If you want a baby, then we will have one. If you don't, then we won't," Cai kissed her after smoothing away a tendril of hair, "can I suggest--can we wait a while until having a little girl or boy? I just found you, and I'm not quite ready to share."

The relief in her face was so profound, that Cai knew he had made the right suggestion. He wrapped his arms around her, "why did this bother you so?"

"I don't know."

"Then we wait. Besides, we need to give our children a safe place to grow up, don't you think?" Cai never thought he would be having this conversation with any woman. He'd had few express any interest in him, seeing his mixed heritage as something that diminished their interest despite his connection to the crown. Rinna hadn't cared about that, only cautious because of who his father was. He wanted children with her one day. That it could be decided for when they were both ready, was a happy surprise.

A few minutes later the six of them gathered to catch up and plan. Elgin and Tolin had returned with news of their own. Elgin speared a slice of ham from the platter in front of them.

"I thought at first the men you killed might have been a scouting party, checking our defenses and looking for weaknesses. I was partially right. They also seem to have been raiding some of the outlying farms and homesteads. They had food, tools and weapons, as well as some coins, probably holdovers from the old kingdom. We brought everything back."

Tolin leaned back in his chair, "a few of the men we took with us offered to visit possible locations the raiders may have visited, to check on them, ask if they needed assistance as well as to see if any of the locations might be hiding spots," he looked at Rinna. "would you know where any of them may be located?"

"No. I stuck mostly to places I could get to in a day, maybe two, except in the early summer when I went into the higher elevations for some berries and plants that didn't grow down here," she made a face at Cai signaling that she had been right about the five raiders, "I knew there were people who preferred the more solitary life, but I didn't I meet any of them."

"That means we have potential threats on two fronts. Terrible odds as usual," Dax joked.

"Things are interesting in Fairshine, and I'll know more once the spies return," Josiah noticed Dax watching Marta walk across the room. He smirked at the look on the big man's face. "They are trying to organize, but there is a lot of infighting. The pirate guild is mad that port fees have risen and that the local government can't quite control the thugs and mercenaries who they've hired to keep the pirates from taking over. As expected, the populace stuck in the middle, sullen and afraid. My spies have tried to see if anyone was talking about us here before I left but neither of them heard a peep. Either we are not important, or we are not yet a priority."

Cai nodded, "that gives us time then, at least on that front. What about enemies on the inside?"

Josiah's grin was feral, "oh, we have one or two. We haven't had time to ferret them out as I've been away. I had just put my little friends on the task."

Rinna who had been listening, spoke up, "would our hidden enemies know about what happened yesterday?"

"I don't know. Why do you ask?" Josiah wondered.

"For one, I think we need to determine just who to trust. How much attention did we get when we came in last night?" she looked to Cai for the answer.

"Not much actually. It was pretty late, and we didn't go out of our way to draw attention to ourselves," Cai could almost see the wheels turning in her head.

"And pretty much everyone saw you and Tolin leave and come back, right?" the question was directed at Elgin.

Elgin grinned, "you want to set a trap. Have them think that you or Cai is missing, or both and see who goes somewhere they shouldn't be."

"Something like that. If we make it seem that we are spreading our people thin, looking for the missing Lord Governor..."

"Then we may just flush out Donner and his thugs while finding out what enemies still lurk in our midst," Dax slapped a hand on the table making Rinna jump, "I sent out three small patrols this morning, all heading to the upper mountains, two to the south, one north. They could easily be taken for search parties. It's a simple task to make it seem that is exactly what we are doing."

Tolin grinned, "it will just mean keeping you and Cai out of sight for a few days. Like that's going to be a problem."

"It won't be," Dax smirked, "they know how to keep occupied."

Cai groaned, "as soon as possible, I'm building a house so Rinna and I can have privacy."

Rinna looked at him in confusion for a moment, then at Dax's knowing grin. She blushed as realization set in, "I'm going to the kitchen, where no one can see me die of embarrassment."

"No, you won't," Eolande who had been sitting at another table stood and walked over, "you are going to sit right there, or somewhere comfortable and stay off that leg as much as possible until I know you aren't going to catch infection. I also want to look at it."

Rinna held her skirts out of the way as the healer examined the wound, lay her hand over it for a healing push, then applied fresh poultice before rewrapping it. Eolande smiled when Marta brought Rinna a mug of tea, and Rinna's face when she took her first sip. The healer had mentioned an herbal solution against pregnancy to both women, which was like what Rinna thought had been used by women in Fairshine. Rinna's questioning expression had Eolande nodding in agreement.

"Lord Governor, I am going to ask that you ensure she

keeps her off her feet as much as possible for a few days. Her wound was deep, and she needs to let it heal," Eolande used a matter of fact voice causing Rinna and Marta to exchange grins. They liked the transformation from the pensive woman Eolande had been. Seeing Eolande adopt what they assumed was a natural demeanor, delighted them.

"Just don't translate, off her feet to on her back," Tolin quipped, Cai glowered as Rinna blushed scarlet.

"I was going to suggest I have you as my advisor today in council, you've not participated yet, and you need to; but I like the idea of using our supposed absence to flush out potential spies," Cai picked up Rinna's hand, kissing her fingertips. He saw Josiah nod in approval, "I think we need a day to plan, to spend in private council just the six of us, and to rest. None of us have had it in a while."

"Spoken like a wise leader," Elgin replied.

Fifteen

A small pavilion was set up on the fortress roof with a couple of benches shoved together for a table and blankets and furs heaped up to lounge upon. The set up was Josiah's idea who had grown up in an arid climate where the use of shade and natural breezes were important. Rinna suggested using some of the time to meet with the former captives and household staff, giving everyone a comfortable setting to ease tensions. Food and drink were set out for people to enjoy as they came and went, creating a welcoming environment. Rajah appeared as soon as Cai and Rinna got to the roof, settling down behind them. He was an exotic and dangerous looking backrest.

Rinna who had taken her first sip from a mug of cool tea, giggled as she heard Marta's shouts. A moment later the protesting woman was sitting on Dax's lap who had plopped down next to Rinna and Cai.

"Tell this bearded oaf to let me go. I have work to do," Marta gave a pleading glace to Cai who grinned, watching his best friend nibble on Marta's ear.

"Marta, when is the last time you had a rest day?" Rinna knew her friend she had found in Dax what she had found in Cai, love and happiness, "or anyone else?"

Marta scowled at Rinna who was leaning back on Cai, then the other men in the group. She then relaxed, but not before pushing Dax's face away, "the day you all showed up and tossed Lord Bannister and his henchmen out on their asses."

"Then that needs to change," Rinna's leg throbbed. Eolande had ordered her off her feet for the day and Cai was happy to help her comply. Spending the day relaxing and in the company of people she'd come to care about was a gift she wasn't going to take for granted.

"She's right," Josiah tasted his mug of ale, finding it acceptable, "everyone has worked hard and has had to quickly adapt. We've just taken in twenty-two people, several of which need our care and attention, and we have enemies we will need to defeat, but we will only weaken ourselves if we don't see to our own needs or to plan ahead."

Cai was content, wishing he could set all the responsibilities and worries away for a while and lose himself in Rinna, but he recognized the need for connection and harmony within the fortress and its residents. He couldn't ignore the wisdom of stepping back regularly for rest and reevaluation.

He watched Marta as he had for several weeks, certain that he was making the right decision, "Marta. Would you be willing to be one of my advisors? Your insight would be welcome. You've already proven yourself invaluable."

Marta's mouth dropped open in shock, "me?" she glared up at Dax pointing a finger in his face, "you put him up to it."

"No cherished one. I did not," Dax glanced at Cai in surprise and pride, "but I agree with his decision. You know the people who live and work here and in Ragan better than the rest of us, and you are a natural leader."

Josiah and the others agreed that Marta would only make Cai's council that much better. Once everyone confirmed Cai's decision, Dax happily drowned out any of Marta's protests with kisses.

Cai was glad for his friend who had finally won over the beautiful Marta, "also, I want Lady Rinna to focus on other duties," he kissed her temple when she looked at him sharply and the others laughed, "not what I am thinking, my love as tempting as that is. You are good at planning ahead, seeing things from angles we may not, and you have the most education and experience in government spending in time in court. I avoided court as much as I could, hated the place. I need you to help us prepare to oversee all Arowana. Marta and Dax can manage Ragan.

"You are putting us in charge of Ragan?" Dax hadn't expected that decision.

"Unless you want to lead elsewhere," Cai had already figured that Dax was quite happy to stay here with Marta and build a life, "I need to discuss it with Rinna, but I'm sure that we will end up in Fairshine."

Dax looked down to the woman in his arms, "what do you think?"

"You are asking me?" Marta couldn't help but tease the man she adored, "you've never asked me before."

"I never had to before," Dax teased back. His face fell when she burst into tears.

"I think she is in agreement," Josiah observed Marta clinging to Dax, as the big man rocked her.

Rinna thought about returning to the home of her childhood. The idea frightened her, yet she'd known since she'd thrown her lot in with Cai, that was the intended goal. It was a future she would have to prepare for.

Cai had felt her tension with the announcement. He picked up one of Rinna's curls, twisting it around his finger. He leaned his head to whisper, "we're not going tomorrow, my love. We will talk about it later."

Rinna nodded glad that it was a topic for another time.

The morning passed spending time with each of the people rescued from the slave caravan. The younger ones had been already been adopted by families in town who'd lost their own children. The adoptive parents had been given assurances of support as well as admonishments to treat the youngsters as precious, seeing how children were few in post conquest Ragan. The parents, several tearful, as they welcomed their new children promised that their new family members would be loved as their own blood.

Today the remaining adults were given the option to try to return home if they wished or to settle in Ragan and the surrounding area. Everyone opted to stay and were asked to agree to recognize Cai and his council as the existing government and to abide by any and all laws as well as to try to help rebuild Arowana as a peaceful prosperous province.

One of the men rescued commented, "although I expected to be shoved on a slave ship and now find myself free, I have no desire to pledge allegiance to the empire that encourages the harvest of its residents for profit or that destroyed my home."

Cai recognized the challenge from the man, "I did not ask you to recognize the Khaetor Empire as your rulers, did I?"

"But you are Kheatorian, and son to its king," the man protested.

"Half. The other half is elven of the Silverwood region that the empire conquered and deforested. One of my council members is of that region and my cousin. Two are citizens of Arowana and the rest from other conquered provinces. We do not intend to follow in the footsteps or practices of Emperor Corbaine."

The others gathered looked at each other warily

"You speak treason. You risk all our lives," the man said.

Elgin spoke up, "what is your name sir?"

"Tova," he was of average height with ebony skin, He was so thin his ribs showed from under his frayed vest.

"What did you do before you were captured?"

Tova's distrust of the line of question was palatable, "I was a papermaker."

Rinna sat up, "what did you use for material?"

"Cotton rags and Jute," Tova took a step back in alarm as she smiled broadly.

"Would hemp, or flax work?" Rinna leaned forward, her focus completely on Tova.

"Y-yes, I think it would," he watched as she detached herself from Cai, then tried to stand. Tova could see pain flash across her face. The couple had a brief whispered conversation before Cai stood and carried her around the table to where Tova stood. He let her down on her feet, then stepped back. Rinna held out her hands. Tova hesitated then placed his larger one in hers noting that her eyes were shining with unshed tears.

Rinna looked into Tova's eyes, "one of our greatest treasures was lost when Arowana was betrayed by the ruler of Khaetor, our library. It had existed for four hundred years, growing bit by bit as new volumes of books, documents and maps were added to it. People came from hundreds of miles away to visit and study in that library. I spent many happy hours there myself there when I was a child. It was destroyed in minutes."

She noted the look of sadness and horror on his face, "I escaped by happenstance with three books from that library. Two, were sold to survive, needing the supplies purchased more, the last was destroyed recently by someone who did not understand or care about its value.

I've seen one new piece of paper in ten years. That was the decree naming Prince Cai as Lord Governor of Arowana. That decree was itself a betrayal, of father to son, king to kingdom. Yes, Cai is son to the king, born to a slave, an elf from Silverwood. Emperor Corbaine intended for the Lord Governor, his son, to fail."

Tova distrust was obvious when he glanced over to Cai who had moved to stand beside Rinna allowing her to lean on him, "you ask me to agree to follow a governor that the Khaetor Empire has no desire to see succeed in his task? Do you realize how audacious that sounds?"

"From the smile on Rinna's face, I can see she likes you Tova," Cai relaxed knowing Rinna had just convinced the man. He just didn't know it yet. "She likes you partially because of your skill, but also because you recognize that what we are trying to do is indeed audacious. She expressed the exact same doubts just a couple of months ago. I still made her a member of my council and my consort."

Rinna turned her head to look up at Cai with an odd expression on her face, "it's true. I was a little girl when Emperor Corbaine and his fire priests murdered my family and most of my countrymen. I know what Cai is trying to do is right. I met Corbaine a month before he destroyed us. I disliked him on sight, he and his magicians. I knew there was something wrong about him. I didn't trust him. My father didn't either but kept his misgivings private. No one listens to little girls who don't look or act like expected and those that could have done something remained silent. Prince Cai is nothing like his father or else I would have done everything I could to usurp him."

Tova stared down at Rinna's pale hands still in his dark ones. No one had touched him in a show of affection since his beloved had died of a wasting disease. The feeling wanted to have him fall to his knees in grief and relief.

"Just one sheet of paper, huh?" he gave Rinna a sad smile, his own eyes shining with tears, "you know I can't rebuild that library."

"I know that Tova. But you can make paper, so we can teach children their letters, to send out proclamations, to draw maps or plans, or even pictures and you can teach others how to make paper as well," she dropped his hands, "I understand if you want to return home and rebuild your life, and I wouldn't blame you, as we cannot offer a certain future here, but I'd be grateful if you considered staying."

Tova watched as Rinna was carried back to her seat by Cai where he settled her into his lap. He couldn't help himself. He laughed, "Lord Governor, you chose well when you picked Lady Rinna as your consort. Her beauty hides a delightful, quick mind, with a touch of the underhand. She is an asset to your council. I accept the offer to stay and the conditions with one exception. I will not take up arms."

"Nor will I ask you to," Cai replied, "I welcome you as a citizen of Ragan. One day, I will offer you and everyone else citizenship in Arowana."

"I'm your consort?" Rinna whispered as he picked up a hand, linking his fingers with hers before wrapping both arms across her stomach.

"You are more," he murmured back.

While Tova and Rinna were talking, Josiah's attention had been drawn away to a pair of children, a boy and a girl who talked in low tones but with animation. When they were done, he handed something to each child. They smiled and scampered off back down the stairs as quickly as they had arrived. Josiah nodded to Tolin. Together they got up and left the pavilion following the children's' path in a more leisurely pace.

"I take it they have news," noted Elgin.

"From the looks on both their faces, I am going to guess that Rinna's ruse worked," Cai noticed the confusion on Marta's face, "Rinna suggested trying to help flush out any spies by making it seem either myself or Lady Rinna was missing. We haven't been seen outside the fortress since we both left yesterday morning."

"Tolin and I made a lot of noise yesterday when we headed out to find them, so most of the village saw us. They also saw us return this morning, riding in without them. Rinna and Cai came in after most people had already gone to bed. Whispers were sent out this morning that they had not returned, and we had found evidence of foul play. We also sent out three teams to check on outlying residents, giving hints that they were actually search parties."

Marta's brow furrowed in confusion, "but I thought Cai and Rinna got rid of the people who had intended harm."

"That's right, darling," Dax explained. He hugged her as he watched her eyes light up with comprehension.

"Ah. But whoever is trying to hurt us don't know what really happened," Marta grinned in understanding.

"And," Dax concluded, "we've kept the fortress closed to outsiders since Cai and Rinna returned last night."

About an hour later, a caravan was spotted, making its way down the mountain. It was soon reported to be a shipment of barrels. Marta asked, "do the barrels have blue painted ends?"

Elgin was using a spyglass to watch the process of the caravan having the best vision, "I can't tell from here. They are still too far away. I just can tell it looks like barrels not cages."

"Several things come here in barrels," Marta was obviously happy with any choice. She held up a finger for each, "wine, vinegar, oil, ale or mead are the most common. Whichever it is, we want all of it."

"Then Lady Marta. I will trust you to negotiate the purchase of the cargo," Cai declared. They then planned what to do once the caravan arrived.

The next morning the caravan pulled into the village of Ragan. The lead driver and his guard noted that the place looked even shabbier than before. The closed taverns were a surprise as were the missing houses that once stood against the fortress. The six wagons stopped outside the gates then four men worked to unload three barrels. Marta and Dax walked out of the fortress while they were unloading watching a few feet away.

"Three barrels is not enough," Marta said, when the men had finished.

"Lady, the price of passage has been three barrels of ale for the past two years. More and we lose profit," the lead driver who was also the merchant admired the pretty blonde in the dark green gown.

"We want all the barrels."

"You seek to rob us? those are unacceptable terms," the merchant argued.

Marta looked at the man with a solemn expression, "no. We want to buy them." She named a price.

"We get more per barrel at the coast. Why should we settle for less here?"

"Because you have at least another four days of travel with no habitation between here and Fairshine, loss of at least another barrel in bribes, then to wait on a return cargo, more bribes to appease those in control at the coast which costs you time and money as you have to feed and house your animals and yourself as you wait," Marta countered, "with us, you get a fair price for all twelve barrels, and far shorter time away from your homes and families."

"But no return cargo," the merchant smiled seeing that he was in for some negotiating. He eyed the large bearded giant beside the blonde woman, understanding that the village had seen a change in control. He hoped this one was for the better, as his profits had been shrinking with every trip. He'd planned on making this one his last. This shift in power had him seeing new possibilities with less risk.

In the end, he sold all twelve barrels of oil, and was taking back a variety of items including three bolts of velvet he was certain he had had to give up as a bribe on an earlier trip. He knew he would have his new cargo sold before he got home, and his cut of the oil profits would be much larger than expected.

Once negotiations were concluded, the doors of the fortress were opened, and the wagons allowed inside, while the other three barrels were rolled in behind them. As soon as the last wagon passed through the entrance, the doors of the fortress shut again.

"I apologize for not having better accommodations than the stables for you," Dax gestured to one of the tables for the men to sit after they had seen to their horses and the barrels unloaded, "we are a fortress under transition and have no spare beds. The former local lord left things in less than pristine condition. The Lord Governor has chosen to make Ragan his headquarters for now as he begins the task of rebuilding the province. He would be here this evening but is away overseeing other matters. He apologizes for the unexpected changes regarding trade and hopes for better trade relations in the future."

"I must say," one of the other drivers said as he tasted his dish of lake trout grilled in herbs, "this is a lot better treatment than we've been used to getting here. We are used to having to stay at one of the taverns; and your slaves, you have them trained so well."

The look Marta gave him was frigid, "we have no slaves here."

"No slaves?" the man stammered, "but how can you get anything done without slaves?"

"As you can see, quite well. Abolishing slavery in this village was one of the first things the Lord Governor did when he arrived. It will be expanded throughout the province in time," Dax winked at Marta as he watched their guests digest the information.

It was well after dark before Dax, Marta and Elgin met with Cai and Rinna. Elgin had spent some time speaking with Eolande and had returned looking thoughtful."

Marta, if I see you in the kitchen tomorrow, I'm going to chase you out, injured leg or not," Rinna warned, "we shoved our roles on to you, and you never did get a proper rest planning for today."

"I enjoyed playing lady of the manor and driving a hard bargain over a man who thought he could cheat me while I batted my eyes at him," Marta said with a laugh, "it was worth it to hear Dax growling behind his beard with jealousy when the merchant kept looking at my breasts."

"Which she had on near full display," Dax grumbled. Marta had adjusted her chemise and kirtle to enhance her breasts. Once they had concluded their business with the merchants, Dax took Marta to the buttery where it took a good half hour to readjust her clothing.

"I still don't like telling them that we have abolished slavery," Rinna said, "I'm glad we did…"

Cai stopped her with a kiss, "my love, it was your first council suggestion, and an excellent one."

"I'm worried about the possible ramifications. What if the slavers decide to send an army after us? Do we want to be on the lookout for a third set of enemies?"

"Is this the most commonly used pass to the coast?" Cai understood her fears.

She shook her head, "no, this is the next to the smallest."

He picked up one of Rinna's curls and twirled it around his finger, "I asked how many caravans on average came from the mountains during the travel season. I was told ten, and about fifteen going the other way. That's twenty-five total groups or about one to two a week which hasn't happened. Trade is down. Of the ones so far, we've gained a more diverse workforce and some necessary supplies."

"You intend to close the route to the coast," Rinna had suspected that is what he was up to, not what he said next.

"No, my love. I intend to control it, build Ragan into a strong border town that has an independent viable industry, then do the same to the next route over. Arowana fell because it depended on the capital for its defenses while the capital assumed the mountains offered adequate protection. You said that when it was attacked there were soldiers coming from the road to Ragan, am I correct?"

Dax was trying and failing to keep his hands where they belonged with Marta, who kept trying to keep them from wandering, "I was fourteen and had just been conscripted when Arowana was taken. Some of the men I served under bragged about how easy it was to take the kingdom, because the borders were undefended. They marched in, and then marched right back out losing almost no one."

"I'm sorry, but your people didn't stand a chance, which is why my father went after you in the first place, it was easy. Those he can't take by force, he makes trade deals with, then proceeds to rob them blind, by sending in the most unscrupulous merchants and officials he can find. He wanted your port, your treasury and to say he did it, nothing more. He didn't even bring back any slaves to show off or add to his harem, just had his troops and magicians destroy everything and everyone they could find on their way in and out," Cai wrapped his arms around Rinna who was trembling, "you and Garrett were very, very fortunate."

"I know," she held onto Cai, "it's just hard to hear how bad it truly was."

Elgin had been listening, spoke up, "Corbaine hates to lose. He's gotten away with what he has, because he has his magicians and has made it sound like he's got more power and might than he really does. He has also kept the court in turmoil, playing people against each other, while allowing his territories to fall into ruin."

Cai, rubbed Rinna's back, noticing that Marta too was distraught, tears in her eyes with her head tucked into Dax's shoulder, "when I, when we decided to stay, I determined that we would not make things easy for him anymore, at least not here. You helped me make that decision, as did Marta, Dax's recruits, Patrick and Ysanne. Yesterday confirmed it when you put hope back in the eyes of a man whose ribs I could count, and Marta did it today when she showed a wily merchant her shrewd negotiating skill."

Dax chuckled, "my golden-haired beauty is indeed a shrewd negotiator. She wouldn't let me buy her heart, so I had to steal it," he stood pulling Marta to her feet. "We'll see you in the morning."

Elgin watched Dax and Marta walk down the stairs from the rooftop. He then sat down right beside them, interrupting their sly touches, "I talked to Eolande about you today," he said without preamble.

"Me? What about?" Rinna wondered.

"She agrees with me that you are like Cai, a half elf. Eolande told me that you two were the second and third half-elves she's encountered," Elgin glanced over at Cai then back to Rinna, "my cousin who loves you very much told me what your guardian had told you, your feeling like an outsider in your family. He knew it bothered you, and he wanted advice."

"There are stories about elves visiting before I was born, and I'm sure my father met them. He didn't trust people who were not human, and he didn't have much use for women. It seems odd to me that he would have taken a non-human lover. He barely acknowledged the female servants in the house, only Momma and me, and the queen when he had to. He didn't like Princess Esmeralda, but few people did once they got to know her."

"Maybe he wasn't really your father," Cai suggested, frowning when she shook her head.

"My brothers all had hair like mine, except blonde, Papa did too," Rinna stared into the forest beyond the portico, "I never fit in with my family or any of the people at court. I was just too different and was told repeatedly that I was not pretty or and I got called some ugly names, by my brothers and some of the girls at court. I ended up thinking I was a foundling my parents took pity on and tried to stay out of everyone's way."

Rinna was quiet as she blinked away a tear. She then

reached over and squeezed Elgin's hand, "thank you. I knew almost immediately that I belonged when I met you and Cai. Maybe my missing heritage is why."

Cai had her sitting on the edge of the bed wrapped in his arms right after he closed the door to their bedroom, "the question you asked me about being pregnant, it was related to your past, wasn't it?"

"Women in court were valued for few things, their lineage through their fathers, their beauty, their ability to keep a good home and entertain, and the number of sons they could birth," she ran little kisses along his chest, "I was not going to survive in that world."

"I value you for your beauty, your mind, your ingenuity, your passion for your countrymen, your bravery, your body," He undid the ties on her kirtle then the ribbon on her chemise. Once there he pushed it all off her shoulders exposing her breasts. "If we have ten children, or none, that will not change what I value in you."

"I value you for your strength, your courage, your honesty, your willingness to seek advice, your passion to right wrong, your beauty and your body," she helped him undress as he had her as she spoke, "I am yours; you are mine."

Cai repeated as he lay her down on the bed and poised above her, "I am yours; you are mine."

Sixteen

The next morning, the gates of the fortress were opened enough to allow Dax, Marta, and three guards out, along with two barrels of oil. Chairs were produced for Dax and Marta who waited silently for the townspeople to notice what was happening. It didn't take long for a small crowd to gather. The population of Ragan had never risen above one hundred in the decade since Arowana was conquered, now it was down to sixty-seven including the thirty-eight people inside the fortress that was feeling the strain of too many people for the space.

When Dax felt he had enough people's attention, he stood and began speaking, "yesterday, we took delivery of twelve barrels of good quality olive oil. The oil should see to the needs of the fortress as well as to the citizens of Ragan. Some will be held back for future trade."

He saw that he had everyone's attention, "every household will receive a jar of oil. Appeals can be made for larger amounts, but they will need to prove the need. Once you have run out, then more can be purchased, either through service or trade. Businesses will receive the same offer with one exception. They will start with two jars."

"You are going to enslave us through access of something we need?" shouted a man in the crowd, "this is worse than what we endured before!"

"How much do you think a jar of oil is worth?" Dax asked the man, "I assure you it is far less than what you were being charged before. We settled on either on an hour labor for unskilled, half for skilled. The labor can be helping to finish helping repair the buildings here in the village, helping dig a new well, or a decent cistern for our bodily waste, building and manning the watchtowers we will be using, adding to our supply of food, lumber or other resources."

"Where is the Lord Governor? Why isn't he saying all this

instead of you?" another shouted.

"The Lord governor is not available today. I am his second in command, in charge in his absence," he had anticipated the question because of the rumors they had spread, so chose to mention Cai's supposed absence and move on. "We also have twenty-two new residents, most of whom have been staying within the fortress as they recover from their harsh treatment by slavers. They will soon be moving among you. We are fortunate to have several skilled craftsmen among them who will help Ragan prosper and become self-sufficient."

"Self-sufficient?" yelled the first man, "we are the subjects of the Khaetor Empire, the Lord Governor resides at Fairshine and we exist at his whim."

Dax stepped forward walking through the crowd that parted before him until he stood in front of the man who spoke. His voice was quiet, with a hint of sadness, "do you think that whoever currently holds the old capital cares about us here?"

"Do you wish to continue that type of existence wondering when someone is going to decide to raze the place again, or would you rather be able to live your life without having to worry about being enslaved, or killed by the hands of oppressors?"

He heard several sharp intakes of breath as those around him understood what he was suggesting. "Yes, it's a bold question, but it's also something all of you should be asking," he turned and walked back to Marta, his hair flowing behind in a breeze him while his beard parted at his chin and followed that on his head. He winked at her before turning back to face the villagers.

"Lord Josiah and Tolin are hunting the fugitive Donner who murdered one of his girls in cold blood. While they look, they are also looking for any we suspect are causing harm to our neighbors in some of the farms and homes in the upper elevations. They will be brought to justice for their crimes. Our intention is a peaceful community, as well as one who can defend our borders," Dax sat down and picked up Marta's hand kissing it.

"What now?" She whispered, "they are going to wonder why we didn't mention Cai."

"Now we wait. Remember we never made an official statement of where Cai and Rinna are. They'll figure it out," he nibbled on her fingers, sending little thrills through her body, "how about a little wager? Who do you think will come forward for oil first?"

They both guessed wrong, as it was the first man who spoke who came forward, prompted by his wife. The doors of the fortress were opened to allow freer passage of people, including several of the recently rescued, who took tentative steps outside the gate. They were immediately greeted by the children who had been captured with them, causing tearful re-unions and the meeting of new families. Dax and Marta went back inside to allow what had become a festive setting to flourish.

Tolin arrived as Dax and Marta were crossing the court-yard. He dismounted, handing the reigns of his horse to some-one standing nearby. He stopped a moment looking back at the queue for oil just outside the gate then went to Dax.

"Obviously we've missed some fun," Tolin said, "if we didn't need extra hands, we'd simply leave you out of it, but..." he grinned as he watched Dax's eyebrows raise.

"Marta? Go get Cai and Elgin. I think we boys are going hunting," Dax smiled wistfully as he watched her hurry inside.

Tolin grinned, "I still can't believe she finally let you into her bed."

"Gave up on that, took her to mine and she decided it was a better place. I'll not be ridding of her easily," he stroked his beard, "not that I mind."

About fifteen minutes later, Cai and Elgin walked out of the keep both armed and wearing light armor. Cai was carrying an upset Rinna. He took her to the spot they had set up for pub-lic council, kissed her then joined Dax and Tolin.

"She's mad that I won't let her walk anywhere. She's mad

that she has a guard assigned so she doesn't get on her feet any more than absolutely necessary while I'm gone."

"Marta strode over to Dax, carrying a bag, "this has food, so you idiots don't starve to death. Don't get killed, hurry home. Rinna and I will be wanting five healthy men riding through those gates," she tugged on Dax's beard, then threw her arms around him, before letting go to join Rinna.

"You are going to get attention the moment you ride out that gate," Elgin watched Marta walk to Rinna. The two women held hands talking to each other, "people will see that we've not been honest about your whereabouts."

"Good. It will also show those who are on the side of our enemies that we are not to be taken lightly," Cai watched as Dax gave orders to the guards who were staying as five others prepared to leave, "Tolin, what did you and Josiah find?"

Tolin had gotten a fresh horse and was tightening the girth on the saddle, "an armed camp. Donner and one of the old lords are running the place. It looks like they've raided some of the farms in the area as there is a decent sized flock of sheep and goats as well as people under guard."

"How well defended?" Cai looked over to Rinna. He hated to leave but he trusted that she would manage things in Ragan quite well in their absence.

"Better than you'd think. It looks like someone has been planning a coup since before we arrived. I wager that Bannister was at risk for being overthrown in the very near future," Tolin got on his horse as Dax and the five guards rode up, "Josiah, being the master sneak that he is, went in last night, found out that they don't know where the five men are that you and Rinna killed, and do think that both of you are missing and that we've been looking for you."

"Excellent," Cai turned Lucky towards the gate, "let's give Ragan something to gossip about, then stop a coup," he kneed his horse into a trot as he rode through the gate. The site of the four warriors leaving the fortress with the additional soldiers made a big impression on the villagers. Cai nodding in acknowledgement to those he passed purposely kept the pace to a trot until reaching the edge of the village. People stopped and stared, clearly unused to a show of organized force. Dax's soldiers got a few waves, and one shouted I love you. Rajah jumped down from one of the roofs of the nearby houses once Cai and the others passed, then bounded into the forest going North East. Within minutes they were gone swallowed up by the trees.

Once in the forest Tolin took the lead. They soon came to a stream and followed it upwards until it branched into two smaller ones. Tolin took the right fork following it until they reached an open glen. Ahead of them were grassy slopes with shrubs scattered about. They could see the stream continuing up in a dip between two hillsides. The mountains loomed over them; their tops capped in snow. Tolin pointed toward the right.

"The camp is in a valley over that ridge. We need to go around to a pine wood just to the east. It's the only approach where they won't see us coming."

"Tolin, How much longer?" Cai heard distant thunder. Looking up, he saw dark clouds coming in from the south east, fed by the warmer coastal waters at the coast.

"About an hour."

"Let's see if we can beat the rain," Cai nudged Lucky forward.

"And let's hope Josiah didn't get bored and is sitting there on a pile of bodies waiting for us," Dax joked, "I didn't ride all the way up here to look at the pretty scenery."

It was raining when they reached Josiah and Tolin's camp. The temperature had dropped with the rain and the waning afternoon. Tolin stayed back with the other soldiers while Cai, Dax and Elgin went with Josiah to see the enemy camp.

It was in a cove with a small creek fed pond. Sheep and goats were feeding on the hillside on the side of the cove nearest the pond. On the other side of the pond men sparred or lounged about watching.

"As you can see, it's a nice cozy little arrangement," Josiah said, "the house is their base of operations. The outbuilding to the right is where they shove their prisoners at night."

"Sentries?" asked Elgin. Josiah pointed them out, all positioned to see anyone coming from the direction of Ragan or from the north or south.

"They don't expect anyone from this direction, because they didn't consider how we got here as a viable way in. Their mistake," Josiah grinned, "they also lost three quivers of arrows, six swords and a ham. Couldn't sleep last night."

"Surely not all of these people are from Ragan," Elgin shook water off his cloak now that the rain had stopped, "it's not that big a village."

"They aren't," one of the soldiers, a man named Manel said. The other soldiers agreed, "we would get people who had worn out their welcome down at the coast, then pissed of someone in charge in Ragan. I always thought they just went on over the mountains. I guess I was wrong."

Cai digested that information. He was expecting someone to show up from the coast any day. Knowing that nefarious types were what to expect just meant one more problem to deal with. They would have to address the matter of visitors and newcomers when they got back.

A little before dawn, Elgin and two of the soldiers who had proven their skill with a bow went to deal with the threat of the sentries, each approaching from a different location to add a sense of confusion. There was no moon. It had set a few hours ago, although a few stars still shone. The air was cool with a slight breeze, rustling through the needles of the pines behind the camp.

Josiah took three soldiers with him. He intended to take care of the guards surrounding the outbuilding and free anyone inside. That left the last guard, Tolin, Dax and Cai to deal with the rest. Rajah was crouched beside Cai, ears turning as he listened to the different sounds of the night.

They waited about fifteen minutes for Elgin and his group to get into position, then made their way towards the house.

They not being spotted gave a good indication that the archers had done their job.

"Hold up a second," Dax whispered, prompting Cai and the others to crouch behind the house. Dax soon returned carrying a large piece of deadfall. Dax walked around the front of the house where he hurled it at the front door. It crashed through the door followed by shouts of alarm. The noise had the intended effect. Men scrambled out of their tents, some armed, some still trying to pull on their pants. Those in the house had to deal with the destroyed door and the large piece of wood hampering their way out. Several men rushed at Tolin and Cai who dispatched them, while Rajah pounced on tents, dispensing of any who had chosen to remain hidden. A few tried to run away but were killed by Elgin and his three archers who had the advantage of a higher elevation and adding confusion to the mix.

The sky was turning pink by the time it was over. Dax had killed one of the men who had made it past his barrier. Of the forty-two men in the camp eighteen were dead, another eleven were injured. There had been six people in the outbuilding, five men and an elderly woman. They huddled under blankets next to a campfire, eating the food Marta had packed.

Cai could see that Josiah was very angry as he walked towards them, leaving his two men with the rescued.

"Those six people are all that is left of eight families who had homes up in this area. They were scattered, came down maybe once a year to get supplies and sell their wool, pelts or cheese. Those that weren't killed outright were brought here. The woman only survived because she threatened to cast a spell on them if they tried then began chanting incantations. She says she's eighty-four; reminds me of my granny."

Cai watched as Donner and the others who were in the house were brought out and made to kneel with the rest of the prisoners. One was one of Bannister's advisors, a man that Manel said was named Thotu. Manel then pointed out the rest of the former residents of Ragan, eight in all.

"You know what you have to do cousin," Elgin watched Cai wrestle with the decisions he was going to have to make, "I will act as your guard and your sword and will stand as witness as you do what you must, dispense justice as Lord Governor of Arowana."

"As will I," said Tolin

"As will I," repeated Dax. The rest of the men who had come with Cai each repeated the vow. They then arranged themselves to stand facing the defeated, with Cai in the middle. Rajah reclined in front of Cai, keeping a sleepy looking watch on the kneeling men.

"Thank you, Elgin," Cai turned his head then nodded to Dax.

Dax's voice echoed across the tiny valley, "all hail Prince Cai Sunspear, son of Corbaine Sunspear, Emperor of Khaetor, duly appointed Lord Governor of the province of Arowana. The Lord Governor has heard the charges against you and has seen the results of your crimes. He is now ready to serve justice upon the accused before him."

There were gasps of shock heard from the cluster of freed prisoners and from several of the men who had once held them. The rest looked back, either in fear or suspicion.

Donner yelled, "you lie!"

Cai waited to see any further responses or comments. There were none. He stood, his hand resting on the pommel of his sword, the end of which was resting point down on the wooden step. "For the crimes of murder, rape, theft, and the harm to the residents of this region who are under the protection of the Lord Governor, your lives are forfeit. The leaders and any who these six can identify as committing the crimes listed will be executed."

He turned to the six people sitting nearby. They hesitated until the old woman stood. Then they each walked to the person they blamed and pointed, then silently they turned away. Cai noted with grim satisfaction that Donner was one of the men picked.

Cai lowered his head, then nodded as Elgin and the two other archers completed their work. Once done, nine remained. Cai looked at each in turn. Finally, he spoke.

"I take no pleasure in what was done here today. I take less pleasure in seeing the lives of innocents destroyed, and livelihoods stolen. This cannot be a land of peace without justice so hear my words. The nine of you will live and you will be allowed to go free. Each of you will be given food, water and a horse and left either on the pass over the mountains or along the road to the coast. There you will be allowed to continue your journey if you do not turn back onto the lands I oversee. To ensure you remember your crimes and our leniency, each of you will be given a brand on your hand."

Cai unsheathed his sword. He walked past the nine and stuck it into the coals of the fire left burning by the tents. He waited a few minutes then approached the first man convicted. Dax held him down, while Elgin held out the man's wrist. Cai lay the flat of the sword down on the back of the man's hand, counting to three before moving it away. The man collapsed, holding his wrist while wailing in pain. One of the men scrambled up, running towards the woods. He didn't get far as Rajah was on him before the man had gone fifteen steps.

"The choice remains the same for the rest of you. I offer you your lives. Choose wisely," Cai, grim faced, moved on to the next man. Once the grisly task was done, Cai walked to the pond where he dipped his sword to cool and to wash off the burned flesh. There he stood staring into the water hating what he had done, hating himself for doing it.

He felt a tug on his sleeve. Looking over he saw the elderly woman. She was stooped over, her head reaching no further than his chest.

"When I was a lass. I saw your father's grandfather deal justice to people who had slaughtered their neighbors over a matter of rights to an oasis. The oasis had enough water for both communities to share, but one community was bigger and had better weapons. The survivors were cast out, forced to cross the desert. Those that survived appealed to the king for justice."

Cai's attention was fully hers. His great-grandfather had been a legendary king, if the tales about him were true. Jordanus was someone Cai had wanted to emulate seeming to be everything his father was not.

"When the king arrived. He executed the leaders of the community and all who were found to have property of their former neighbors on them, the rest he branded like you did just did," the woman stared at the water herself before looking back up at him, her eyes black and sharp.

Cai remembered being told the story about the desert people and how Jordanus dealt with the matter. It hadn't occurred to him that he had just merited the same justice.

"Thank you. And I'm sorry for what has happened here, and that you had to live through this horror twice," he blinked in surprise when she started laughing then stared as she pulled up a sleeve revealing her own brand across her skinny arm.

"I was six. I deserved to be killed for my crimes but was spared because there was no proof of my participation having already eaten it all," she dropped her arm, "Your great-grandfather wept for what he had to do, and that people could be so cruel over so little. He was a good king, and Khaetor prospered under his rule. It is a shame he only lived a year longer." She patted his arm then walked slowly back to the others she had been rescued with.

The newly branded were made to help gather the dead whose bodies were loaded onto a cart to a clearing free of trees or grass and piled along with firewood for a pyre. The survivors were given the offer of shelter in Ragan until they could rebuild their lives. All refused.

"We chose this life and we wish to remain to rebuild it," one of the men said, "However, we would welcome aid. We have scattered flocks to gather and homes to repair or rebuild."

"We will send anyone willing as soon as possible," Cai promised.

It took well into the evening of another day to complete

what needed to be done, including repairs to the farmhouse door where the survivors would be staying until their herds could be gathered. The next morning, they left, taking a different route to the road. All the branded chose to go over the mountain pass.

"I need a drink," Josiah said as they approached Ragan, "hell, I need to get fucking drunk."

Tolin nodded. The trip had been necessary. None of them had enjoyed what they had to do, "I am in complete agreement. Come on old man. I'll buy the first round."

The village was quiet, people settling down for the evening when they arrived. Cai noticed lights on in the Putrid Boar. He started to stop to see what was happening, but he wanted to see Rinna more. He walked into the great hall a few minutes later. There were several people eating the evening meal. Marta who had just walked in from the kitchen stopped in mid step. She ran past Cai, blonde hair flying behind her.

"Welcome home Lord Governor," someone said. Cai turned seeing Tova standing nearby, "she's on the roof with the healer."

"Thank you," Cai headed to the roof. Rinna was sitting under the pavilion they had made almost a week ago. Eolande was handing Rinna a cup.

Rinna saw him, "Cai!"

She started to get up and was firmly pushed back down by Eolande. A guard was two steps closer as well.

"My love. Your being held down by Mistress Eolande does not have me feel like you are healing like you should," Cai sat down beside her, wrapping an arm around her shoulders.

"I was doing just fine, taking my time and my damned leg…"

"It's her womanly time, so she decided to take herself to the kitchen garden in the middle of the night and in the rain for something for cramps instead of asking and slipped in the mud," Eolande was looking at Rinna with a stern expression.

"I just landed on my bottom."

"And sprained your ankle. Welcome home, Lord Governor. We will leave her into your care," The guard offered Eolande a hand to help her stand.

Cai gathered Rinna in his arms, "you were supposed to stay off your feet."

"I know. Everyone was asleep, and I was going slow. I just slipped," she kissed the base of Cai's neck, "I am glad you are back. I was worried and I've missed you."

"I've missed you too," Cai kept holding her, not saying anything else, just needing her presence.

Rinna could feel the tension in his body, and his fatigue. She saw him staring out into space, "tell me Cai. Whatever happened, it bothered you. I can't be a good advisor, or a good consort if I cannot listen, so let me listen."

"I want to protect you from that," he protested.

"I know," she reached up, placed a hand on the side of his face turning his head towards her, "tell me anyway."

Cai got up. He undid the straps that held his sword to his back and set it aside, then he stripped off the rest of his armor, then finally his shirt. While he undressed, Rajah appeared having gained access to the roof as he always did, by climbing up the side of the building like a tree. The big cat flopped down to begin washing himself.

Rinna watched Cai enjoying the play of his muscles as he did the simple task of undressing. She waited, knowing he was very unhappy with what had transpired. Finally, he sat back down. To her surprise he lay his head on her lap, wrapping one arm around her back. In a quiet voice, he told her everything, needing to unburden himself of what he had to do. She stroked his hair giving him assurance that she was listening and was there for him.

They lay quietly after he finished, listening to an owl hooting in the distance, wrapped up in each other.

Cai thought she had gone to sleep until she spoke, "I could not have done what you did. The old woman was right. You showed eighteen people that you are capable of not only being able to rule, but to do so wisely. I doubt they will be silent on the matter."

"I hope so. I would rather not have to repeat that ever again," Cai blew out the candles set up around the pavilion, deciding that a night on the roof with the woman he loved would suit him just fine. "I know we will face conflict, and quite possibly future battles, I just have no stomach for it. I never really did. I'd rather have a peaceful life."

"So, do I," Rinna held him close, knowing how tired he was, "we will have that. We already do. I know I am at peace when I'm in your arms."

Cai had no words to express how he felt about what she had just said. He allowed himself to slip off to sleep, known he was just as at peace in hers.

Seventeen

Cai led the members of his council plus the five soldiers who had gone with him out of the fortress the next morning. He carried Rinna who with a sprained ankle had again lost the fight to walk until she was healed more completely. She was set down on a chair set out for her beside Marta who winked at her friend, handing her a cup of tea.

The villagers, already curious about where Cai and the others had gone gathered. A mist covered the lake, that would burn off as the day warmed, seeping into the village as it often did this time of year.

Cai didn't wait for the formal preamble from Dax, instead deciding to get right to business, "a few days ago, we went to confront the former owner of the Putrid Boar and his companions to bring him to justice for the murder one of his people. What we discovered was a farm converted to an armed camp. The residents of the camp had six prisoners, the living survivors of eight families who had lived along the lower slopes of the mountains."

He told them what happened and how justice was dispensed then waited while the villagers digested the news, gauging the responses of the villagers. There was a mixture of shock, sadness and anger among them.

The survivors need our help. We were asked for volunteers to share in their rebuilding and in their livelihood," Cai concluded. "We want Ragan to grow and prosper. Hopefully the actions taken will see us go a long way to accomplish that. Today however, is to be a day of mourning for those that were lost. Tomorrow we continue the work to protect ourselves and our future, knowing that there are others who will seek to harm us, if we let them," He waited as Dax and the rest dispersed, some going to speak with the villagers, some going back into the fortress. He bent to pick up Rinna.

"Wait. There is someone I want you to speak with," she stopped him. Cai turned to see who she was talking about when she looked beyond him and smiled. Three women approached. One looked vaguely familiar.

"Good morning Darla," Rinna looked up to Cai, "Cai, Darla and her companions once served under Donner."

Recognition came to Cai, "you served us our food, our first night here."

Darla bobbed a quick curtsy as she nodded, "yes, Lord Governor, I did, and I will never forget how well you and your men treated me," she glanced to Rinna who smiled and nodded her encouragement, "we wish to reopen the Putrid Boar."

"And I'd been thinking of burning the place to the ground," Cai frowned at the news, "but I am very curious if you can talk me out of it."

Darla blanched; her brown eyes widened in her pretty light-gold face. She was a bit younger than Rinna and not much taller. She stepped back, intimidated by Cai.

Another of the trio stepped forward. She was a few years older, her skin and hair darker, "I'm Junia. Donner bought me and my sister right off a slave caravan two years ago. She is the one he murdered. I hope he was one of the people who met your justice and is not currently climbing over the mountain pass."

Cai did not expect her matter of fact manner but saw why Rinna was encouraging them in their venture. She recognized tenacity.

"Donner would have received punishment anyway for the crime of murdering your sister. He added to it by participating in the murder of our neighbors in the outlying farms. I regret that we couldn't kill him twice."

Cai hid a smile at the flash of satisfaction in Junia's eyes. She then placed a hand on the arm of the other woman with her.

"This is Meera. We were the ones who kept the doors open, us, cook and the kitchen boy, Joel. We were all slaves, even though you freed us. Donner wouldn't let us leave. Despite the horrors, the Putrid Boar is our home. We know how to run a proper tavern, and how to turn it into an inn to provide shelter for visitors and guests. According to cook, Donner stole the place by murdering its former owner."

"And I take it my love, that you approve of this?" he slid an arm around Rinna's waist who had stood to stand next to him, hanging on to his waist to keep from putting weight on her injured leg, "of course, you approve of it. Knowing you, you've already figured out how to convince me if they could not."

"You won't let me walk, so I have to scheme," Rinna retorted. Cai's laughter startled the three women.

"My consort is shrewd. I approve on three conditions," Cai took Rinna's free hand, bringing it to his lips for a kiss, "you change the name; you always keep a room available for guests of the Lord Governor and that the sale of sex is willingly earned and fairly compensated."

The three women looked at each other, then hugged each other in delight and relief.

"Thank you," Junia's relief was evident in her voice.

Cai learned that a caravan had come and gone in his absence. It brought beeswax candles, woven rugs and hammered shields with the Sunspear royal crest worked in. The merchants had been thrilled with a successful trade with Marta and had spent their visit making smaller trades with the villagers.

The next one was sighted two days after Cai's return. This one had a human cargo. The merchants this time were given an option of releasing those imprisoned and returning from where they came from or death. They chose to fight thinking that the four soldiers blocking the narrow gap would be easy to overtake. They never saw the archers above them. Ragan then welcomed fourteen newcomers including three little girls. All were given the same option as the first group and like before all opted to stay. Three of the women and five of the men asked to be taken to the farms that had lost their residents, having skill sets suited for life in the farms. They were welcomed gladly by the survivors.

Once her stab wound healed, and the swelling in her ankle went down, Cai took Rinna to the place where they had defeated the murderous raiders, knowing that the old woman had decided to settle there. They brought with them some supplies and a young couple who were part of the volunteers. Rinna was enchanted by the old woman whose name turned out to be Lucinda reminding her of Garrett's wife and her former nursemaid. The two spent several happy hours talking herb lore as Cai chopped wood for Lucinda's fireplace. The couple they had brought with them were delighted with the little valley, ensuring that Lucinda would be well taken care of for as long as she needed them. They left soon after to help guide a small flock of sheep back to their owner's home.

Promising to return in the Spring, Cai and Rinna toured several of the other homesteads, discovering that most were abandoned. Rinna stood just inside a house that looked like the occupants had just stepped away. The house was close to the same size as hers and Garrett's had been except for a loft.

She picked up a rag doll, "they had children. How can…"

She couldn't complete the question. Cai held her as she wept.

"Your tears match my fury," Cai noticed the small loom in a corner, a weaving project nearly done, "we should have checked on people here sooner."

"It's a terrible way to learn from our mistakes," Rinna sniffed as she stepped away from Cai, "I don't think either of us want a repeat."

"I still feel like I'm making things up as I go along," it was raining outside, the sound pattering on the thin stones that made up the roof of the house. "I hate that it cost innocent lives."

"Cai," Rinna stood behind him, wrapping her arms around his front. The temperatures had dropped with the rain, "I knew that what you intended would be hard, if not impossible. You and your--our friends have accomplished more than I imagined possible. We are having to undo what others have gotten away with for years."

"So, what do you suggest?" Cai dislodged her hold, walked outside to sit on a rough wooden bench on the tiny porch of the house. Rinna sat next to him.

"We support those that come here," she saw a trio of deer grazing at the edge of the forest. Rajah had disappeared several hours ago to hunt. "they liked being isolated, but they were too isolated. They had to come to Ragan for supplies and to trade. I don't think anyone came to them. If you want to oversee Arowana, you need to make sure all of it is looked after. King Senneck forgot that."

"I think we can make that happen, my love," Cai slipped an arm around her, "I wouldn't mind making this trip again."

They spent the night in the house. While Rinna prepared a meal and straightened up the inside, Cai found the remains of the family the house once belonged to. The ground was too rocky to bury them, so Cai covered was left of them under a cairn of stones. As he finished, he saw Rinna approach with the doll and the weaving cut from the loom. She placed the items on top of the cairn, setting a rock over the woven cloth to hold it in place. They stood silently, hand in hand unable to find the proper words to honor the family they never met. The next morning, they began the trip home.

"As much as I've enjoyed having you all to myself, even with the sadness we encountered, it's good to be home," Rinna said as they saw the village in the distance. Rinna had never explored that far north, so enjoyed finding a few plants she didn't recognize as well as a few she did. She filled a bag with carefully gathered seed pods and a few rhizomes to take home.

"I agree," Cai watched Rinna as she looked at the panorama before them, "have you given more thought to my question?"

She laughed, "I have. I just don't know how to do it. We certainly need to discuss it."

"I do want a marriage, or something like it. I want it clear that we intend to spend our lives together," Cai urged Lucky forward.

"Cai, I want that too. But how your people did it, and how mine did are different. And then how others who have come here are different still," it was one of the things they had discussed on their trip along with other plans for each other, for Ragan and beyond.

"We could still try to steal a ship, and let others figure out how to write laws for governing a nation," Cai quipped.

"Tempting, but no," Rinna watched Rajah bound down the hill knowing there were children and treats in the village, "we are both too responsible."

In their absence two more caravans had arrived, another slave transport adding another twenty-three people to the population of Ragan. The slavers opted to abandon their cargo rather than fight after seeing Dax and Tolin waiting on them. A merchant sending expensive cloth, two kinds of grain and a sow with a litter of piglets was the other. The merchant went home with nuts, a supply of quality fur pelts, as Patrick had more than enough to work with and some gold Bannister had hoarded.

The council met to construct basic laws and matters of civic order. As there were no religious presence in the village, they decided to make matters of marriage, property transfers, etc. something handled mostly by local officials, and that electing them from the population was a priority.

It was a clear late summer morning when the Cai called the village for a public meeting. The air had begun to cool in the evenings, and flocks of waterfowl began to visit the lake on their way south, which kept hunters busy.

Cai stood, "the council and I have put together a set of laws and rules that should work to make Ragan and eventually all Arowana a prosperous province for many years."

The villagers looked at each other in curiosity, muttering amongst themselves.

"We will post copies of the laws for any who can read, and make sure everyone understands what it means. Matters like marriage, births, deaths, transfers of property and such will be included. But first, we have something to ask of you. We ask that you choose among yourselves representatives to act as your elders who will work with Dax and Marta. I've designated them as Lord and Lady of Ragan. This is your village; you should be able to have a say to what happens here."

Cai nodded to Dax who spoke, "there are many things that we have considered and are putting into place and will share with your representatives who will then share them with you. But for now, let's set that aside. I know of at least one couple here who wishes to proclaim their intention to marry."

Cai and Rinna smiled at each other then stepped forward. Facing each other they clasped hands. Cai started, "I am Cai Sunspear, son of King Corbaine which I cannot help, Lord Governor of Arowana and resident of Ragan. I give my heart, my life to Norinna, daughter of Gregor Tessenae, former advisor to the once king of Arowana, council member of the Lord Governor. All I have, and all I am is yours."

Rinna blinked back tears, "I am Rinna, who was found by the saber cat of the Lord Governor, was made a member of his counsel and his consort, who has found a home among his people and mine. I give my heart and life to Cai, son of Corbaine, who's deeds, horrible as they were, made it possible for us to be together. You are my heart, my love, we are forever."

Cai had his own tears as he heard her words. He embraced her lifting her feet off the ground, "my love," he said as he kissed her.

"I love you," she answered.

"Okay you two, out of the way," Dax said. Cai and Rinna broke apart, seeing Dax and Marta hand in hand, and three other couples behind them.

The day ended with dancing, music and a bit too much ale. Tova supplied some freshly made paper to record the five weddings. By nightfall, Patrick, Junia, Manel and an older woman named Priscilla were named representatives by the village.

#

Rinna was forty feet up a tree, she could see the yellow

flag Elgin was waving from his own tree on the next ridge. She stretched out waving her own flag in response. Even though the terrain was hilly and heavily forested, if one chose the right spot, it was possible to see a good distance away. They had found a way to send messages from the road to the coast in a quick, covert manner. All that was needed was to build shelters in the selected trees and recruit watchers to rotate. Once done, Ragan would know if anyone was coming from the coast in a matter of minutes.

She leaned back against the trunk enjoying the sensation of the bark against her back, the sound of birds nearby and the breeze that blew intermittently, rustling the leaves around her. It was the first time she had been truly alone since meeting Cai at her old home. She found that although she enjoyed the moment of solitude, she did not miss the loneliness that had been a companion for so long.

She missed Garrett wishing he were alive to see the sparks of his dream coming to fruition. While it was quite possible that all their plans would still end in disaster, what had been accomplished in less than a season would have been impossible for her and Garrett to imagine. Rinna had never given herself the luxury of contemplating their plight before, instead diving into preparedness, caution and the tasks of every day.

She now had the love and support of Cai, their friends and others whose life she had entered. Their presence was allowing her to feel like she belonged, something that had always eluded her. She looked down and saw Cai approaching on Lucky. It only took her a minute to climb down out of the tree and be standing by the road as he rode up. He smiled down at her as he dismounted, then let out a surprised oof when she threw herself into his arms.

"Rinna my love, what's wrong?" she had dressed in the tunic and trousers she preferred for working early that morning. As she cried, he picked a leaf and a few tiny bits of twigs out of her hair, her curls having been left unbound. She had washed it that morning and was combing out the tangles to let it dry when they decided to look at possible watch locations. She got her tears back under control.

"Nothing is wrong. I've not had much time for thinking things over in a while. I needed it. I just realized a few things up there. One of which is how glad I am that I have you."

"You are a gift I never thought I'd have, so I think we are both grateful for each other," Cai stepped back from her with a grin, "I know we have a little while before Elgin catches up to us, and there is no one about…" He lifted the hem of her tunic, pulling it off, then dropping it to the ground as his hands cupped her breasts. "I see a patch of ferns over there. I think it would make the perfect spot."

Her look was sultry as she stepped back, stepping out of her trousers, after pulling off her boots. She then walked naked towards the place he had indicated. It was set back a few yards from the road, surrounded by trees that soared fifty feet into the air. Just enough sunlight filtered from overhead to dapple the ferns in light. Rinna reached the ferns and turned to see if Cai was following. He led Lucky, tying him to a nearby tree, before shedding his own clothes by his horse.

He knelt on the ground tugging on her hands till she knelt facing him. They reached for each other falling into a tangle of arms and legs as their hands and mouths found purchase. Cai kneeled back, seeing Rinna's hair spread out under her, her arms thrown back over her head, he thought her the most beautiful creature on earth. He leaned over to kiss her, rolling over on to his back as he pulled her up on to him.

"I want to see your face. I want to watch as you come undone," Cai helped her sit upright so she straddled him, "mount me," he said. He gasped as she found him, sliding down slowly until she had encompassed all of him.

"Like this?" she asked feeling him fill her.

"Yes! Now ride, my love ride," Cai reached down, grasping a hip with one hand. With the other he found her clitoris to encourage her to rock against him as he sent waves of pleasure through her with his fingers. She leaned back enough to put her hands on his thighs, threw her head back, and lost herself to the sensation of his hands, his penis and their movement, her breasts bouncing as she rode, faster and faster. Just as she thought she could go no further, her climax hit, and she cried out his name as he hurried right behind her to his.

She fell back in between his legs, boneless and content, but he wasn't done. Sitting up he pulled her up, so she faced him both still seated, still connected. They kissed as he circled her breasts with his thumbs, causing the nipples to pebble. She found the scar on his shoulder and ran her fingertips over the contours as her other hand tangled itself in his hair. Rinna felt her desire build right back up and began moving against him.

"Cai, Oh Cai. Please don't stop."

"I have no intention to," he twisted so she was under him, her legs still wrapped around his waist. He found her hands and placed them above her head, then leaned in thrusting fast and hard as she thrashed her head with her second climax. As she rode the waves, he too fell, collapsing onto her, replete from his own.

"There is a good chance that I may never be able to walk again," Cai murmured against her neck, "But damned was it ever worth it, my love. I can't wait to do that again, if I can remember what it takes to move." he smiled at her giggle.

Well you have squashed me, and I'm content," she ran her fingers through his hair. She didn't care if they didn't move for a while.

He raised his head as he heard an approaching horse, "that must be Elgin," he got up and walked to Lucky where he picked up his pants. He'd just had them pulled up when Elgin stopped his horse and looked down on the ground then back over to where Cai and Rinna were with a grin.

"Cai? Did you leave my clothes in the road?" Rinna cried to Elgin's laughter. He watched with amusement as Cai walked over to the road, picked up Rinna's clothes then walked back to the clearing where Elgin could see an arm reach up and grab the items out of Cai's hand.

A few minutes later they were both dressed. Rinna wouldn't look at Elgin, "Lady Rinna. I promise I saw nothing, heard plenty and knew that the two of you were doing what people in love tend to do. So, I went back down the road for a few minutes."

Rinna's face turned red, "I'm just embarrassed by it all."

"I'm not," Cai said with pride, "I'm quite happy. She is too."

"We did learn that we can use flags from a decent distance depending on terrain," Elgin said as they rode back towards Ragan, "the question remains on how far we want to go?"

Rinna, who'd been quiet, said, "two to three signal spots would give us a decent head start, and the ability to send someone out to see what we are expecting. I just wish we had a way to let each other know if its friend, foe or trade."

"Different colored flags?" Cai suggested, "we will figure something out.

Eighteen

The flag system was crude but effective. After debate, it was decided to have two sets of messages, one going to Ragan, and one going back to the nine watchers along the road to the Arowanian coast. Incoming would relay people coming in, and if they were a caravan of cargo, or a group of armed men. The messages would then be acknowledged at each station by a white flag. There were plenty of volunteers for the job among the children and youth, who saw it as a grand adventure. They had to be reminded that the flags were for important messages only, after a few false ones were sent. Undeterred the watchers developed their own system of communication, improving the original and reducing boredom during the long hours up in their trees.

It didn't take long for the system to prove itself beneficial when the signal for armed men approaching from Fairshine was received and acknowledged by the watchers. The moment the first message arrived Josiah left with his scouts, while Elgin stood at the parapet waiting for new signals until darkness fell. Josiah returned three afternoons later, tired from the trip where speed mattered over rest.

He sat down at his spot at the table and poured himself a mug of ale. He confirmed what the watchers had reported with added details. "It's about fifty men, a couple of supply wagons. Our bog slowed them down a bit."

Josiah ate, then went to get a few hours of sleep informing Cai that his scouts would be reporting in as the group advanced. Rajah had disappeared soon after the news of the incoming soldiers was made. Cai didn't know what the big cat was up to, as Rajah tended to make his own plans, but he sensed that Rajah was doing something to help, not hunting and exploring. Rajah always seemed to follow the needs of Cai and now Rinna when it mattered, something Cai was thankful for.

The incoming group sent out scouts of their own to report back on the lay of the land and the condition of the village.

They were captured by Josiah's scouts who brought them to the assassin for questioning. They were fed, examined by Eolande for illness or injury then placed in a storeroom with a guard.

While Marta planned for extra beds and worked with Eolande to prepare for injuries, Rinna spoke with the villagers. She offered them the chance to head to a safer location and burst into tears when every one of them refused.

Patrick spoke for the villagers, "when the Lord Governor and his council came, we were enslaved, living in fear and suspicious of him and of you. We thought that he would be just like the others had been, and that you had decided to cut your losses and use your body to stay safe. We were wrong. We will help you defend our home, your home."

The council debated on how to meet the contingent. There was no place where Ragan or its people had the upper hand and thanks to the scouting reports the people coming were indeed planning taking Ragan for themselves. They had taken a break without a solution. The rooftop of the fortress had become a favorite spot, especially in the evenings. Everyone was frustrated and tired so Tolin's outburst of laughter was unexpected.

"Mind sharing on the joke?" Dax asked. Tolin was doubled over in laughter, tears rolling down his cheek.

Cai scowled as he walked to Tolin, "What the fuck is so funny?" Tolin pointed down. The spot he was standing overlooked the fortress courtyard. A narrow walkway ran along the walls of the courtyard. Cai could see a couple of guards and someone working in the stables, "I don't get the joke."

"It's been right under our noses the whole time. That is where we meet them," Tolin wiped tears from his eyes.

Cai looked in shock at Tolin, "you want to invite them inside? Are you insane?" he shouted.

Beside him Rinna said, "oh. That could work. It would work."

"What would work? What is it I am not seeing?" Cai demanded.

"Lord Governor come sit down, we shall explain every-thing," Rinna winked at Tolin.

#

Prince Azuul would have preferred to let others deal with the problem with the Ragan road. The merchants had complained that supplies and slaves were not arriving as expected. Others expressed dismay that the road itself was impassable, and they were forced to use alternative routes. Bannister, the former lord of the Ragan route had complained the longest. He and his lacky, Hovind still lived because they had enough clout in Fairshine to help Azuul solidify his position. It was now time for them to go back to Ragan. Azuul brought enough forces to subdue the rebel village and his half-human spawn of a brother. He had been angry to learn his father had also given Cai the province.

They had been delayed at the section of road turned into a bog a few hours into the trip. Azuul spent several minutes screaming at anyone who would listen for letting the road get to such a state. Passing through the fifty yards of knee-deep muck was miserable as they were also bombarded by midges and mosquitoes. They lost the rest of the day thanks to the delay.

The third night was interrupted by a scream. The entire camp went on alert expecting an attack. When none came, it was assumed that the sound was a wild animal. None with the prince were natives of the land. Bannister and Hovind had never heard of any wild animals that had a habit of attacking travelers, nor could a source of the scream by found. The next morning the disemboweled body of one of the horses was discovered not fifty feet from Azuul's tent, nowhere near where the scream had been heard.

By noon the next day, the commander of the troops reported that none of the scouts had returned. That night, few slept worried about the mysterious creature who had killed one of the horses. The next day their fears were realized when another horse was found, its head sliced almost completely off. The body of a guard was found on the opposite end of the camp with great tears in his clothing that did not quite hide the gashes in his body.

The group was relieved on the sixth day when they saw the lake as they climbed the last hill. Every morning they'd discovered a dead horse. The night before something large had defecated inside Bannister and Hovind's tent. Everyone was spooked and glad to see civilization again.

A bridge crossed a stream, the road continuing past through the village. A mill could be seen downstream, its wheel turning lazily with the current. To Azuul, the fortress was un-impressive, two stories, made of stone and wood, with a crude parapet along the top. The village stretched out beyond the fortress set on a rise overlooking the lake.

Azuul could see the road beyond the village as it rose up into the high mountains. He looked at the fortress seeing no sign of life as they passed it, needing to enter the village to gain access to the entrance. He had no use for the pristine beauty of the lake, the forest that surrounded most of it or the mountains with their white peaks. He just wanted the road to have traffic back on it again.

His commander ordered a halt at the bridge, "I don't like it. There should be people here. It's too quiet."

"Then drag them out of their houses," Azuul's patience was at an end, his nerves frayed by the actions of the mysterious beast. His father had ordered him to bring the province under control, and it was proving to be a waste of time. The only value to the place was the harbor and the money gained by taxing everything thing bought and sold or delivered. There wasn't much of that, as the pirates who should have been allies to the empire openly defied Azuul's rule and the soldiers he had brought. There had been several scuffles resulting in an uneasy truce. Azuul wanted the pirates gone but didn't yet have the resources. Bannister promised he had the means and the man-power to restore the trade route and doubted that Cai remained in Ragan.

"There's no one here. It looks like they all left, and in a hurry," one of the soldiers reported back.

Azuul sneered at Bannister, "well that will be your job to get them back. They are all in hiding, the cowards. I'm leaving you enough men for the job," he looked at the fortress with its closed doors, "now let's see this fortress you've bragged about."

Bannister rode up to the gate then pushed the it open. He rode in followed immediately by Azuul. The commander tried to shout a warning, sensing a trap, but was ignored. When nothing happened, he nodded and went inside with the others, ordering two men to remain outside. The courtyard of the fortress looked like no one had been there in some time. Moldy straw was strewn about near the empty stables and was a variety of debris scattered about the space. The door to the keep stood partially open. Azuul watched as a pigeon walked out the door into the courtyard.

"This is a strong defensible fortress?" Azuul exclaimed as he threw his head back and laughed. The sound echoing off the walls of the courtyard, startled the pigeon who flew into the air rising above the parapet before falling to the ground with an arrow through it. Seconds later the gates leading to the outside slammed shut. The bang got the attention of those caught inside, many of whom turned to see where the sound had come from.

"Hello brother."

Azuul turned back to the sound of the voice. Cai was standing at the door, his sword drawn. He was wearing his battle armor. Rinna stood beside him, a crown of flowers her own head, her unbound curls ruffling in the slight breeze, arrow notched in her bow and aimed right at Azuul.

"Cai. I didn't expect you to still be here. Everyone at court knows how ruling is an aversion to you. I'm impressed with how you've managed to hold an empty village and a useless fortress. Give up this pretense. You won't last five seconds. You are outnumbered and will soon be dead," Azuul gloated. He narrowed his eyes as he looked at Rinna. "I may keep your bitch alive for now."

"My bitch will have an arrow through your eye before the first man steps forward," Cai's voice was calm as he glanced upwards, "besides, you are completely surrounded."

Azuul and his men followed Cai's lead, looking up to see that they were indeed surrounded. Dozens of men and women had arrows trained on those down below. Rajah jumped down from the roof landing a few feet from Bannister whose horse reared up spilling the overweight man to the ground.

"Gods above and below, what is that?" the commander cried in alarm as everyone shuffled backwards and away from the large cat.

"That is my saber cat. Azuul here killed two of our brothers trying to take it, meanwhile Rajah chose me," Cai tilted his head, "you may have met him on the road." He smiled grimly as several men looked in fear between Cai and the cat.

Dax stepped out next to Cai followed by eight of his guards who lined up in formation to one side. His beard lifting slightly in the breeze, he surveyed the men facing him then bellowed, "soldiers! Drop your weapons."

Dax's own soldiers stepped forward, as two thirds of Azuul's men dropped their weapons compelled by the authoritative command.

Trying not to smile Dax's bass echoed off the walls of the courtyard, "who among you is conscripted? If so, raise your right hand"

The men shuffled on their feet, glancing at their commander and the officers until one, then another raised their hand. Fully half of the men Prince Azuul had brought were conscripted. The officers saw the wisdom in keeping their mouths shut for now.

Dax then addressed the first one who had raised his hand, "you, are you paid for your work?"

"They aren't paid, you dolt," Azuul sneered. He was furious that his commander was just sitting on his horse. "they are slaves."

"Piss off asshole. I didn't ask you," Dax said, dismissing the prince who hissed in fury.

"No sire, we are not," the man replied with awe in his voice.

"Slavery is banned here. The moment you crossed into the territory I control; you became free men. Those of you who wish to stay to help rebuild Arowana into a prosperous, peaceful province, please go stand by the stables," Cai touched Rinna's arm holding her bow taut, smiling as she sighed in relief.

"Sorry, my love," he whispered.

"You can't do that!" Azuul yelled, "these are my slaves. This is my province." He started to dismount from his horse, then stopped when Rajah turned from his watching of Bannister to him. Azuul's tanned face paled when he realized that the big cat's head likely reached to his hips.

I think our father you the same decree that he gave me," Cai pulled his copy out from under his chest plate and read it aloud, "does it say the same thing mine does? From the look on your face it does."

Cai rolled up the decree, "I am Lord Governor here. I intend to oversee the entire province. You are welcome to try and do the same, but not here. These are my people and I am theirs. You and your company are to return home except for the men you once enslaved and Bannister and Hovind who will be answering for crimes committed during their time as Lords of Ragan. If you insist on remaining, your number of men will be further reduced."

The villagers roared their approval shaking their bows in triumph, "Ragan, Ragan, Ragan!" they shouted over and over.

Azuul's face was red with rage. Pulling hard on the reins of his horse, he rode out in a gallop with his officers following close behind. The soldiers who were not conscripted followed.

"Dax, you got some new recruits. Question is, how are we going to feed them?" Josiah asked.

Cai looked up seeing the villagers still watching, "people

of Ragan, today we celebrate a victory we couldn't have had without you. I and the council thank you."

"We didn't have to kill anyone," Rinna leaned into Cai as the villagers cheered.

"Not yet, my love," Cai led her inside, then stepped out of the way as those on the wall made their way out of the keep, "my brother thought he would be able to walk in and just take over. He's lazy, but he's also ruthless and greedy. He's never seen me as a threat because I wasn't interested in playing father's games. The only reason I ended up with Rajah, was because I happened to be in the city at the time. I have tried to avoid the place since I was old enough to walk out under my own power."

"He does now. Your brother sees you as a threat," Rinna shuddered at the thought of death and destruction coming to the people she had grown to love. Losing Cai was unthinkable.

Cai stopped in the middle of the great hall and held her, "we've been very lucky, my love. We won't always be."

Elgin interrupted their interlude, "well, Azuul vented his spleen on his commander and two of the officers who attempted to defend the man."

"He killed them?" Rinna watched Rajah stroll in and curl up by the fireplace. The residents of the fortress had gotten used the big cat and ignored him.

"Yep. They didn't make it a mile away, and half of what Azuul had left mutinied on the spot," Elgin turned hearing running feet. One of the messengers assigned to the roof stopped in front of them.

"Riders approaching sir," the girl was maybe thirteen, lanky and would never be beautiful, save for her smile which was already stopping hearts of the boys her age.

"How many Kiva?" Elgin glanced at Cai.

"About a dozen. The mean prince and what's left are going the other way," Kiva replied. She smiled shyly at Rinna.

"Thank you, Kiva. You can go. I'll watch until your replacement comes," Elgin dismissed his messenger. He watched her leave the great hall to the courtyard, "that girl is smart. She also is in awe of you Rinna."

Rinna did not expect to hear that, "Of me? Why?"

"I'll tell you later, my love," Cai stepped out onto the roof, hand in Rinna's. They'd made it to the roof in time to see the Azuul's former soldiers ride right past the village their destination the pass.

Elgin watched them go, "Rinna, how long until the pass closes for winter?"

"In about two months, why?"

"I think my cousin is calculating the time we have to make sure Ragan is prepared for whatever comes over that pass in the Spring," Cai smiled when he saw Elgin's nod.

Rinna watched the riders disappear around a bend in the road. She then turned to look east where Azuul and his remaining soldiers had gone, "and what about from that direction?"

"Unless Azuul has some very capable allies in Arowana City, he's going to have a hard time keeping the place," Cai rested an arm at her waist, "I think in the meantime, we need to consider looking at the other roads and what our options are there for our controlling all the passes."

"About Bannister and Hovind," Dax held Marta close, "I'm of the mind that we should let the village elders decide their fate."

Marta laughed, "should we set rules so that those two don't end up in pieces and poisoning the lake with their corpses?"

Bannister and Hovind were found guilty of theft, cruelty and extortion. Taking their cue from Cai, Ragan's elders ordered the two men's hands branded, were given horses and told to never be seen in Arowana again. Cai and his council were asked to act as observers.

That night Cai and Rinna were curled up together. They could hear crickets outside their window.

"Cai?" Rinna had snuggled up as close as she could.

"What is it?" Cai had thought she had fallen asleep.

"How long until you go?"

"Go where?" He drew light circles on her lower back, "Fairshine?"

"Yes. I know you need to soon, at least to see what it looks like on the inside," she pulled the covers up closer to her neck. The nights were beginning to cool although the days were still warm.

"I do. It is the capital. I'd like to see what it's going to take to turn it back into one and at least get a feel for its defenses," Cai's hand stopped, "you want to go?"

"I do, but not yet."

Cai's laughter was soft, "now, I'm confused. Then why are you asking?"

"I was thinking about what happened today," Rinna took a breath then continued, "your brother doesn't care about Ragan, or who lives here. He probably doesn't care about Fairshine either."

"His priorities are more personal."

Rinna laughed, "that's a funny way to say he's selfish. I don't want us to be like that." she was quiet for a while, "what we've done here is nothing compared to what is needed to be done in Fairshine. The other passes are probably at least as bad off as Ragan is. It's just a bit overwhelming when you think of it. If you decide to board the nearest ship, I'll understand."

Cai rolled so she was under him, "if I do board a ship, I'm not going without you." he dropped a kiss on one of Rinna's eyes, "I know Fairshine is a disaster and has been as is the rest of the country, but we are going to try to fix things, you and me, and everyone else who is willing." He dropped a kiss on her other eye.

"And I'm not going to do something stupid when I go and let Azuul get anywhere close to me," Cai felt her tremble as he kissed her nose then her mouth, "I'm also going to make sure that my family never gets to destroy anything else here."

"I know, and I love you. Today just frightened me a little," Rinna whispered as she slid her arms around his neck, lifting her head to join her lips to his.

Cai took much longer than Rinna to fall asleep. He knew she had witnessed their usurpers taking what they wanted for half her life. Today had frightened her more than a little yet had once again set her fear aside and did what was needed despite it. He admired her warrior spirit, her sense of honor and her keen mind.

He tried to think of what would have happened if they had never encountered Rinna and had boarded ships to leave the continent. He found that he didn't want to, having found what he had been looking for in her, love, home, family. He knew they both deserved it, as did their friends. He fell asleep imagining what Fairshine would look like after they accomplished what they intended.

Nineteen

The newcomers were readily welcomed and soon found places in the growing community. Some decided to reoccupy the abandoned homes and settlements along the road to Fairshine. Rinna's old home was occupied by one of the former conscripted scouts who had been a farmer in his homeland. He had been carrying seeds from an apple taken when he had been captured and wanted to try to cultivate them. He also found out about the grape vines Rinna had wanted to get. A few weeks later he had two rows of vines laid out in Rinna's former garden and was begging anyone he could for chickens.

Dax's little army swelled its ranks as did Josiah's scouts. The men were thrilled to be in a much better environment and to be offered opportunities to settle. The village craftsman found welcome apprentices among the younger former conscripts. Some of workers for the other tavern in Ragan joined forces with the new owners of the former Putrid Boar, renamed the Dancing Boar. The Brass Shield closed the same week Cai and the others arrived, its owner deciding to seek his fortune elsewhere. Work was done to clean up the inn to turn it into a place that travelers and locals would feel welcome in.

They were still hours away from Fairshine on their fourth day, fording a stream when Cai asked, "I thought you had one of the streams dammed up. Have we not come to it yet?"

"We are crossing it now." Josiah had been told of what happened by Elgin's watchers, "Azuul ordered the repairs. His first and from what we can see, his only actual project on improving anything. That's because the idiot thought he'd have his horse run through it to avoid the mosquitos on his way back and the horse refused to cross, tossing your brother right into the muck. The watcher about fell out of his tree, he was laughing so hard."

Cai grinned, "it seems that the watcher closest to the city has the most interesting time of it."

"They do," Josiah agreed, "it was a brilliant idea. Won't

help us much in winter, but I don't think we will have to worry about trouble from Fairshine that time of year."

"I figured you'd find it amusing that there are guards at the gates," Josiah told Cai as they entered through a gaping hole in the wall after nightfall.

"And a guardhouse. It makes no sense. Completely useless," Cai could see the structure just inside. Few people were out after dark. A fog had settled in from the harbor making it easy to enter the city unobserved.

They spent the night in a place Josiah's scouts often used. A half-burned house, it offered good shelter for everyone and the horses and was far enough away from other people to avoid notice. Rajah who had tagged along, disappeared as soon as they had reached the house to do his own exploring.

The next day they took a tour. They started at the docks. Cai saw that they were in good shape with warehouses, taverns and brothels the most common establishments. Rinna told him that the weather here was less harsh in winter, the summers muggy, with occasional storms wreaking havoc on shipping. He was unhappy that much of the city remained as it was the day Corbaine's magicians destroyed it.

Josiah and Cai watched the activity from atop one of the warehouses by the docks. They had already had a look inside, seeing that the contents were well organized, and the doors guarded. There were three ships moored at the docks two more floating offshore. A few fishing boats and other small craft dotted the water. The harbor could handle three times the traffic.

"What do you see the most of?" Josiah passed Cai a skein of wine. The day was warm and humid, the aroma of sea and fish pungent in the air.

"Other than sailors and workers, armed men," Cai knew that one of the ships moored nearby had a human cargo. It angered him that they could do nothing to help those whose futures were so dire, "I know the slave trade has been falling off, so what else is being stored here that needs so many guards?"

"Everything to keep a city running and then some," Josiah

lay down on his back and closed his eyes, "Those controlling the docks control what enters and leaves them. We already know that the pirates are wreaking havoc on shipping off the coast. Fairshine is their base of operations and their treasure city."

"And my brother?"

"He still can't get the pirates to recognize him as Lord Governor and their ruler," Josiah yawned, "I'm going to catch a few. Wake me in an hour.

Josiah reaffirmed what Cai already knew, that taking Fairshine meant eliminating the pirates' hold on the city. They didn't have any hope of doing it from the sea. It would only be possible by making the sea the only way anyone could get things in and out. They had much to learn and do before taking what they had started in Ragan to Fairshine.

When Josiah woke up, he told Cai to watch the guards on the closet ship to their vantage spot, "if they make a move to board or if anyone else decides to show up to, bark like those little dogs you endured in Porgorlon."

Cai frowned in confusion, "Lord Thasher's dogs? When I wasn't wanting to throw that man out the nearest window, I wanted to murder his dogs. They never shut up and used my saddlebags as their personal toilet. What in the fuck do you want me to bark like one of them for?"

"Because you know what they sound like; and because the pirate that acts as harbormaster owns three of the little bastards and takes them with him whenever he goes out. They bark at anything and everything when he comes to inspect a shipment."

Cai never saw Josiah board the ship. Twenty minutes later he saw a man strolling casually down the gangplank a sack tossed over a shoulder. A large brimmed hat, with three ostrich feathers and trailing ribbons adorned his head. Josiah had stolen clothing that was a bit too small for his frame, the quality and style suggesting it belonged to the ship's captain. He said something to the guards then continued walking like he had all the time in the world.

Cai met him back at the house they were staying in a few minutes later. Rajah was curled up in a corner sleeping off meal. The saber cat's stomach was distended from what had been a feast. Josiah was pulling items out of the bag.

"I've watched you steal out in the open like that before and still can't figure out how you manage it," Cai saw Josiah's clothing set to one side; the other items are what drew his interest, "I'm very curious why you chose this particular pirate to steal from. I do love the hat."

"It's ugly and everyone can see it coming with those feathers waving on top."

"It certainly gets one's attention," Cai laughed.

There were a pair of matched daggers with jeweled encrusted hilts, a gilded candle sconce, five bottles of liquor, a box holding jewelry and what appeared to be the ship's captain's entire wardrobe including toiletries.

Josiah stripped out of the clothes he was wearing putting his own back on, "despite their alliance here, none of the captains trust one another. There is no real leader because of that. I've had my boys looking for a way to sew discord. They learned that they steal and cheat from each other vying to end up at the top of the heap. The harbormaster controls the warehouses but not shipping. All the captains hate him, but he makes them too much money, despite his fees."

"Stealing from one of them will cause an uproar," Cai picked up a shirt made of a soft fabric he'd only seen once because of the vibrant yellow color. It had been an emissary to a nation that visited his father's court when Cai was twenty. The yellow had stood out.

"Naturally. We can't fight them openly," Josiah adjusted his vest, the knives embedded throughout clinking, "so, we just help create a little mayhem."

"What are you going to do with what you stole?"

"Some we will take back with us," Josiah grinned, "if I could figure out how to do it without them yapping their heads off, I'd give the hat to the harbormaster's dogs."

"Alas, your skills have their limits."

"I learned that humiliating lesson when I was tripped by your fucking kitten," Josiah retorted causing both men to laugh.

"I hadn't planned on doing anything about them yet as we discussed back home, but I can't fault your methods," Cai put the yellow shirt back down, "I think we could expand what you've started in the future, but we don't have enough people yet, certainly not enough trained to do covert raids."

"We will Cai."

That afternoon, they went to the main market. It was in a large square that had once served a different purpose, the advantage it being its access to all the city's gates. Most people lived in squalor living to serve a wealthy upper class, the pirates, and the variety of armed guards and soldiers. Cai had seen similar environments in places all over the Khaetor empire. He knew it was bad, but for some reason had held out hope that it wasn't as bad as everywhere else he had traveled.

"I had to see this for myself, I hoped it wasn't, but you were right, Josiah," Cai and Josiah stood on the edge of the market square. It lacked the bustle and noises one would expect in a community of at least two thousand.

"Fairshine reminds me of the slums in Khaetor City and we know your father didn't care one bit what happened to the people there other than the cheap or free labor they provided. We've got our work cut out for us once we get here," Josiah had his hands to his sides, a knife palmed in each. They were watching five soldiers loitering nearby. Residents gave the soldiers a wide berth.

"I can't argue that observation. I've yet to see anything here that just doesn't make me to strangle my father with Rocnor's entrails," hearing Josiah's guffaws, Cai went to a small stall selling grilled fish. He bought some, placing two copper coins into the hand of the boy manning the stall. Cai almost missed the boy slipping one of the coins into his mouth, as the other went into a box on the ground.

"Some things never change," smirked Josiah. He'd seen

what the boy had done as well, "he may be willing to hide a few more coins."

"Another spy?"

"I take them where I can find them," Josiah sheathed one of his knives, "after all, I got my start when I was a little younger than that boy."

Cai grinned, "I still can't imagine you as a street urchin, no matter how many times you've told me of your growing up."

He waited while Josiah had a brief discussion with the boy, then the pair went to the center of the city. Cai wanted to see where the palace and the library once stood. Rinna had told him where her old house was in relationship to those buildings. The palace was a blackened shell with broken balconies and turrets. If it could be rebuilt, it would take decades. Of the library, only two half fallen walls remained. Cai explored the ruins looking for the basement level Rinna had mentioned. It didn't take long to find it. The fire magicians had been thorough in their destruction, their fires hot enough to crumble the stone stairs leading down. Blackened foundation stones among weeds and small trees was all that was left of Rinna's house and those around it. Cai was certain that Rocnor made sure that no one in this part of the city had escaped.

They spent the rest of the visit observing activity at the main gate. Cai and Josiah knew that the route connected most directly to Khaetor City, although it was a several weeks long journey. They saw a trickle of travelers entering and leaving by that gate. To the south lay fields. There was more livestock near the southern gate and barracks for slaves to work the fields that dotted the landscape. Josiah suggested they explore a cluster of buildings inside the gate. They turned out to be barns being used as warehouses from everything like hay and sacks of grain to farming tools, lumber and bales of cotton and flax.

"This is—wrong," Cai had pulled a piece of cotton fiber from one of the bales and was rubbing it between his fingers, "there is no farming inside the city even though there is plenty of space to do so. I know nothing about running a city and keeping it supplied, but I do know this is not how to do it.

"You've noticed where most of the items leaving the area are heading?" Josiah was rummaging through a box that contained tools, pulling out an item now and then to set aside.

"Yeah, right out that gate heading out of the province or to the docks," Cai pushed the piece of cotton back into the bale. They'd been watching the area for two days, trying to determine who they could talk to about possible future trade. "What makes it to the people who live here, is probably sold at a premium. I wouldn't be surprised if having a cow, or a pen of pigs is considered illegal."

"We will fix this," Josiah finished his foraying, picking up the burlap sack he had been carrying with him for days. There was a stash of supplies at the house where they were staying.

"We can't carry all this stuff back home, you know," Cai and Josiah walked out of the barn after making sure no one was nearby.

"I know. My scouts and I will need to be able to pay the people we talk into helping us," Josiah smirked when Cai stopped walking, "building a spy network isn't cheap."

Cai laughed, "I never thought of it before. It just proves how much I have yet to learn."

She was waiting on them when they returned, standing by a horse, a guard on his own horse several feet away. Rajah who had beaten Cai and Josiah home was crouched at her feet.

"Were you afraid I wasn't coming back?" Cai asked as he wrapped her up into his arms as glad to see her as she him. The afternoon was cool with a light drizzle.

"No--yes," she held him as tight as she could as she reacquainted herself with the scent of him.

"My love, I will always come back."

"I looked after him just as you asked me to Lady Rinna," Josiah said as he gave her his own embrace, "he didn't really need me to babysit him, but it was worth him finding out now just for the look on his face."

Rinna laughed as she kissed Josiah's cheek. They all rode

the short distance back into Ragan together.

"What did you think Cai? How bad are things?" Rinna's curiosity wouldn't wait.

"As bad as we've been told," Cai watched Rajah be greeted by three little girls who giggled as he rubbed against them, "I went to where the palace and library once stood."

"Garrett would never tell me if he ever went to see it. The one time I went back, we kept close to the harbor as that was the only place any people were," Rinna took a breath, "how bad?"

"Most of the palace is still standing, but that's only because it was built of stone. It will take a very long time to rebuild it," Cai glanced over to Josiah who nodded slightly, "the library, your home...the fire magicians purposely made sure there was nothing left. I'm sorry Rinna. If there is a way, I will make sure Rocnor and my father pay for what they did."

Rinna didn't say anything as they rode into the courtyard. She dismounted waiting under an eave of the stable as Cai gathered his gear. Josiah smiled at her as he left towards the village. She watched Tolin meet up with Josiah, then the two of them left through the gate together.

"Rinna?" Rinna turned her attention to Cai.

"Thank you for telling me what you learned," she slipped her hand into the crook of his elbow, "I've avoided thinking about my old home considering how things were there for a long time. Every time I do it makes me sad and very angry. I need to change that if we intend to make it our home one day."

"And you don't like it one bit," Cai hurried them both inside. The rain had changed from a light drizzle to a steady fall.

"Of course, I don't," Rinna admitted while her nose wrinkled, "I never really felt like I belonged there. I do here. But I also know it's because I have people who love me here, even though I'm..."

"Even though you aren't like what you think many expect you to be," Cai finished for her, "you are who you are, who I fell in love with and who everyone here respects and admires."

Rinna started to say something but Cai placed a finger on

her lips, "before you say it, I know it's something I'm having to accept as well. We have much in common, my love."

"We will figure it out together then," Rinna stood on her tiptoes to kiss him.

"Welcome home, cousin," Elgin said as Cai and Rinna entered the great hall, "I can now stop trying to talk Lady Rinna into going in search of you. She's been most insistent."

"I have not," protested Rinna.

"No, you haven't," Elgin grinned at her as he bent to kiss her cheek, "you've just spent every moment you could spare bugging the watchers or staring hopefully over our battlements for his return."

"Well seeing how she missed me so badly, I'm going to give her a proper hello," Cai swept Rinna up into his arms, not stopping until he reached their room. There he sat down on the bed with her.

"I kept wanting to ask your opinion, or what you remembered from when you were a little girl. At the same time, I was glad you weren't there," Cai undid the tie of her cloak so she could wriggle out of the damp fabric.

"I've been very curious what you have discovered and at the same time not wanting to know," Rinna was concentrating on the ties of his leather gauntlets. She got one loose, pulled it off his arm, tossing it behind her.

"Which one won that particular battle?" Cai smiled as his other gauntlet joined the first.

"My curiosity of course," She pushed him backwards, then reached for his leg to pull off a boot.

"My love, I can get all these things off myself."

Rinna slid off the bed to tug off the boot then peel off the sock, making a face when she caught a whiff of a garment that had not been washed in a while, "I know. Give me your other foot."

Cai propped himself up on his elbows to watch Rinna. Once his shoes and socks were off, and set by the door, she picked up a small bundle off their dresser.

"These are for you."

"You got me a present? The last present I remember ever getting was…"

"Elgin," Rinna held out the bundle, "he told me the story. He was in awe of you for a very long time. Now he loves you because you are family and a friend. You deserve presents now and then."

The bundle contained a pair of shoes, a larger version of the ones Patrick had made for Rinna but with detailed stitching showing the Sunspear crest in blue and yellow.

"I know I had asked Patrick to ask me some shoes I could wear indoors or for when we're holding council. I did not expect this," he turned them over in his hands admiring the workmanship.

"You expected something functionable," Rinna took them out of his hands, setting them on the table by the bed. "There's more. I know everything you own. All of it is practicable and the garments of a warrior, not a prince or the Lord Governor of a nation. If I must dress the part, then so do you."

Cai couldn't help but laugh at his demands to her being thrown back at him, "is there a similar threat to the one I once gave you? If so, I'll take the threat."

Rinna joined him with her own laugh as he undressed, throwing his clothes in every direction in his haste. It only took her a few moments to be as nude as he was when they both heard the scratching at the door.

"Should we let him in?" Rinna who was laying kisses on his chest paused to ask.

"If we don't, he will try to climb in through the window," Cai reluctantly disentangled himself to let Rajah in, "as you can see, he got fat on those lizards he caught in Fairshine. He'd just get stuck."

"Sand Dragons. He ate them?" Rinna watched as Rajah found his favorite spot under the window where Rinna had made him his own bed, "I heard they'd taken over some places. Some people used to catch them for food and for their leather. I also know they can grow to be bigger than he is."

Cai got in the bed. Rinna pulled him closer, "I saw him at the palace district dragging one out of an old fountain. It was about half his size and why are we talking about Rajah's diet choices when there are far more pleasurable things we could be doing?"

It was well after dark when Cai heard Rinna's soft sniffs, "my love, what's wrong?"

Rinna turned to tuck in close, "I was just remembering what growing up in Fairshine was like. I hated everything about the court, but then I was just a child, finding it all boring. I was thinking about how beautiful it was and that it and all the people who used to be there all gone."

"Did you like anything about Fairshine?" Cai kissed away the tears he knew she had shed.

"I liked watching the ships sail in and out of the harbor and watching fog roll in. I really liked it when there were festivals. People came from all over. Some were not human. Once a group of Minotaur visited, their ship needed repairs following a storm. Their men were huge and had fierce looking horns. The women were slightly smaller versions of the men. They all had the most beautiful eyes and were very kind to me. I found out they liked the taste of rose blossoms. The palace gardener was furious to discover how many I'd stolen."

"You were quite the wild one, weren't you?" Cai laughed, "did you get caught?"

"No, but I couldn't go back the next day to get more," Rinna smiled at the memory, "I also talked a traveling minstrel out of one of his baby griffons. I wanted it for a pet."

"They don't stay little and would have eaten everything in your family's stable."

"Papa made me take it back. I cried all the way back to the inn where the minstrel was staying. My brother Emil was mad because he had to take me and that he couldn't have the griffon either. Lucinda was mad because I refused to dress like a girl or brush my hair."

"How old were you when all this happened?" Cai heard something in her tone of voice that tugged at his heart.

"Seven," Rinna wrapped her arms around him, "nobody really cared what I did, as long as I stayed out of sight, didn't do something to get my parent's attention, and was available for family functions and appearances at court."

"No wonder you survived so well here; you'd been training most of your life." Cai kissed her nose, "you had an interesting but lonely childhood. My intent is that you never feel lonely again."

"My intent for you is the same," Rinna tilted her head to kiss him back.

Twenty

A week later, the scouts who had gone with Cai and Josiah returned with interesting news which Josiah relayed over dinner.

"My boys confirmed that the pass next to ours is closed and had been for a very long time, as is the one furthest south. The locals don't know why. They just know that anyone who goes to Avengee doesn't return," Josiah said between bites of fish, "they learned that Prince Azuul was sending slaves out to fix the problem. He doesn't seem to care about the southernmost one at least not now."

"The southernmost road goes through farmland that turns into salt marshes near the border. I wonder if the marshes took over," Rinna sipped a cup of watered wine, "Avengee, the one next to us has an old mine, but I don't think it's active. I remember some talk and my father not liking what was being decided, but not why. The one next to it is the biggest road, and the one King Corbaine arrived from. Its name starts with an S. I can't remember the name of the last road."

Elgin chuckled, "he's been here less time than we have and has already lost three trade routes," he looked at Cai, "I wonder cousin. I know you wanted to control access to the port, think this provides an opportunity?"

"It's worth a look," Cai replied. He'd finished with his meal and had pulled Rinna into his lap, playing with a curl of her hair, a habit he had picked up when he was thinking. "I think we need to rebuild or build roads to connect the border communities independent of Fairshine first, choke off all access to the outside except the port. After what I saw there, it's the best way."

"There used to be a trail," Rinna offered, "Garrett used it once to see if things were better at the next pass. All he said was that it wasn't and insisted I drop it. That was years ago. "

"Well, I'm curious," Tolin refilled his mug with mead, "I wonder if there is anyone here who would know what used to be there."

"It would be nice to know, but I think it's not as important as finding what's there now and gaining control of that territory," Cai decided, "we will need it, if for no other reason than a place to put people. Even with some going to replace those lost at outlying farms, and some of the places we found along the road to Fairshine we are running out of room. This village is not that big, and I suspect that there will be more people over time."

"And with the loss of the shepherds, our stores are going to be even tighter this winter. It's going to be a challenge just to feed everyone in the fortress," Marta complained. She was sitting next to Dax who had insisted she spend more time out of the kitchen. "It's work keeping all you big men full."

They deliberated well after the supper dishes were cleared away. They knew they had about six weeks before the snows returned to the passes and could expect at least two more caravans before then. Josiah sent replacement scouts to Fairshine to keep an eye on the coast. Elgin's watchers had organized themselves so well that he let them take things over. The village was prospering with a range of skill sets to see to most of the needs of the population, plus to be able to begin stockpile things, like leather, lumber and a variety of dried meats.

Josiah decided to go visit the people they had rescued from Donner's group, wanting especially to visit the Lucinda who reminded him of his grandmother. He took a group of ten with him along with some tools and a supply of herbed tea from Rinna promising to be back in a couple of weeks. Tolin and Elgin took twenty men with them to scout out the next mountain pass as well as to see if the old trail could be improved upon for a proper road. The fortress was much quieter once everyone was gone showing just how crowded it had been.

"I dread all those people underfoot again," Marta complained the next morning, "This place is just not big enough for everyone."

"I agree," Rinna was helping clean up from breakfast. She

planned on spending time in the Stillroom mixing ingredients for a poultice that Eolande favored, "it makes me miss my and Garrett's little shack. It was tiny, but it was also private. Now I can't even set out herbs to dry on the roof without having to step over sleeping bodies." Without warning, tears filled her eyes. She set down the bowl she had been washing and ran out of the room.

He found her at the spot where she had dived into the lake the day, he first kissed her, "I thought I'd find you swimming towards the middle."

"The fabric of skirts gets all tangled in my legs. I almost drowned myself last time." Rinna dashed away her tears.

"Last time?" Cai pulled her back against him. The lake had small ripples from the breeze. An eagle dove at the water several feet from shore, coming up with a fish in its claws. "When was that?"

"When you and the others went to deal with Donner. It was raining, I missed you, my leg hurt, and I wanted to punch Marta who wouldn't stop crying over Dax. I was also scared for you. After everyone went to bed I went to the garden. I had started my monthly and chewing on a bit of fennel helps with the cramps. I couldn't stop thinking about you, dreading you coming back injured, or not at all. I decided to go swimming," she leaned back, feeling his love and anger.

"You snuck out and tried to go swimming in a dress, in the middle of the night with a stab wound in your leg?" Cai turned her to face him, his expression fierce, "do you realize how dangerous that was?"

"Not until I dove in. All that damned fabric weighed me down, and my leg wouldn't cooperate. I managed to get back to shore, and up the garden path when I slipped on a wet step with my muddy feet and tumbled right back down the damned hill. I had to crawl back up. I made it as far as the kitchen door, when I was discovered."

"My love, that was a foolish thing to do, and I know you are not foolish," Cai kissed her nose. He found that he wasn't angry at her, instead proud of her tenacity despite the risk she took. He was glad he was finding out now instead of when she had first done it. He would have probably threatened to lock her in their room which would have not gone well at all, He appreciated that they could be honest with one another, and be safe in that knowledge.

"I got yelled at by Eolande, but she didn't know what really happened. She just assumed and I didn't try to correct it. She and Marta wouldn't let me out of their sight even to go to the privy. Also, the garden can't be seen from the roof. I've checked, which is why no one saw me. We need to fix that."

She picked at the fabric of his shirt, "I'm sorry. I deserved what I got. I was dishonest to you and to everyone else. I know better. I was embarrassed by how stupid I'd been. I just needed to run away for a little while."

He stepped back and pulled off his shirt, then sat down and pulled off his boots. Then he pulled out two daggers from sheaths worked into his pants. He stood up, pulling his hair out of the tie he usually kept it in, looked down at her and grinned.

"Are you going to stand there gawking all day, or are you going swimming?" he dove into the lake resurfacing several feet beyond.

Rinna kicked off her shoes and removed her apron then her dress. She dove in staying under long enough to swim just past him before resurfacing to splash him. Laughing she swam away. When he caught up to her, she was floating on her back, eyes closed, her hair floating behind her, undulating in the ripples of the lake's surface. Cai flipped over on his back, found her hand and floated beside her, finding the sensation of bobbing on the water soothing.

"Cai?" She said after a few minutes.

"Yes, my love."

"You didn't yell at me. Why?"

"I would have if I'd been there at the time. Your safety is too important to me and you tend to take risks without thinking them through," Cai squeezed her hand.

Like I did when I decided that a pitchfork made a perfect weapon?"

"Exactly. It was brave and caught those men off guard, but you acted first, thought about it later," Cai was feeling the chill of the water. He knew they would need to swim to shore soon, "I know you will be going inside and apologizing to Eolande and Marta because I know you are a woman of integrity, just like I know that you won't hesitate to take another risk and not think about the consequences, especially if it's to help or protect those you care about."

They floated silently for a few minutes, watching fluffy clouds float slowly by above them.

"Why don't you ever get scared?" she turned her head to look at him, "you just do what needs to be done, even when it's hard, or dangerous. You listen to people; you frighten our enemies. You said you didn't know what you were planning to do when you first arrived, but everything has been effortless for you."

"The day I met you and decided to fight for this place, I was terrified. The first time I kissed you, I was certain you'd slap my face and forever be my enemy. The night you fell out of the tree, I was afraid to come near and find your dead body. The first time I walked into the fortress, I thought for sure I'd be shot in the back with an arrow. Taking on the slavers and Donner, standing up my half-brother, winning over the people of Ragan, taking on the role of fucking Lord Governor with only four friends and a beautiful woman my saber car found in a tree..." Cai tugged on Rinna's hand causing her to float closer, "I've been scared through all of it. I've talked myself dozens of times out of taking you, stealing a boat and not getting back off until we found a place that had never heard of Kheator."

"You hide it well."

Cai laughed, "and you don't? You are far more willing to take chances than I am, more adaptable to changes, are very astute in reading people, gifted in earning their respect, too damned quick with that devious mind of yours. I know my brother about pissed himself when he saw you with that arrow pointed at him. He thinks women are good for only one thing. Your standing there staring him down, solid as a rock, upset him greatly."

"He has no idea how close I came to shooting him. He looks a great deal like your father."

Cai saw the eagle from earlier circling above them, "maybe if all this didn't scare us, we wouldn't be trying to take this on. I knew I couldn't do any of it alone, and I often pinch myself that my friends agreed to help. Then I met you and knew that whatever the outcome, it was worth the effort."

"I just wish Garrett had lived to see this," she watched little fluffy clouds hurry by, the wind stronger above them than on the lake's surface.

"Ah, you're missing him."

"He complained constantly, and towards the end was unable or unwilling to help, and I miss him," Rinna inhaled, "he would have griped how you are doing everything wrong and insisted that you and I, mostly me, dress and act properly for the roles we got placed in and would have been thrilled to see it all. Then he would have moved heaven and earth to find a priest."

"Oh, if you want…"

"No!" Rinna stopped floating, treading water as she faced him, "you are stuck with me without some priest and his assistants dressed up in their finery and jewels throwing powder, chanting and pontificating on our sins. I liked how we declared our marriage. If we had a priest, he'd want to sanctify your position, with rituals and offerings to his god which actually went to him, then demand that the villagers pay homage to the gods, or rather his upkeep, while insisting the gods know better at how to be a ruler so he, the priest needs a prime position on the council…and why are you laughing?"

"You are funny and exquisite at the same time," Cai was also treading water as he got his laughter under control, "I take it you don't like priests."

He thought of the fire magician priests that had such influence in his father's court hating everything about them. Her description fit them well, as it did most of the people who served the various gods in the empire. He heard splashing and noticed Rajah swimming towards them.

"No. They dictated life in the courts, and Garrett thought they or rather their gods were the key to the nation's success. One of the many things we argued about. He was convinced that I was losing my moral core because I refused to spend two seconds at his shrine or give offerings to the gods and had abandoned all my lessons of proper female decorum. I knew how a lady of the court was supposed to act, I just didn't see the point when we lived in a shack and I spent my days trying to keep us from starving."

She saw Rajah and watched as the big cat swam circles around them, "he kept hoping a priest would show up in Ragan, I kept hoping one wouldn't."

"Do you feel better now?" Cai saw that Rajah was circling closer, "your lips are a lovely shade of blue and I think Rajah wants us on land."

"I do. I needed to unburden a bit. I love you Cai," she turned watching the big cat nudge Cai with his head as he swam past.

"And I you, my love. Grab his coat, we will let our impatient cat help us get to shore," Cai had a grasp of Rajah's fur behind the big cat's neck. He had just enough time to grab Rinna's hand before the cat headed for shore, pulling the humans along.

They were brought back close to where they had dived in. Marta was waiting on them, with a cloak for Rinna and Cai's shirt, shoes and daggers. Rinna hugged Marta grateful for her thoughtfulness.

"We have incoming," Marta said as they walked back towards the fortress.

"Slavers or regular traders?" Cai stopped and picked up Rinna's shoes and dress. He tried to see what was on the road on the pass but couldn't from that vantage point.

"Neither. We have armed men."

Cai heard Rinna's sharp intake of breath. He put an arm around her, "Khaetor army or private?"

"It looks private. They should reach the rock fall in about an hour," Marta said, her nervousness as obvious as Rinna's, "we should get a better idea of who they are as they get closer."

"The caravan that left the other day. Do you think those people met them?" Rinna's anxiety was climbing as she noticed Dax riding out with his troops.

"Where's Lucky?" Cai used Rinna's shoulder for balance as he pulled on a boot.

"You are staying," Dax said, "we don't know who or what these people are, and we do not have Elgin, Tolin or Josiah with us. Your job is here as Lord Governor. Let your general handle things," he blew a kiss to Marta.

"General now?" Cai shook his head as he smiled, "recruit them if you can, kill them if you must. Don't get killed yourself."

"Where are we going to put more people?" Rinna had to almost run to keep up with Cai. Marta followed behind at a slower pace, turning her head every so often to see Dax get further away.

"I have no idea, my love," Cai waited for her, so they could walk into the courtyard together.

Dax returned a few hours later, minus his troops but with two from the incoming ones. By the time they entered the courtyard, Cai and Rinna were sitting in their chairs for court. They both wore diadems, on their heads. A shield with the Sunspear crest stood on a stand next to Cai's chair. Marta was standing next to Rinna was holding a jewel encrusted goblet. Dax smiled understanding the display was for the men who accompanied him, seeing Rinna's hand at work.

Marta stepped forward till she reached Dax, holding the goblet upwards, "welcome home Lord Dax, general and council to Lord Governor Cai, son of Corbaine Sunspear king of the Khaetor empire."

Dax nodded. They had discussed using the guise of diplomacy and pageantry when unsure of what the situation with newcomers were. Rinna had explained that it served two purposes, to control the pace of how things proceeded, and to give an impression of power and dominance. He grinned as he dismounted, taking the goblet from Marta, drank the wine it contained, before returning it to her with a wink.

"Thank you, Lady Marta," Dax bowed to Cai whose lips quirked, "Lord Governor, lady, I introduce you to Commanders Lucien Carbot and Allen Dunwale of the Khaetor army, sent to assist the Lord Governor with the subjugation of the province of Arowana."

"You are not dressed as Khaetor commanders. Neither are your men. Where are your uniforms?" Cai's voice had a bored, haughty tone to it.

The commanders looked at each other. Lucien opted to speak for both. Lucien was six foot, with the dark skin and reddish-brown hair common of Khaetor natives, broad shouldered with a touch of grey in his and the stubble on his face.

"Lord Governor, we were under the impression that you would be at the capital. We also had to turn around at Avengee pass and take this one instead. It cost us time and men."

Cai waved a listless hand at the commander's civilian style clothing, with only the capes of command designating their ranks, "you still don't explain this."

"Lord Governor. We lost most of our supplies at Avengee, which unfortunately included our uniforms. The conditions there had us in cold weather gear, as there's snow in the passes there. We were forced to stop near the top of the pass thanks to a storm. We hadn't had camp set up for long when there was an avalanche that I still wonder how any of us escaped from," Commander Allen stammered. He was younger, an inch taller with coloring like Tolin, except his hair was a darker blonde. "We have had to make do with what has remained."

"The avalanche. Did it close the pass completely?" Rinna watched the two in interest.

The commanders stared back in surprise that a noblewoman would ask such a question, especially in the presence of her lord, who was her master.

"Answer her," Cai ordered.

"We, we think so," Allen answered.

"You think so? Did you not examine afterwards to see if the way was still passable? Did you not see if you could recover your supplies or rescue the injured? I see from your expressions that you did not," Rinna's voice had taken a tone that let the Khaetor commanders know that she was not what they assumed.

"That is most disappointing," Cai observed, "we had heard recent rumors that the pass had become inaccessible and have sent scouts to assess the situation from our side of the pass."

He took Rinna's hand. Together they stood, "your men may camp beside the lake nearest the pass. Please do not wander too deeply into the lake, the waters only look placid." The commanders hastily bowed as Cai turned and went inside the fortress, his retinue in his wake.

"It was all I could do not to burst out laughing at the warning about the lake," Marta said once they were inside and had been thoroughly embraced by Dax, "I still don't understand why you decided to dress up and play snooty king and queen with them."

"Blame Rinna," Cai held her close, knowing that the whole encounter had rattled her, "we had just discussed diplomacy. Then I saw that Dax was making the commanders' men stay on the other side of the rockfall. She suggested that we get them to tell us what we wanted to know, by a show of pageantry."

"Remember when Prince Azuul showed up? He was the only one all dressed up, was wearing the most ridiculous shoes, "Rinna explained, "he was trying to impress everyone with his get up and attitude. It didn't work because we saw him coming a long way off. He would had done the dazzle and sneer with these guys and they expected it."

"I take it their capes tipped you off that they were Khaetorian?" Dax asked, "it was the only thing that did me. Those men are tired and it's obvious something traumatic happened. They were expecting an easy trip. They got us instead."

"The look on their faces when you told the one to answer Rinna," Marta said, "utter shock, but not disgust. I found that interesting."

"I did too," Rinna smiled at her friend, "I know the Khaetorian nobility give women far less value than the Aworanian nobility did. Their reaction was not what I expected, but then my experience with the Khaetor army is limited."

"Now the question is what to do with them. I'm half tempted to have them reopen the Avengee pass, but I wonder if we want even want it opened right now," Cai sat down on a bench in the great hall, taking Rinna's hand in his and placing it on his thigh as she sat down beside him.

"I'm for waiting to see what's on our side first," Rinna offered.

"I agree. But in the meantime, more mouths to feed," Marta complained finding herself on Dax's lap who had sat on another bench.

Dax scratched his chin under his beard, "well we certainly can't send them to the coast, and we can't let them know they ended up with the wrong prince, at least not yet."

Twenty-One

Early the next morning Cai and Rinna went to visit the camp where the Khaetorian troops had settled. They had chosen a spot near the road along the northern shore. It was a small meadow that offered shelter from the winds blowing off the mountain slopes and a picturesque view of the lake and the village to the east. It didn't take them long to see that the two commanders had been honest about one thing, the men had clearly suffered something. There were several injured and all looked emaciated.

"Unless I missed someone, I counted thirty-seven men. How many are there supposed to be?" Rinna asked as they were noticed. The two commanders were waiting just outside the camp. Several of the other men were standing about, looking with curiosity.

"There should be close to a hundred," Cai said.

"Good morning Lord, Lady," Lucien and Allen both bowed in a manner like how Elgin did, something Rinna found amusing. She filed it away for later, wanting to know where that custom originated.

"Good morning Commanders," Cai responded as he dismounted, then helped Rinna down off her own horse, a piebald gelding she had named Turnip, thanks to a tan colored patch on his flank that was the shape of the root vegetable.

"We discussed it last night and decided that we want to know more about what happened, in a more informal setting before deciding what to do with all of you," Rinna smiled up at the men. They had talked it over with Cai and Marta thinking that it would be also disarming to the soldiers. They knew it was a risk, which Dax had argued against, but he was outnumbered, especially when he realized that Rajah was coming along.

"Please forgive my rudeness from yesterday," Lucien gestured to an array of camp stools around a fire. He had assumed Rinna was taller, "I am unfamiliar with the customs of this province. In Khaetor, noble women are not allowed such freedom of expression."

Rinna tilted her head at the use of the term noble women, "I find that hard to believe seeing that most of the men I've met from Khaetor since your king destroyed my homeland have been quite willing to converse with myself and other women in Ragan, albeit not always with respect and kindness and have expected us to reply."

Lucien blinked, hearing Allen's gasp, "Lord Governor, your consort--" he looked at his co-commander, "is she as shrewd as she just hinted?"

Cai smiled, "if she had been old enough, and a man when my father decided to wreak havoc, Arowana would have likely still been a free kingdom, not a province of Khaetor."

"Upper class women, as I grew up, didn't seem to fair much better than the women in your home country, commander. The lower classes had it better until after the conquest. None of us have fared well in the duration until recently," Rinna took Cai's arm, her face displaying a quiet challenge, "the Lord governor decided that both genders have much to offer in making a home, and a province succeed."

"That's it. I like her. She reminds me of my Ma," Allen burst out, grinning, "my Ma is tiny, tenacious and easily underestimated."

"Good," Cai smiled, seeing how well the description fit Rinna, "Lady Rinna and Lady Marta have been vital into the successes we've seen in the past few months. We value their wisdom and input."

Soon the four were sitting around a fire, steaming mugs of tea thanks to mixture of herbs Rinna had brought. The mornings had started to be cool. Rinna knew from experience that the higher elevations would already be experiencing frost, the mountain tops seeing fresh layers of snow.

"We know that there was more to the story than what you told us yesterday, and we did not give you the opportunity to do so," Cai sipped his tea. It wasn't something he usually drank. He found the flavor more appealing than he expected.

"I assume you were testing us," Lucien sipped his own tea, blinking in surprise then taking another sip. Rinna beamed. It was a blend she'd been experimenting with, so was happy that her new testers found it to their liking.

"We were testing you," Cai said, "nothing personal. Knowing who to trust is necessary these days."

"It took us a while to figure out that we may have just been had," Allen set his mug down on a stone near his stool, "smart set-up, using the rockfall on the road like that. Gave your people plenty of time to check us out, plan your defenses, while you had pulled us away from our troops."

Cai smiled into his mug, recognizing a compliment from someone who understood defensive strategy, "thank you. We'd like to hear what brought you to us, if you don't mind."

"we'd been patrolling the Sandhar desert region when we got the orders to come here," Lucian started.

"Sandhar?" Cai interrupted, "who did you guys piss off?"

"It was my brother who did the deed, by marrying the daughter of a regional governor, a love match," Allen said enjoying the aroma of the tea, "the governor griped to someone important, and the next thing we knew the lot of us were sent to roast in Sandhar. I heard that my brother and his bride took a ship out of Khaetor control as soon as they could."

Cai nodded, "that would do it, especially if the governor had bidders for her virginity."

Rinna stared at him in horror, "and your father called us uncivilized."

"My love, my father is an arrogant ass, who wouldn't know a civilized people if they bit him on the nose," Cai watched her as she observed the two commanders staring slack jawed at Cai, "he is my relative. I don't have to like or respect the man, especially as I've too often seen his brutality."

Lucian was the first to recover, "I met your father once, or rather he made a point of stopping by on his way to or from some place or thing he wanted. I'd always thought kings were special until then."

"Bravo, Commander Lucian," smirking, Rinna reached for his cup, then poured him more tea, "that was tactful and yet scathing."

Allen continued the story, "Luce and I, well we were glad to get the hell out of Sandhar and hopefully be doing something useful for a change, besides scratching sand flea bites, killing scorpions the size of ponies and running off the odd bandit. The Avengee road was the closest so we headed there, made good time until we got near the top of the last peak. We started losing men. Stragglers mostly, but we couldn't figure out what was happening or why."

"By then the weather had turned on us, so we opted to camp for the night and wait for the storm to pass, fucking cold too. We did a head count and saw that we had lost twelve men during the day, including one of our best junior officers."

"We'd barely pitched our tents when we felt a rumbling under our feet, like an earthquake, and then the one side of the mountain simply slid down and covered everything up. We left with a hundred and ten, we lost twelve going up the pass. The avalanche took us down to fifty-three. The rest?" Lucian shuddered, "something hunted us. They didn't follow us far, but whatever or whoever they were, they were relentless."

"You never saw them?" Cai asked.

"No," Lucien held onto his mug tightly, "most of my men have been with me for many years. Allen has been for four. Most of us started out as slaves. I'd freed all the conscripts left because they are good men. They didn't deserve this."

"They will remain free as well," Rinna's voice was gentle, "the Lord Governor abolished the practice here."

Lucien and Allen again looked at each other in surprise, "how?"

Cai took a breath, "believe it or not people contribute more readily, are happier, healthier when they are free. Ragan was a village of slaves, barely hanging on when we arrived."

"It certainly looks like well on its way to recovery," Lucien observed.

"There has been a lot done in a short space of time. We've been fortunate," She looked up to Cai who nodded, "we wish to invite you to be a part of our community and to help us rebuild Arowana into a vibrant, healthy and free province."

"You wish independence," Lucian whispered. Allen just looked frightened.

"Wouldn't you?" Rinna retorted.

"What you ask for is treason," Lucian warned.

"No. What was treason was your king using a wedding as a ruse to murder my people and plunder my home, destroying the one true item of worth Arowana had, its library. I watched as the king's magician priests burned Fairshine to the ground," Rinna was standing, "I came here immediately after and saw that everyone here was dead, and the village burning."

She stopped, tears sparkling in her eyes, her hands fisted by her side, "Forgive me," she whispered as she turned and hurried away in the direction of the lake.

Cai watched, making sure she didn't decide to keep walking to end up in the middle of the lake to cry things out, "she was eleven. She and her father's majordomo were the only two survivors that they were able to find, and only because they were outside the gates when it happened. She recently lost him."

"It's a wonder she doesn't hate you," Allen observed, he watched as Rajah approached Rinna, butting his head against her for a pet. She sat down, arms wrapping around the big cat's neck as he curled up around her, "I saw that beast on the roof yesterday. I thought we were dead for sure, and yet…"

He glanced between Rinna and Cai, "who is he bonded to, you or her?"

Cai saw that Rajah had found Rinna, sensing her distress. He knew she was in good hands, "me. He took right to her, made her his own, as he had done to me. I don't dare take her for granted. Doesn't hurt that I did the same to her as Rajah."

He turned back to the commanders, "my goal is to restore Arowana, at first as a quiet, healthy province. Eventually, I hope to see it as an independent kingdom again, as I doubt the empire will survive my father. We are a long way from that, only having control of this small region."

"We were under the impression that you held the old capital, which was why we were going there," Lucian marveled at Rinna with the saber cat. He'd seen one in battle before and had been impressed with its quick lethal abilities.

"The old city has changed hands several times since it fell according to what we've learned as has Ragan," Cai was glad to see that the two commanders were smart, curious and quick to adapt. He decided to take a chance, "currently it is held by my brother Azuul. How long, remains to be seen. His brief visit here didn't go well, as he lost most of his men, without anyone having to raise a hand against him."

"Prince Azuul? That's the bastard who forced my brother and his bride to flee," Allen glowered, "I can't figure out how he has managed to stay so long. He makes enemies very quickly."

Cai laughed, "it's one of his better talents. My father probably sent you to Azuul, knowing it would piss my half-brother off, which would cause more chaos, which would further ensure the province was not a bother to anyone."

The men moved on to terms of what would be expected if they stayed along with a witnessed allegiance to Arowana, its leadership and its people. The offer to leave military service was given to everyone, as well as the freedom to return to their homes. Cai didn't expect anyone to take him up on the second offer. He offered a third, a welcome to family members of those who stayed. By the time the sun made its presence fully known, an accord had been made.

Rinna returned her eyes more on the men who had been watching with curiosity and suspicion. She spoke without preamble, "we have an excellent healer here who can help treat some of your men's injuries. I was also thinking. One of the taverns has not been reopened. I wonder if it would be useful as housing, at least for now. The weather will be turning much colder in a few weeks."

She stopped and took a breath, "I also apologize for my

outburst. I know that you are not responsible for what happened here a decade ago. It was wrong of me to…"

"Lady Rinna," Lucian stopped her, "we, Allen and I, we had discussed limping home and taking our chances of not getting sent back to Sandhar or executed, but the two of you showing up here, unarmed, unescorted, well we didn't expect that. After listening to you, and Prince Cai, you have willing allies in us."

"Thank you," Rinna was delighted at the turn of events as Azuul's visit had scared her more than she was going to let on. She knew that they needed people like the two commanders if their recent successes had a hope of continuing.

"We need allies, and friends. I'm glad you are willing to be the first, and I suspect soon you'll also be the second."

Cai's attention was drawn to cries of distress, seeing the soldiers backing away as Rajah approached who then lay down beside him, "Rajah knows the difference between friend and foe. He will harm no one who hasn't earned the mauling."

Rinna smiled fondly as she scratched Rajah's head at the base of an ear, a favored spot, "he's terrifying in battle, and yet is adored by every child in Ragan."

"General Dax will meet with you later today. All of you who remain in service will be under his ultimate command. The rest of the council is away but should be returning soon. They are all good men, and good friends. You'll like them," Cai placed his hand at Rinna's back, signaling that it was time to depart.

"You may camp here as long as you need while your men make their decisions. They may need to earn our trust as we do theirs. I don't think it will take long," Cai waited as Rinna gathered up her pot and the little bag of tea, then handed the bag to Lucien.

"For later."

"I hope you are not giving me your only supply," Lucien took the little bag.

"Oh no. I have enough to last a while yet," She smiled up at him, then Allen, before allowing Cai to lead her back to Turnip.

On the short ride back to Ragan, Rinna was quiet, her expression somber.

"My love, should I have insisted you stay home and taken Dax instead?" Rinna shook her head as fat tears slid down her face. Cai reached over catching Turnip's bridle.

"I'm sorry Cai. I should have not reacted as I did," she squealed in surprise as he pulled her onto his horse.

"Something about this morning bothered you. I need to know what it was," Cai felt her wrap her arms around him, burying her face into his neck.

"It wasn't this morning. It was your brother. He's bothered me more than he should have," Rinna was glad he was willing to listen, "I couldn't help thinking of your father sending more troops using other passes or sending a full army and a fire magician with them here and then they showed up. It frightened me and I've not been able to get it out of my head."

"Would you believe that your outburst impressed those commanders more than just about anything else we said?" Cai kissed the top of her head.

"You are joking."

"No, my love, and then Rajah arrived and stole your thunder," Cai felt her laughing as he joined her.

"As for my father giving that type of attention to us, I think it's possible, but not very likely. He's not known for needing to retake a territory as he strips it of all he can then leave it to its reduced fate with whomever he can waste to toss in and keep it in the empire's fold.

"Then why send Azuul, and the ones before him?" Rinna asked, "you don't count. It was the one smart move he made."

Cai barked out a laugh, "if there is money to be had, to keep it flowing. I don't doubt the slave trade is profitable, but it's too small here to matter much, based on what we've seen elsewhere. The harbor is in a good location for travel to ports along the eastern side of our continent and to the continent across the one to the east, the name escapes me. It's being used as a pirate base not as part of a trade route.

"Balandar," Rinna offered, "at least that's the nearest country to the east. I don't remember that much about it."

"I think there is something going on in Arowana that is making someone a lot of money or keeping the interest off something else. We simply do not know enough yet. I intend on that changing," they rode into the village. People were up and about curious about the soldiers camped nearby. Cai stopped to explain to the village elders what had been decided and to prepare to welcome new residents.

"Can you trust them?" Patrick asked.

"They dislike the king, and they hate Prince Azuul," Cai replied, "both are advantages. Plus, they were dazzled by my wife's beauty and her brains."

Rinna rolled her eyes, "they lost most of their men, and the commanders freed all who were conscripted immediately after. To me that mattered. They also seemed quite content not to have to go back to Khaetor."

The elders satisfied, they continued to the fortress, "I am going to talk with Dax, my love. Then I want to spend the day, just you and I." Cai held her face in his hands.

"That sounds wonderful. I'll pack us a lunch and a blanket." She gripped the front of his jerkin, to pull his head closer to her so she could kiss him.

She watched her husband walk inside looking for Dax as she stroked Turnip's nose. He had trotted back to the fortress along next to Lucky, his reigns sitting on his neck. He was a very accommodating horse. Rajah had bounded off somewhere, likely to raid a fishing net. He had discovered they made for easy fishing. He didn't even look guilty when she scolded him on it. She realized just how happy she was, and she had no problems resting the blame on a saber cat with golden eyes, who linked her to the handsome man he was bonded to.

Josiah returned a few days later to report that the shepherds were doing well and had appreciated the help and influx of people to help restore their flocks and homes. He and Lucian quickly became friends, finding that they had both grown up a few miles from one another. The empty tavern was rejected by the newcomers. It took a matter of days for them to help raise a log barracks behind the fortress for a more permanent solution. Meanwhile, everyone that could did what they could to gather as much food supplies as they could before winter.

The last caravan of the season arrived on a blustery day, two weeks after the Khaetor soldiers had. The leaves surrounding Ragan were in full color but had already fallen off the closer one got to the tree line.

The merchant leading the caravan was the first one that had arrived with the barrels of oil. This time he brought four wagons filed with sacks of a dried bean, oats and barley, something that thrilled Marta as they were running low. He and Marta were both well satisfied with the transaction when he left two days later. A week later the pass was hidden behind clouds that dumped snow on the mountain sides. Elgin and Tolin returned the same day.

"We found an abandoned castle almost directly across the road from where the old trail let out. Parts of the trail were cobbled, what you could see of it," Tolin said, relaxing with a mug of ale and a full stomach.

"Is it habitable?" Cai was glad to have all his friends back in one place again

"It would take work, but yes," Elgin said, "it looks like people just got up and left. We decided to look at the pass later, as the weather turned nasty right after we got there, so we headed towards the city. Parts of the road are being reclaimed by the forest confirming that it's not being used. We also saw signs of old habitation on that road, but like everything else, long abandoned. The one to the next pass was open. We did see traffic there."

"We know there was an avalanche recently thanks to our new friends, but that's too recent to have make the pass inaccessible," Dax smiled as he watched Marta talk to Rinna and Eolande.

"I also suspect there are people in the forest between us and the road. We saw the remains of a settlement. Elgin had sensed that he was being watched but could never confirm it, "I'd like to go back, winter on its way or not. Something bothers me about Avengee. I want to look at the pass."

"I'll go with you," Offered Allen. He and Tolin had hit it off. They were from the same region and had discovered they were distantly related, "I'm sure some of my boys will want to go too. I'd ask Lucian, but he's found a new campaign."

They all chuckled as they saw Lucian approach the women. Marta and Rinna exchanged a smile, then quickly excused themselves before Eolande realized what was happening.

"Playing matchmaker?" Cai settled Rinna on his lap, breathing in the scent of her hair.

"Hardly," Rinna reached up and ran a finger along the line of his jaw, "Lucian and Eolande have been sneaking looks at each other for a couple of weeks now."

Cai looked around the room as he played with a curl of his wife's hair. "My love, are you happy?" Cai asked.

Rinna pulled his head down for a kiss. As their lips parted, she said, "a few months ago, I was living on the edge of despair knowing that I was headed to a shortened life of slavery, then your damned cat decided to visit my treehouse. You gave me hope, a new life and your love while considering me valuable for my mind and abilities. Even Garrett didn't do that, and he educated me. I am happy. I'd be a fool not to be."

"You are no fool," Cai rested a hand on her hip as he turned all his attention to her.

Twenty-Two

There was a trickle of people traveling from the coast for several weeks following Prince Azuul's failed attempt to take Ragan. Cai was alarmed by the exodus until he was told that such travel occurred about the same time every year. He ordered for the bridge to be guarded so that each traveler could questioned over and to pay a small toll.

"There's a lot less this year," Marta told him and the others. "we also didn't get near as much traffic as usual coming the other way. It's slowed in the past few years."

"Slowed?" Cai found that interesting, "that could partially explain why those vying for control in Fairshine are unhappy. Any reason why?"

Marta didn't know, only expressing gratitude that they had been able to keep everything coming over the pass for themselves, plus some trade to keep the traveling merchants happy.

The attack came nine days after Elgin and Tolin returned from their expedition to Avengee. The weather had turned chilly, with a cold drizzle encouraging everyone to stay indoors. Cai and Dax were discussing whether to add on to the fortress next year when the rooftop watcher ran down the stairs to the great hall, his face ashen.

"Soldiers, lots of them, left the city heading this way," he gasped, his body trembling.

Cai sat the boy down, handing him a cup of mead, "do you know how many?"

The boy shook his head, "No not yet, just that there are a lot."

"We will know soon. You and the other watchers are doing your job and doing it well. Go back and keep us informed. Get yourself a couple of runners while you are at it, Archie, so you don't wear yourself out," Cai patted the boy on the shoulder.

Dax was already heading out the door, barking orders

when Cai heard Rinna's frantic cry. He turned seeing her on the balcony, "Rinna, my love, we have time--"

"The bridge! The bridge is on fire!" she shouted running down the stairs as fast as she could.

Cai had barely processed what she had said when the door to their bedroom, the one nearest to the stairs exploded outwards with flames shooting into the great hall.

"Everyone out! We are under attack!" Cai yelled. He picked Rinna up who had fallen the last few steps with the force of the blast, running out to the courtyard. They heard a loud thud then the groaning of wood as they fled.

Flames could be seen shooting from the roof of the keep as they exited into the courtyard. They heard shouts and screams outside the fortress walls. Dax, already on Devil ordered his men to grab someone and get out to safety. He himself looked frantically for Marta, who came out with Eolande, both women coughing. He rode to the women pulling them both onto his horse then out the front gates. Rinna found herself pulled onto someone else's horse as Cai ran to the stables to get his own. She screamed in desperation not wanting to leave him.

Outside it was chaos. The buildings nearest to the fortress where fully engulfed in flames as were all the trees near them. People were running to the lake, jumping in to get away from the fire. She caught a glimpse of Elgin, hair flying behind him as he rode by on his horse loosening an arrow towards a target, then reaching behind him for another. She turned her head to see what he was shooting at and saw the fire magician, hands bright with fire, the bridge a backdrop of orange flames and black smoke as Elgin's arrows hit him. Then everything was lost to her view by smoke and trees as the horse she was riding on continued, turning into the forest.

Her rescuer stopped at the entrance of the quarry used by the ceramic makers near the village. It was only then that she realized that Lucien was the rider who had scooped her up, his face grim as he helped her down, "don't you worry about your husband, Lady Rinna. I saw him leave the fortress."

Rinna sank to the ground, her legs unable to hold her upright. Dax had already arrived with Marta and Eolande. The three women clung together, watching as Dax and Lucien rode back the way they came. Other men on horses deposited women and children before turning and leaving again.

Rinna forced herself back to her feet, turning to see those gathered around her. The sound of crying echoed against the rocks of the small quarry. She walked silently through the group of frightened people, Marta and Eolande trailing to a shed where they climbed the steps onto the small porch.

"Please, everyone let's get out of the rain," Rinna said as loud as she could, not quite able to keep it from trembling, "we've planned for worst case scenarios. This is one of our gathering spots. You know that and what to do. We should have news soon."

She went inside, opening the chest that contained blankets, handing them out to people as they came inside and found a spot to sit. She counted fifteen people in all, far too few. Of those gathered, only she Marta and Eolande were from the fortress. She hoped others were coming or had found somewhere else to shelter too distraught to consider the alternative.

She watched as Eolande went around the room checking for injuries. The shed was unused being built as an overseer's hut under Bannister's rule. It was large enough to hold people for short stays, containing food, a small cache of tools and weapons, along with bandages and healing tonics and salves. It looked like any injuries were minor, so she left the Eolande to her work.

Rinna took one of the blankets, a bow with a quiver of arrows and stepped back outside. Even though they were sheltered, there were no men to act as defenders with them as had been planned. As far as she knew, she was the only one with any experience with weapons. Marta stepped outside wrapping an arm around Rinna's waist.

"I'm scared. We are all scared," Marta rested her head against Rinna's as Rinna clung to her, "what if there's nothing left? What if…"

"I can't think about it right now," Rinna was fighting the desire to either run back to help or collapse into a ball of terror and grief, "I've got to go stand guard. Someone has to defend the entrance of the quarry."

"I'm coming with you."

"Marta. I can't ask that of you. You've never had to…" Rinna couldn't say kill a man. Her doing so twice still gave her bad dreams, although she had never told anyone, not even Cai.

"Yes, I have," Marta stepped back inside, then out again, carrying a short sword, "my grandparents were natives here. My father took my mother and raised us in Khaetor City. I was the youngest so was born there. My father worked as an emissary for the cloth merchant guild in Fairshine. He got into trouble, and some bad people came. They killed my mother and were hurting my big sister. I took a kitchen knife and stabbed one of them in the back. I got three good stabs in the man before they threw me off and began to kick me. When I woke up, I was in a cage waiting my turn to get sold."

Rinna and Marta watched the rain fall as Marta continued, "I was six. I got lucky, even though I was scrawny and black and blue when I was placed on the auction block. I was sold to a woman who had lost her little girl to a sudden illness. She owned a bakery, taught me everything she knew, until she herself got sick. I got sold again when she died and sent here, to where my parents were from, of all places. I was working as a cook at the Brass Shield when Bannister and his bastards showed up."

"Why didn't you tell me?"

"It took a while for Dax to get it out of me," Marta admitted, "it was just hard to trust anyone with my past until him and you."

"You are my best friend, and we will be mighty and brave together," Rinna gazed around her as the rain fell steadily, hearing it hit every surface, it loudest on the terracotta tiles that made up the roof of the hut.

"You are my best friend too, and we will cower under the trees and only pretend to be brave," Marta shot back causing Rinna to snort out an unexpected laugh.

The two women found vantage spots within easy sight of one another and settled down to wait. The entrance to the quarry was a wall of boulders piled up long ago as workers cleared away earth and stone to access the materials for the ceramics Ragan had once been known for. The forest surrounding the quarry was quiet, the only sounds the rain falling steadily and dripping off the branches and leaves onto the forest floor. The day marched on, the rain ebbed and flowed in intensity while Marta and Rinna waited. Every so often someone would step out of the shed, either to relieve themselves or to see if anything was happening. After what seemed like hours Marta perked up.

"I hear something," she hissed.

Rinna stood, hearing horses approaching, "get out of sight until we know who it is," she climbed into the tree she had been sitting under knowing the height would give her a better advantage.

"Lady Rinna, Lady Marta," someone called out, "it's Commander Lucien, we've come to fetch you home."

Rinna climbed down out of her tree, seeing the commander and others approach the shed. He had six men with him. By the time she and Marta got back inside the quarry, Lucien had Eolande in his embrace who wept against him as Rinna and Marta walked over.

"Commander?" Lucien turned his head, looking down on Rinna, Marta close behind.

"Your men are fine. They've taken the bulk of our forces to engage the army that was going to finish what the fire magician had started," he kissed Eolande's temple then released her. She joined Rinna and Marta who both slid an arm around her.

"The fortress took damage, but it can be repaired. We lost two other buildings and the bridge. As soon as Elgin shot that damned fire priest his fires snuffed out," Lucien shook his head in near disbelief, "I would have never guessed that they could be killed."

"How many people?" Marta asked, her hand gripping Rinna's.

"We don't know yet," he watched as his men began putting people on their horses for the return trip back to the village, "we know the two at the bridge and probably anyone on the roof of the fortress. Your bedroom is gone Lady Rinna. Hell, all the second floor and part of the roof is gone."

Rinna swayed against Eolande who held her friend upright. If Rinna hadn't happened to be watching the lone man waiting to cross the bridge as she brushed her hair, she would have likely still been in the room when the fire magician hurled his fire. Eolande began whispering, sounds Rinna couldn't decipher. Whatever magic it was, it seemed to help shore her up.

The death toll was seventeen. The two guards at the bridge had been the first to die. There had been six people on the roof of the fortress, including the boy who had just told Cai of the incoming army. Four more perished on the second floor, two more watchers sleeping off their time on duty and the two sisters they had taken in from the first slave caravan. They had been returning downstairs from taking hot tea to the guards on duty. The other five had died in the two houses the fire priest destroyed, never having a chance to escape when the buildings exploded into flames.

The people of Ragan were grieving, in shock and furious, knowing that an army was coming. Those that weren't injured or on their way with Cai to engage with that army gathered as dusk approached in front of the damaged fortress.

"We thought you were going to protect us, yet we are having to bury people, and an army is heading to kill us all," a man yelled.

"Where did all the soldiers go? Did they run away?" asked another.

"We can't defend ourselves. You've doomed us all," yelled a woman.

Rinna looked to Lucien who had gathered the soldiers assigned to stay. He nodded to her. She squared her shoulders and stepped forward.

"I know you are frightened; I know you are angry. I am too. I know that we've just lost friends and family and are grieving," she cried out. She waited until people quieted.

"We've known all along that we could, and likely would be attacked. You've helped us defend our home; you've helped us prepare. We tried to think of everything, every possibility to defend against an attack. We did not expect a single fire magician determined to murder us."

"What he did not expect was that we were anticipating trouble. The guards at the bridge prevented him from walking right to the heart of the village and burning us all before we knew what happened. The watchers have told us of every single person who has passed on the road. Without them we would be unaware of the additional threat that our brave soldiers have gone to deal with."

Tears slid down her cheeks as she continued, "everyone we lost today, was helping us to be a peaceful village. We were robbed of them, people who'd become our friends, our family, not because we weren't prepared, but because our enemies fear and hate us, so sent a horror to defeat us. They failed," she pointed to the body still lying to itself near the destroyed bridge.

"That fire magician will never kill again. We proved they are not invincible as we have long thought, and that they cannot destroy or control us," Rinna bowed her head unable to speak any longer, overcome with grief.

"We can provide shelter for any who need it in the barracks while our soldiers are gone. We will also need to organize a sharing of duties. Let us meet in the morning to plan and begin," Lucien turned, giving a slight bow to Rinna and Marta, before moving to join his men.

Rinna and Marta were taken in by the patrons of the Dancing Boar who fed them, gave them dry clothes and put them in the biggest guest room. There the two women curled up together trying to avoid speaking their fears but addressing them anyway. Exhausted they slept.

#

Dax sat down on a log with Cai and the others watching Josiah talk to three of his scouts. They had travelled a day and a half till reaching what they felt was a defensible position to wait for the enemy to approach. Once camp was set up, Josiah joined them. He and several others had gone to scout the approaching army.

"The enemy is not as large a group as we feared, about a hundred. It looks to be a mixture of pirates and mercenaries, and from what we can tell, the pirates are the ones leading it. They are well armed and organized."

"I still can't imagine them using a fire magician as a pre-emptive strike," Tolin turned a small piece of wood in his hand whittling slivers away with a small knife as the wood began to look vaguely like a bird in flight, "I thought they worshipped a water god."

"I think they want control of a port and trade routes and aren't picky about their methods," Elgin considered, "they know that what passes for leadership in Fairshine is useless for getting the roads cleared for them again. I guess they decided to take matters into their own hands, or your brother talked them into it, deciding to let others do his dirty work."

"It sounds more like something he'd do. He probably made promises he had no intention of keeping just so he could get the road opened back up. I didn't know there were any of those fire magicians anywhere near Arowana," Cai stared down at his mud-splashed shoes. They were the ones Patrick had made for him. His boots had been in his bedroom along with his armor.

"I do know that Azuul thinks those evil magician priests were useful tools for keeping a populace compliant. I've not known him to deal directly with one. I do know he was terrified of Rocnor as we all were."

"Your brother is an idiot," Tolin spat. He hated fire magicians. One had killed his older siblings when he was a child.

Dax finished with sharpening his sword, ran an oil cloth over the blade, "no argument there. We knew we'd have more trouble from the city, just not when or how."

Cai scratched the top of Rajah's head. Both he and Rinna had been in the bedroom moments before the fire magician threw a fireball at it. She had left it seconds before Rajah had, jumping off the balcony to the main floor. Cai tried not to think about how close he had come to losing them both.

They decided to divide their forces into three groups. Cai and Elgin would take one, Allen and Tolin another, approaching from the flanks. Dax would take the third, presenting an obvious target, waiting for the enemy to come to them. By nightfall, everyone was in position just waiting for their target to arrive. Rajah disappeared as soon as the strategy meeting broke up.

Dax stayed seated. He had been quiet during the meeting, "worried about your lady?"

He looked up seeing Josiah, "yeah. She's had enough horror in her life. I hated having to leave her."

"I'm sure she's just as worried about you. She and Rinna will be fine, well as fine as things can be. They'll join forces as they usually and do what they must, just as we are doing what we must," Josiah pulled one of his knives out, turning it over and over in his hand, "Cai is just as worried about his Rinna. He will spend the night pacing. It's normal when you have a mate who is so well suited for you. Both of you chose well. They are like daughters to me."

"I never had anyone to come home too, and I really want to go home to her," Dax stood up to stretch, "I'd challenge you to a race of who gets drunk first if we didn't have a battle to fight in a few hours."

"Let's save it for then the snow is to the rafters and we are bored out of our minds," Josiah put his knife back up, "I'm going to try to get some sleep."

The morning dawned with a light fog that burned off as the sun began to show through the trees. Dax had chosen a spot on the top of a hill, keeping the bulk of his men just over the rise, giving them the advantage of being able to see the enemy sooner than the enemy could see them. The forest was close in at that spot as well, making it easy to hide the flanked troops. Elgin had sent all the archers into the branches of trees lining one side of the road. Behind Dax was a break in the forest, giving them room in case a retreat was needed. The pirates had no such room from their approach.

Josiah was sitting on the ground under a tree watching the enemy approach. He could tell they were confident and not expecting any trouble. A short train of wagons brought up the rear, holding supplies, something Josiah would have been surprised if they weren't included. It confirmed by the scouts and the watchers that the invaders intended to take Ragan for themselves and try to hold it.

He waited until they started up the hill, before standing up and stretching, "I suggest you boys turn around and go back," He pulled a knife out of his vest, using it to scratch his jaw, "there's nothing up the road worth wasting your time or lives over."

"Who the fuck are you?" shouted a large man with a shaved head, riding a horse too short for his frame.

"Me? I happen to be a council member of the Lord Governor and the commander of the Governor's spy brigade. The village of Ragan and this road are under our control."

The man laughed, "Brave words for someone alone and defenseless. We know what Azuul sent ahead of us. The halfbreed should be dead by now and the survivors ready to be transported to market."

"The village was still standing and the magician lying dead on the ground with two arrows in his chest when I left," Josiah put his knife back into its space as he watched the man dismount then begin to walk forward moving his sword in an intricate pattern. The other men hung back until another commanded them to move forward.

"You lie. Fire magicians can't be killed by mortal men," the man sneered.

Josiah faked a yawn, taking a few steps backwards, closer to the tree line, "Your sword technique needs work. I'd laugh at your waving that thing around if it wasn't so pathetic."

"You are dead old man," the man growled. He stopped the pattern he'd been attempting to weave with his sword walking closer to Josiah.

"Turn around and you will live," Dax boomed as he crested the hill a line of shielded soldiers behind him. The man with the sword stopped in surprise before roaring as he began to run forward the others behind him. He lasted three steps before falling forward a thrown knife in the side of his neck. The moment the man hit the ground; Elgin's archers released their arrows. The forward movement of the pirate army stopped as they shifted away from the unexpected onslaught raining down on them, only to be met by Tolin and Allen's well-trained swordsmen. Dax held his men in reserve.

The pirate army realized they had walked into a trap. Those in the back kept trying to press forward until they saw what was happening. They hindered those in front from escaping. Chaos ensued as they were overwhelmed by the superior skill and fury of the Ragan defenders. Rajah chose that moment to join in, adding a level of panic. The battle took less than five minutes.

"Damn," Allen walked out to survey the battlefield, "I didn't even break a sweat."

"That's because we let our men do their jobs," Cai shifted the strap on the sword he'd never unsheathed as he joined Allen, "They did it very well. Let's just hope we don't ever have to do it again."

Ragan lost two of their fifty-five defenders, and another five had injuries. Of the enemy the body count was sixty-two, most killed by Elgin's archers. The rest escaped with their injured coast abandoning their wagons and the slaves driving them.

"It could have been a lot worse if we hadn't known they were coming," Dax passed a flask of water to his friends as their little army celebrated their success.

It took three days to do the work of burying the dead and collecting weapons and other items of value. Elgin and Tolin went in search of the escaped slaves, finding all eight, six men and two women hiding nearby, terrified of their fate. They were brought to where Cai and Dax were overseeing the work of looting and granted their freedom, along with an invitation to join the community of Ragan as citizens.

The two Ragan defenders were buried at the top of the hill with piles of stones to mark their graves. They had been once been part of Allen and Lucien's forces. The next morning Josiah's scouts returned, reporting that the retreating enemy had not stopped until they got to the city.

Twenty-Three

Rinna climbed the ladder to the roof. The stairs to the second floor had survived the fire, but not the rooms or the balcony, all being constructed of wood. A long ladder accessed the roof, the bottom end perched on the top step. She and Lucien met the morning after the attack, agreeing that the fortress needed to be repaired as soon as possible, ready to be defended and to act as a shield for the people of Ragan. She wanted to see the damage for herself, but had been unable to until today, because other duties kept her too busy, but mostly because of grief.

The damage to the roof was not as bad as feared, thanks to the rain that had fallen, but still significant. All the wooden parts of the keep's roof were gone. Thankfully the wall walk remained unscathed and any part of the roof that was stone.

The keep would be uninhabitable for months. Some of the outlying rooms downstairs suffered damage as the fire destroyed the ceilings above them. Marta and Rinna were relieved that the food storage areas suffered minimal damage. The buttery and larder were both underground. The kitchen had survived intact but was only accessible through the garden thanks to the fallen debris.

Rinna leaned on her hands against the blackened parapet and looked past the destroyed bridge. Lucien suggested rebuilding it with stone, which she agreed was wise, then asked him to see to what would be needed. She had had to make hundreds of decisions over the past week.

One of the decisions Rinna had to make involved Marta after she was discovered passed out in the kitchen of the Dancing Boar. Marta had broken down in tears when she was revived and ordered to bed. Only then did she admit that she thought she was pregnant. Eolande confirmed it soon after, thinking that Marta was a couple of months along.

"I wasn't sure. My cycles have never been consistent and honestly, I wasn't paying attention," Marta sniffed as she sat up in the bed, she shared with Rinna, "I stopped drinking the tea after we married. I hadn't told Dax yet. I wish I had. What if I never get to?"

Rinna hugged her best friend thrilled with the news, sharing similar fears, "the day I met your handsome giant, he and his friends defended me against a bunch of Bannister and Donner's thugs, and I swear the man was grinning while swinging that gigantic sword around as men dodged to get out of his way. The five of them were terrifying and sent most of those bastards running back to Ragan as soon as weapons were drawn."

"But you had to shoot one of them, because they had snuck up behind Elgin."

"Yes, because that damned Rajah was sunning himself and wouldn't move," Rinna smiled at the memory, "I had one arrow, and a lot of luck. Josiah had a knife thrown into the other so fast, it was like we both hit our targets at the same time. Then that man of yours picked me up, threw me on that monster of a horse who is so well named and laughed as the two of them proceeded to have me fear for my life all over again by tearing through the forest."

"He told me that you pulled hair out of his beard, you were holding onto it so tight," Marta smiling, pulled away from Rinna, "he's like something from a legend, they all are. They will come back, won't they?"

"They have to," Rinna had said.

Rinna turned away from the bridge and her recollection of her conversation with Marta. She could see the two destroyed houses, their blackened husks standing as a testament to just how close they had all come to dying. There hadn't even been enough left of most of the fire magician's victims to bury.

She wiped the new flow of tears away with her hands, wishing she could scream her anguish out while floating in the middle of the lake. If Cai didn't return, she knew that is where she would want to go and stay until the waters claimed her. But she also knew that she had a responsibility to the people who had decided to look to her for guidance and strength. She realized that she had gone from someone who lived on the fringes of a community, to helping to lead it. That had her thinking as she often had over the past few days of Garrett wishing she had him beside her for guidance. Sighing, she climbed back down the ladder avoiding looking to her left and the place where her and Cai's bedroom once stood.

"Lady Rinna?"

It was Anna, the woman who had once called her Cai's concubine. Anna had fallen in love with one of the former slaves named Trey and blossomed as a result. Anna had been taken under Eolande's wing who was training her to be a healer.

"Yes, Anna."

Anna handed Rinna a mug of tea and a small meat pie wrapped in a cloth, "Eolande put me in charge of making sure you eat," She crossed her arms, "if you didn't, I was supposed to insult you until you got mad enough to do so."

Rinna smiled, "for such a sweet looking woman oozing compassion, she sure can be a bully."

"Yes, she can," Anna pointed at the pie, "so, get to it."

"Yes ma'am," Rinna unwrapped the pie. She sat on the stairs sitting her mug down beside her. True to her word, Anna didn't budge until Rinna had eaten and finished her tea.

"Eolande is teaching you more than how to bully patients into compliance, is she?"

Anna laughed, "she is. I just don't have her magical extra."

"Few do."

"True, but if you are part elf, you have to. All elves have magic," Anna protested.

"If true, then Cai and I both got robbed. Elgin has no magic at all, unless you count being an amazing archer," Rinna closed her eyes as she spoke willing the tears to go back where they belonged. She was so tired of weeping.

"They'll come back. I know they will," Anna touched Rinna's shoulder.

Rinna nodded, unable to answer. She followed Anna back downstairs, then outside. She went to where they held public council her time of quiet reflection over. The space had been transformed into a central command area. A shelter from the weather had been hastily constructed to protect her and those working with her from the elements.

Rinna sat in Cai's court chair, seeing Tova approach grateful for the brazier that gave off heat nearby. The day was overcast and chilly. She had asked him to help record everything that was transpiring, and to assist with updating inventory. He sat down beside her as people began to queue up to ask for advice or directions. After they were done, she took Turnip, riding with an escort to her old home. She had promised a visit, something Marta had reminded her of, seeing the fatigue and strain taking its toll on Rinna.

"I can hold court downstairs for a few hours, seeing how no one will let me lift a finger to do anything else, or go past the front steps of the damned inn," Marta insisted, "Zedra is quite proud of his orchard. You should go see it."

Rinna ended up being glad she had taken her friend's advice. Not only had her old garden been taken over by a small grape arbor, he had added blueberry bushes. On the porch of her former house sat five cups filled with dirt and a tiny twig sticking out of each.

"Those are the apple trees you helped me plant. Every seed germinated. They've lost their leaves. If they survive the winter, then I'll plant them in bigger pots. We won't see fruit for another few years," Zedra informed her as he proudly showed off the work he had done.

He was hoping to hire an assistant next Spring and had begun clearing away some land to expand. Rinna saw that the treehouse was gone. She didn't ask about it. Its absence felt like a loss, along with the rest of the changes, a part of her life set firmly behind her. She saved her tears for the ride back.

Ragan's defenders returned two days later, arriving on a bright sunny morning that was burning away the hard frost that had fallen the night before. They were all tired wanting to get home as soon as possible.

Cai and his friends stopped in front of the destroyed bridge looking towards the village as the rest of the defenders forded the stream for home. The wagons would stay for now until a temporary bridge could be built. The eight newcomers asked to stay with the wagons. Cai fully expected them to try to cross the pass, and informed them that the weather might not cooperate, leaving them to decide for themselves whether to stay.

"You think they'll make a run for it?" Dax watched the group talk among themselves by their wagons.

"They are thinking about it. I hope they don't," Cai wasn't watching them. He was looking at the village knowing there was a lot to be done. He was relieved that most of the men they took with them had returned. All would be needed in the months ahead.

"They've been busy. I didn't think anyone would be able to get up there seeing the flames and smoke when we left," Elgin noted. They could see guards manning the top of the fortress, the sides still bearing the blackened marks of the fire magician's assault. Lucien waited for them on the other side of the ruined bridge.

"That they have," Tolin agreed, "maybe the damage wasn't as bad as we assumed." He and Elgin had been on the archery range Elgin had set up getting in some practice time with Allen and a few of the soldiers the morning of the attack. Josiah had returned that morning and was watching when they heard the first explosion.

Josiah shook his head, "It's going to be bad enough that we will be working our asses off trying to get things habitable before we are buried for the winter."

"I just hope the loss of life was minimal," Elgin wish he could have reacted faster, before the magician's fire struck the two houses. He would never forget their going from standing structures with thatched roofs and a woman running inside to fully engulfed in flames in seconds.

"Welcome home." Lucian greeted them after Cai and his

friends forded the stream, "we are looking forward to details of your victory."

"What about here? What is the status?" Cai braced for the news.

Lucien informed them of the loss of life and the extent of the damage to the fortress. 'The village elders have suggested using the Brass Shield as your home until the fortress gets rebuilt. It needs some work, but it has five bedrooms upstairs and a couple smaller downstairs."

"I'm surprised the thing is still standing considering how much of the place has been picked off for use elsewhere," Elgin stopped, looking down at the charred circle where the fire magician fell. Someone had stuck a pike in the middle and put the magician's blackened skull on top. He started to reach for the pike.

"Leave it," Tolin said, his voice husky with emotion, "let it serve as a reminder that fire magicians can be killed just like the rest of us, and it was proven here."

"I think we all are ready for some much-needed rest," Cai frowned at the display but didn't disagree with Tolin's thoughts, "I'm going to find Rinna and a bed. Knowing her she's worked herself near to death."

"I just want Marta and to disappear for a while myself," Dax said with a grin, "I'll find you when we can no longer stand to be in bed."

Cai thought the idea was a grand one. Tolin, Elgin and Josiah headed to the Brass Shield to examine their new accommodations. He rode to the fortress, greeted and congratulated at every turn. Seeing Tova waiting he dismounted at the courtyard door, handing his reigns off to someone, "where is Lady Rinna? Where is my wife?"

"She's in the hall helping move as much of our stores into rooms that haven't suffered damage as she can," Tova gave a slight bow, "she has barely left the fortress except to tour the village, once to see the progress at her old home, or to check on Marta. She took charge, made decisions and probably has shed a lake's worth of tears. She had to be bullied into eating or sleeping. Last night she fell asleep eating supper."

"Marta? What's wrong with Marta?" Cai's stomach dropped in alarm.

"Nothing that about seven or eight months won't cure," Tova laughed as Cai realized what was meant.

"Dax is going to an insufferable braggart," Cai grinned, delighted for his friends.

Crossing the courtyard Cai entered the great hall. He was horrified by the damage and that any of them had survived the carnage. He needed to find Rinna, hold her, tell her he loved her, and try to forget the past several days.

She was sweeping out a room, her head bent to her task. He thought she'd never been more beautiful. She turned away, to continue sweeping down the hall where she had gathered up a small pile. There she stopped resting a moment as she rested her head against the handle of her broom

"Good morning my love. What's this I hear about you working yourself to exhaustion?"

Rinna's whirled around, her eyes opened wide.

"Cai!" She threw herself onto him, causing him to stumble back into a wall as she showered his face with kisses and tears until he caught her face with his hands, capturing her lips with his own.

"You act like I wasn't going to come home to you," he teased when he finally let her speak again, "I would never do that."

She looked up into his eyes seeing them as liquid as hers, "I kept telling myself that. I kept telling everyone that. I was so afraid. I couldn't have stood it if you didn't."

"And I'll wager you fooled everyone into believing otherwise," he held her close, relieved to be home and her back in his arms.

"There's so much. So much I need to tell you, so much I need you to tell me, so much to do," she whispered into his chest.

"I know. Let's see if the Dancing Boar has any empty rooms left," he whispered back, "we can hold each other, comfort each other and then tell each other everything."

She tilted her head up to look into his eyes, "they saved us one."

They made it just outside the Dancing Boar when a shirtless Dax flung open a window, then shouted to the world the news of his pending fatherhood as his hair and beard blew in the autumn breeze. The village stopped what they were doing to watch Dax until someone shouted back, "took you enough tries!"

That made everyone laugh, including Dax who shouted down, "and now I'll be having several celebratory attempts!"

"Dax!" Marta cried as she tried to pull him from the window. That just had him pull her into his arms and kiss her to the cheers of onlookers.

That night, they gathered in a corner of the Dancing Boar. They were left alone by the village who seemed to sense that with the return of their Lord Governor and his companions, they could rest easy again.

"We were very, very lucky," Lucien said, Eolande fighting sleep in his lap.

"We were, but we also were well organized and prepared," Tolin countered, "I think we sent a strong message that we are not to be underestimated."

Cai was thoughtful. He had Rinna in his own lap, a strand of hair curled around his finger, "I agree, which is why I think we should proceed with our original plan."

"I was hoping you'd say that cousin," Elgin sipped his ale, "I'm still curious as to the state of the pass in Avengee, and why the road there has not been used in a while. If that idiot brother of yours wants to know, then so should we."

"And we have the advantage of knowing how much Azuul has to do right now to keep his head on his shoulders," Josiah smiled watching Dax idly stroking Marta's stomach, "our new residents were happy to relay the deteriorating political landscape in the city. That's why I'm going to take a few men and see what is happening for myself. I suspect that the pirates suffered a big setback in manpower and influence, that is if attacking us using a fire magician as a preemptive strike was their idea."

"You don't think it was?" Tolin took a sip of his mug of ale, then set it back down.

"I don't know, but I don't think so. That one of those fire magicians was even in Fairshine bothers me. It bothers me even more that he was connected to what we assume were pirates," Josiah got the attention of one of the barmaids for more ale.

"I tend to agree," Rinna was sleepy and for the moment content. Something about sitting on Cai's lap just had her feeling like she was home, "the pirates could have corroborated with someone else, or they were hired. They would have no interest in taking over a mountain village. Not enough profit for them."

"I should have some answers when I get back," Josiah assured everyone.

Allen spoke up, "at least their slaves have decided to stay."

Marta nibbled on a piece of bread. Her stomach seemed to accept food in the evenings more readily, "I'm glad. Ysanne said that two of them used to be weavers and that there are flax fields on the far side of Fairshine. She is going to want some for linen."

"Are you sure that old castle is habitable?" Rinna moved the topic back to the pass next to theirs, "if you plan on moving there soon, it will be rough going. Winters here are cold enough. Avengee is higher in elevation so it will be colder and for longer."

"Enough of it is, that a small group can manage until Spring when we can bring more people over," Elgin said, "but not until we look at that pass. What Allen and Lucien experienced on the other side bothers me."

"Yeah. Someone one was there. They were not at all welcoming," Allen said, "which is why I want to go too."

"In the meantime, the fortress is uninhabitable, we have even more people, and I'm still wondering how to feed everyone," Marta complained.

Dax kissed his wife, "Marta, darling. You will be letting other people do the worrying about that, or you order and point. You will not be allowed to burden yourself."

"Allowed?" Marta's eyes gleamed as she glared at her husband, "for that I should throw you out of my bedroom."

"Ah, but you'll just let me back in."

Two weeks later Elgin, Tolin, Allen and two volunteers left heading southwest towards Avengee. They planned on being gone long enough to explore the pass and what might be there. Josiah and his group had already left escorting the watchers back to their posts on their way to Fairshine.

Repairs to the Brass Shield were completed a few days after Elgin, Tolin and Allen left on their expedition. The building had the roof fixed; the kitchen rebuilt to meet Marta's standards. All the window glass, fixtures and furniture had long been looted when the tavern closed. Some things could be replaced from the stores in the fortress, the rest would be over time.

"This was the tavern I worked in when I was first brought here," Marta beamed the day they moved in. She walked around the main room, touching the mantle, the bar and a brass shield that was said to have once belonged to a long dead Arowanian knight. Dax hung it over the mantle where it had once been.

"This will do nicely," Josiah who had just returned, was delighted with their new home, "I can come home and go to the tavern at the same time," He had made sure the bar was stocked with all the beverages they might need, raiding the fortress stores for supplies. He took a small room downstairs for his own.

Cai and Rinna took the biggest bedroom. It had a small window looking out over the lake. The room had a bed and a fireplace. It shared a chimney with the room next door. Dax and Marta had taken a room on the far end of the hallway.

They lay together with candles set on the mantle. Rajah was curled up on a blanket by the fire. Outside a sleeting rain fell, turning into snow as the liquid hit the higher elevations of the mountains.

"I've been thinking," Rinna's fingers traced the outline of the scar on Cai's' back.

"My love, you are always thinking," his hands were entangled in her hair, as he undid her braid.

"I'd like, I'd like a child with you."

Cai's hands went still, "are you sure?"

She nodded, "we may never live long enough to make Arowana a peaceful province, but that shouldn't stop us from trying. It should also not stop us from giving this land a future people to populate it."

"Is this because of Marta?"

"Yes--No."

"Which is it?" Cai continued unbraiding her hair.

"I've been thinking about it for a while, mostly wondering if I'd be any good at being a mother. Marta just had me deciding," She held him a little tighter, "I just don't want to be like my own mother."

"Nor I like my father," Cai kissed the shell of her ear, "I'm certain we can surpass their parenting skills."

She giggled, "I agree. Besides, I want a little one who has your eyes and your courage."

"And I wouldn't mind one with your hair and your canny brain."

"Then let's make one," She said as she felt his hands leave her hair.

"Let's indeed," his lips found hers.

Coming early 2021

AVENGEE
Chronicles of Arowana
Book 2

Biography

Stories have always fascinated Sylvie Parris. She used to lay awake long after she should have been asleep as a child reworking stories she'd read or seen in a movie, imaging herself in the story, the princess or heroine of course, or what would happen after the end, that is if she wasn't reading. Sylvie was always reading. Both habits stayed with her long into adulthood, except that she began to find herself making up new characters in her head and trying to figure out what to do with them. Once she started writing all the story ideas, lines of verse or dialog down, she found she couldn't stop.

Sylvie lives in the upstate of South Carolina with her cats Miko the Merciless and Baffi, the Junior Writing Assistant.